OTHER CITIES,
OTHER WORLDS

OTHER CITIES, OTHER WORLDS

URBAN IMAGINARIES IN A GLOBALIZING AGE

EDITED BY ANDREAS HUYSSEN

Duke University Press   Durham and London   2008

© 2008 Duke University Press

All rights reserved

Printed in the United States of
America on acid-free paper ∞

Designed by Heather Hensley

Typeset in Minion Pro by Tseng
Information Systems, Inc.

Library of Congress Cataloging-in-
Publication data appear on the last
printed page of this book.

CONTENTS

ACKNOWLEDGMENTS

The essays that make up this volume were first presented as formal lectures in a year-long graduate research seminar in 2001–2002 at Columbia University, conducted as a Sawyer Seminar and funded by the Mellon Foundation. All of the essays have been updated and rewritten since they were first presented. The seminar was concluded two years later by a follow-up conference which generated further discussions and several more essays. Both the seminar and the conference featured architects, urban historians and theorists, anthropologists, sociologists, literary and cultural critics, curators, and writers, most of whom came from those non-Western cities they spoke about. Two essays were commissioned at a later time to round out the volume.

My first thanks go to the Mellon Foundation for the generous funding and support that made the seminar possible. The Sawyer Seminar itself was developed in close cooperation between the Center for Comparative Literature and Society, which I directed at the time, and the Graduate School of Architecture, Planning, and Preservation at Columbia University. Special thanks are owed the Graduate School of Architecture, Planning, and Preservation and its deans Bernard Tschumi and his successor Mark Wigley, the Temple Hoyne Buell Center for American Architecture and its director Joan Ockman, and my colleagues at the Center for Comparative Literature and Society. I am especially grateful to the students who made the seminar such a success — an engaged and imaginative group from a variety of disciplines in the humanities, social sciences, and architecture. Together we read and discussed the published work of the invited speakers before they came to Columbia. In closed sessions after the public lectures, the students engaged the lecturers, peppering them with questions and comments, many of which resonate in the rewritten versions of the original presentations. I am pleased to acknowledge the significant input of Zeuler Lima, Esra Akcan, Sjoukje van der Meulen, Eric Bulson, and Salomon Frausto all of whom helped in a variety of pedagogic, intellectual, and organizational ways to make the seminar, its regular sessions and biweekly public lectures, and the final conference a major event on campus. Thanks must also go to the colleagues who provided engaged formal responses to the lectures — each one of them a trigger for ensuing lively discussions which in turn also fed into the revision of the essays assembled in this book. Unfortunately and due to lack of space, these comments by George Baker, Bruno Bosteels, Jean Cohen, Manthia Diawara, Jean Franco, Mahmood Mamdani, Reinhold Martin, Gyan Prakash, James Schamus, David Scott, Gayatri Spivak, and Mark Wigley could not be included in this volume.

Going back to my own first engagement with the theme of urban imaginaries beyond my own focus on urban narratives, I must thank Ackbar Abbas, Benjamin Lee, and Mario Gandelsonas for the intense discussions about urban imaginaries we had in two seminars in Hong Kong in May 2000 that later fed into the planning for the Sawyer Seminar. Unfortunately, Lee's and Gandelsonas's lectures could not be included here since they have already been published elsewhere. I also want to thank Neil Brenner for several stimulating discussions about world-city theory which helped me get a handle on a complex field of study that lies rather outside of my own scholarly research, though well inside my literary interest in urban culture.

Finally, I want to thank my editors and production staff at Duke University Press, Ken Wissoker, Courtney Berger, Pam Morrison, Patricia Mickelberry, and Heather Hensley. Thanks also to Christopher Manning, who prepared the index.

I dedicate this book to the Columbia students, an international and cosmopolitan bunch whose curiosity, imagination, and engagement with city cultures in a globalizing age made the Sawyer Seminar such a rewarding experience for all participants.

Andreas Huyssen

WORLD CULTURES, WORLD CITIES

"From now on, I'll describe the cities to you," the Khan had said, "in your journeys you will see if they exist." But the cities visited by Marco Polo were always different from those thought of by the emperor.

—Italo Calvino, *Invisible Cities*

Most cities of the world have undergone major transformations in recent decades. Processes of urbanization have greatly accelerated across the world, and cities have grown closer to each other economically and culturally. Transnational corporations, with their effects on local and global economies, have created new networks of cities, and the spread of the global and regional culture industries, heritage foundations, mass tourism, labor migrations, academic exchanges, and cultural spectacles such as biennales, sports events, and blockbuster museum shows have made "other cities" part of the way we live and perceive the world. Together with these developments, a new vibrant literature has emerged among political economists, sociologists, anthropologists, and urban theorists across the world. It seeks to capture the emerging thrust of urban developments in their changing relation to nations and regions, to social movements, and to the effects of a globalizing economy and world culture. While many of these terms, like *globalization* and *global city* themselves, can legitimately be questioned as to their historical, hierarchical, and propagandistic implications, there is no doubt that some new understanding of cities and world culture is on the horizon of the early twenty-first century.[1] Scholars need to take advantage of the new knowledge about cities produced in the context of globalization while putting more pressure on the ways in which globalizing processes are understood in different disciplines.

WORLD CITIES AND URBAN IMAGINARIES

My main motivation in putting this volume together is the conviction that as citizens in the Western academy and critics of the neoliberal triumphalism of globalization, we often do not know enough about the deep histories and current developments of urban areas elsewhere in the world. Thus, the title: other cities, other worlds, and the bracketing of cities in the territories of the northern transatlantic and the member nations of the Group of Eight (G8). To bracket the cities of the northern transatlantic is not to diminish the impact of the urban imaginaries of Paris or London, New York or Los Angeles in other parts of the world, let alone to forget the history of empire, colonial conquest, and domination. Bracketing is a necessary but insufficient way to dislocate accounts of modernity from the West, a move analogous to, but slightly different from Dipesh Chakrabarty's attempt to provincialize Europe.[2] It is simply based on the pragmatic idea that we need much deeper knowledge about the ways in which modernity has historically evolved in the cities of the non-Western world, what urban constellations and conflicts it has created there, and what such developments might mean today for city cultures at large.

Apart from my wish to assemble a group of writers from different social-science and humanities disciplines, all of whom are working in cross-disciplinary ways, and to compile a volume of essays on cities in Latin America, Africa, the Middle East, and Asia, my choice of scholars and places could not help but reflect my own connections to intellectuals abroad, my participation in international conferences outside the United States, and the knowledge I have gained through travel to those "other cities," which have left me with a deep sense of wonder and fascination. The more diverse my experience of cities has become over the years, the more I have begun to wonder what it is that makes up the urban imaginaries both of the cities one inhabits and of those one visits, and how such very distinct urban imaginaries reflect and contest the notion of cultural globalization.

So what is an urban imaginary? Italo Calvino strikes a deep chord with his marvel of a book entitled *Invisible Cities*. Calvino himself once described his book somewhat nostalgically as "something like the last poem of love about the city."[3] Beyond its fictional premise, however, the title suggests that no real city can ever be grasped in its present or past totality by any single person. That is why urban imaginaries differ depending on a multitude of perspectives and subject positions. All cities are palimpsests of real and diverse experiences and memories. They comprise a great variety of spatial practices, including architecture and planning, administration and business, labor and leisure, politics, culture, and everyday life. They consist of a cacophony of voices and, more often than not, feature a multiplicity of languages. In some deep dimension all cities remain invisible just as all cities today are world cities in the sense that there no longer is any pure, uncontaminated, monocultural, or monolingual locality—which historically may have been the exception rather than the rule anyway. And yet, locality is constantly produced anew by our very visible movements through the urban sphere, our recognition and negotiation of the built space of our environment, and by all of our interactions with urban life.[4] An urban imaginary marks first and foremost the way city dwellers imagine their own city as the place of everyday life, the site of inspiring traditions and continuities as well as the scene of histories of destruction, crime, and conflicts of all kinds. Urban space is always and inevitably social space involving subjectivities and identities differentiated by class and race, gender and age, education and religion. An urban imaginary is the cognitive and somatic image which we carry within us of the places where we live, work, and play. It is an embodied material fact. Urban imaginaries are thus part of any city's reality, rather than being only figments of the imagination. What we think about a city and how we perceive it informs the ways we act in it.

It has always seemed to me that talk about globalization and global culture is either vastly premature or simply a category mistake. Clearly, there is no one global culture shared by all inhabitants of the planet Earth, and there probably never will be such a unified culture. The very notion of culture implies contestation, critique, conflict. Local and national histories, religious affiliations and customs, languages and modes of cultural expression are simply too vastly divergent to ever melt down into some kind of Esperanto culture. This is what I mean by category mistake. The dystopian view of one hegemonic global culture taking over is articulated by those in the United States or abroad who lament cultural Americanization via consumerism, media, and McDonald's, who blame Western modernity in general for all the ills of the world, and who usually do not bother to learn about other cultures and languages to begin with. Articulated within the United States, the critique of globalization simply as imperial cultural hegemony risks lapsing into an ahistorical politics of guilt combined with what my colleague Gayatri Spivak has called sanctioned ignorance.[5] Articulated abroad, it latches on to deep national and cultural currents of anti-Americanism that often betray equal levels of ignorance. In both instances parochialism reigns supreme. At any rate, neither the triumphalism of market economics, privatization, and the cyberfuture, nor apocalyptic laments about homogenization and cultural imperialism under the signs of Disney and McDonald's have been able to offer persuasive models for understanding the current urban transformations of a no-longer bipolar world.

Another definition of global culture, however, seems more promising and perhaps even cosmopolitan in a new way in that it embraces and maintains a dialectical tension between the universal and the particular rather than opting for one against the other. This view acknowledges all cultural articulations extant in the world in their very differences and affinities. It neither denies nor exaggerates the considerable impact of Western mass culture, technology, and lifestyles across the world. But it emphasizes plurality by focusing on spatial diffusion, translations, appropriations, transnational connections, and border crossings that are not per se new, but have accelerated and intensified greatly in recent decades.[6] By not taking Western cities as the inevitable jumping-off point of analysis, this approach also broadens our geographic imagination. This is an extremely rich field for scholars interested in cultural translation, but the difficulty remains how to reconcile the universal and the particular in the practice of cultural criticism without lapsing either into empirical particularism or abstract universalism.

In order to get a better handle on "the global," this volume focuses on the primary production sites of what is called global culture. Cities have always served to condense and thicken cultural developments and their dynamics, and they still do so today. In the wake of Charles Taylor's use of the term *social imaginary* and Henri Lefebvre's argument about the social production of space, the notion of urban imaginaries has become quite commonplace.[7] However, there are different usages of the term. Some focus more on media images, cyberspace, and global popular music that connect cities with each other. Others focus on translocal social movements around land rights, squatting, and housing or on transnational Web-based grassroots efforts concerned with human rights or ecological issues.[8] Yet others see the linkages between local embeddedness and translocal business connections and practices as key for urban imaginaries.[9] Indeed, all of these are key dimensions that, together with the *longue durée* of customs, languages, and everyday practices, generate the urban imagination today.

To be sure, utopias of the good life and haunting specters of crime, corruption, and decay have always existed side by side in urban imaginaries. Think of the shining city on the hill and of the hard-edged modernist urban utopia or, alternatively, of the great whore of Babylon as a long-standing gendered metaphor for the city. Think of the glittering metropolitan centers in glass and steel or of the sprawling megacity of the twenty-first century with its slums, ghettos, and shantytowns. Both the shine and the darkness are today present everywhere in their specific early-twenty-first-century form: the modernist utopia in its current corporate and consumerist hubris, with its suburbs, ex-urbs, and gated communities, right next to a modernity noir of ghettos, shantytowns, and favelas extending mile upon mile into the countryside.

But urban imaginaries are also the sites of encounters with other cities, mediated through travel and tourism, diasporas and labor migration, cinema, television, and the Internet. The global and the local invariably mix, a fact captured with the neologism *glocalization*.[10] Such linguistic acrobatics, which actually originated in a Japanese car ad before becoming popular in academe, remain as abstract as the preceding approach that simply opposed the local to the global in binary fashion. It, too, risks covering up more than it reveals. It discourages questions about the specificities of the global-local mix in any concrete urban imaginary. However useful it first was as a critique of the earlier global-local binary, the glocal risks becoming a mere abstraction without historical depth.

The World's Fairs, for instance, held primarily in the industrializing world in the later nineteenth century and early twentieth century up to World War II, already produced such local-global encounters, and some of their cultural forms are preserved today in events such as the Olympic Games, the World Cup, and, for more limited audiences, biennales and specialized commodity fairs (automobiles, electronics).[11] Some economists have argued that the world was already as connected economically around 1900 as it is today.[12] Their economic argument is persuasive. But as any comparison of World's Fair culture from the Crystal Palace in London in 1851 to the Century of Progress exhibitions in New York and Chicago in the 1930s with urban experiences in the contemporary world would show, connectivities in the mind and in reality now exist on a different scale and for an ever-increasing number of people. At the same time, this increased proximity in space, facilitated by the movements across national borders, by travel, and by legal and illegal immigrations, has generated new fears and ethnic conflicts across the world. Both distance and proximity have entered into a new and volatile relationship.

In his analysis of modernity and of the postmodern condition, David Harvey has spoken eloquently of the time-space compression that modernity has brought about in the world.[13] He argues that the organizing of the spatial world as a grid of longitudes and latitudes and the introduction, in 1884, of time zones based on the Greenwich Meridian were the visible signs of the need to manage the relation between temporal and spatial distance and proximity on a global scale. In the wake of ever-faster travel and communication technologies, he continues, distances and temporalities have shrunk and human perception itself has undergone a historical shift. What this thesis neglects, however, is another major shift in perception that is the direct consequence of time-space compression and that can also be traced back to the late nineteenth century. Even then, as the enormous popularity of the World's Fairs demonstrated, the very real compression of time and space, brought about by new technologies and imperial expansion, was accompanied by the simultaneous expansion of time and space in the imagination. World's Fairs—or Universal Expositions, as they were called in Europe—focused not only on technological and urban futures, but they also staged encounters between the West and its others. The "Streets of Cairo" was a favorite attraction at several World's Fairs, drawing on and exacerbating what Edward Said has described as the "imaginative geography" of the West.[14] These always temporary and very theatrical events were themselves a primary mise-en-scène of time-space compression. World's Fairs functioned ideologically as a major device to popularize the presumed superiority of the West over the Orient or the primitive, a maneuver that became ever more urgent and questionable as worlds converged. But they also were sites of cultural encounters across borders, opening an unknown world beyond the familiar, beyond scarcity, and full of possibilities.[15] Even though it shipwrecked in practice, socialist internationalism was one of the major political manifestations of this expansion of time and space in the imaginary. Its legacies are still to be explored and rewritten for our times.

This simultaneous contraction and expansion is what I would call the time-space paradox generated by modernity. Urban imaginaries were, and remain, a key site for such expansion even as distances between cities seemed to shrink. Today, the direct encounter with other cultures, the weakening of national borders and national identities, the clash of religions at a time when stable territorialities are being dissolved both via concrete migration and media representations—all of this brings about imaginary expansions of space and of time with very contradictory effects. People in our globalizing world are not just getting closer to each other and thus potentially becoming more communal, as Marshall McLuhan had it in his catholic and ultimately anti-modern fantasy of the global village.[16] They carry with them memories of conflicts and incompatibilities with deep historical backgrounds, animosities rooted either in imperial domination, both past and present, or simply in fears of otherness, instilled by histories of war, religious conflict, and ideological manipulation. Despite the newly found exuberance about the potentialities of urban life, the specters of destruction and decay haunt urban imaginaries today as they have in the past. That is why among Europeanists Dickens's and Dostoevsky's city novels, Poe's "Man in the Crowd," Döblin's *Berlin Alexanderplatz*, and Kracauer's dystopian prose miniatures about urban scenes in Berlin, Marseilles, and Paris still have such a hold on the imagination.

GLOBAL CITIES DISCOURSE

Something else must be said about how the study of urban imaginaries emerged from world-systems theory and the new urban geography and how one can think about its relation to cultural and historical issues, the primary focus of the humanities. In the 1990s processes of globalization as radically novel phenomena were studied primarily in terms of economics (financial markets, trade, transnational corporations), information technology (television, computers, the Internet), politics (the waning of the nation-state, civil society, the rise of nongovernmental organizations), and international human rights. While much of this work suffered from the short-term horizons of social-scientific model building, world-systems theorists such as Immanuel Wallerstein and Giovanni Arrighi have appropriately insisted that capitalism can only be understood on the largest possible spatial and temporal scale—that of a world economy, which did not spring from nowhere in the 1980s or the 1990s, but has deep historical roots.[17] Together with Lefebvre's pathbreaking work, in the 1960s, on urban space and the sociology of everyday life, the world-systems approach to political economy made its mark on the new urban geography and sociology of scholars such as Manuell Castells, Edward Soja, and David Harvey, whose work has done so much to make globalizing processes visible and understandable as a new stage in the development of capitalism from Fordism to post-Fordism, from national economies and their linkages via internationalism to global financial flows and the network society.[18] All of this work confronted the demand to understand globalization according to a deeper historical frame and to compare it to earlier phenomena such as internationalization, empire building, and colonization at least since the eighteenth century, if not before, not to speak of other forms of globality that thrived before European modernity even appeared on the world stage.[19]

By the mid-1990s globalization discourse had entered into a close relationship with research on cities in the social sciences. In the humanities as well intense scholarly interest in city cultures had been emerging since the 1970s. Much of this work seems to have been energized by a critical nostalgia for a kind of urban formation that really belonged to that earlier stage of a heroic modernity, rather than to our own time: the Paris of Baudelaire and Manet, fin de siècle Vienna, the London of Bloomsbury, Weimar Berlin, and the New York of the Harlem Renaissance. Its predominant spirit is captured by Hegel's dictum that the owl of Minerva begins its flight at dusk. As valuable memory work, these studies of the classical modernist cities and their culture stand in the shadow of the urban transformations of our own age.

Thus it is no coincidence that they often betray a sense of loss, if not a nostalgia for the modernist city, a nostalgia that is no doubt fed by the insight that these prototypical modernist cities, with their sense of vibrant futures, are fast becoming part of history, rather than representing the cutting edge of global developments. Even New York, since 9/11, is no longer "delirious," the term Rem Koolhaas proposed in 1978 to reclaim a dimension of modernism against both postmodern architectural populism (Robert Venturi) and traditionalism (Léon Krier).[20] In recent decades some classical modernist cities in Europe have taken on a veneer of museal cities in which preservation reigns supreme. Clearly, the modernist city in the West has become historical, but one should not underestimate the importance of the museal dimension for urban economies and urban life. Cities depend on "cultural engineering" more than ever to attract capital, business, and power. Even small cities depend on such "imagineering," the creation of a cultural image and legacy that will attract both tourists and new residents as well as satisfy the desires of the local elites and inhabitants.

The cultural dimensions of urban transformations in the West understandably were not the primary focus of global-cities researchers in the social sciences, whose work was primarily driven by the logic of recent economic and technological developments. With the fast growth of transnational corporations, a network of global cities had emerged, since the 1970s, as key to the expansion of capitalism. When corporations became transnational, they of course established themselves in cities rather than in the countryside. The trend to transnational economic networking accelerated significantly after the fall of the Berlin Wall in 1989, the collapse of the Soviet Union, and the opening up of China to capitalist investment. With the triumph of neoliberal economics, U.S. cities rebounded, although they had been largely written off in the 1970s as centers of crime, drugs, and decline. At the time, the urban crisis, combined with the rise of new informational technologies, led many researchers to the mistaken assumption that cities as bounded and centered space within national borders would lose their traditional function and that real space would yield to virtual space. Much of the exuberant language of global flows and networks can be traced back to that constellation of dystopian urbanism and the utopianism of technological communications.

The predictions, of course, did not come true. Processes of urbanization everywhere intensified and accelerated. Real cities took center stage in social-scientific investigations of globalization. The result was a body of world- or global-city research that distinguished cities in terms of their place in the Wallersteinian hierarchy of metropolitan core, semi-periphery, and periphery. In this first phase of world-city research John Friedman thus distinguished among "core primary world cities" (New York, London, Tokyo, Paris, Los Angeles, and Chicago), "semi-peripheral primary world cities" (Rio, São Paulo, Singapore), "core secondary world cities" (San Francisco, Houston, Miami, Toronto, Madrid, Milan, Vienna, Sidney, Johannesburg), and "semi-peripheral secondary cities" (Mexico City, Caracas, Buenos Aires, Seoul, Taipei, Hong Kong, Bangkok, Manila).[21] Saskia Sassen in turn focused only on a few global cities, such as London, Tokyo, and New York, defining them primarily as the major centers of finance management and control.[22] Despite the differences in focus in Friedman and Sassen, most large African cities and many other Asian, Middle Eastern, and Latin American cities fell through the cracks of an approach that opposed the genuinely modern city to the developmental city and that still seemed predicated on the idea of globalization as a new version of the modernization theories of the post–World War II era.

Scholars began to worry that the "regulating fiction" of the global city could have dismal consequences for urban populations when a city's success was measured by its participation in globality, just as the threat of not becoming global might mean stagnation and immiseration. Clearly, the notion of the global city as telos for urban ambitions across the world still rested on the earlier division between the First and the Third World. The "global city" was increasingly recognized and understood as a scholarly construct, rather than a real place, a tangible object. Independent of the scholarly aims of its early proponents (Friedman, Sassen), the global city had become a slogan serving either to claim avant-garde status for certain, primarily Western centers of finance and services or to articulate ambitions elsewhere to join the urban upper crust. Typically, such ambitions manifested themselves in the national symbolism of laying claim to the world's tallest skyscraper, even if horizontal building was the prevailing mode, as in Kuala Lumpur (the Petrona Towers) or in Shanghai (Pudong).[23] Certainly until 9/11, if not beyond, the skyscraper has maintained its image as master signifier of modernity and of the global city. However, one must heed critics such as Jennifer Robinson who argue that the conceit of the global city has itself become a way of reasserting Western notions of advanced modernity and urban developmentalism which ignores many vital aspects of urban life that fall outside its purview.[24] London, New York, and Tokyo are, to be sure, global cities in the specific sense of being centers of stock markets, global finance, and services, but the point is to recognize with Anthony D. King that today all cities are world cities.[25] Indeed, all cities are affected by the structural realignments of capitalist economies across the world, the changing role of nation-states in political economy, the ever more complex negotiations between globality and locality. This alternative notion of world cities would include cities in the older industrial core states (Detroit, Manchester) and industrial cities in the former Soviet bloc that have been left in ruins as a result of deindustrialization. It would also include the cities in the marginalized zones of the world economy which feature their own brand of vital urban life (sub-Saharan African cities), but remain largely excluded from Western-style globality.

In an attempt to expand the field of urban research Peter Marcuse and Ronald van Kempen speak of "globalizing cities," Simon During speaks of "regional world cities," and Robinson advocates shifting the discourse toward "ordinary cities."[26] Such semantic strategies are intended to suggest that urban transformations are not limited to the world centers of finance, services, and media, but that they resonate everywhere, even if to different degrees and in clearly asymmetric fashion. Nevertheless, Robinson's and During's suggestions, while laudable in spirit, don't strike me as semantically or theoretically satisfactory. In some sense even the world's most influential urban centers of finance and services are also robustly regional, and they produce their own locality. The notion of the ordinary city in turn risks veiling the vast asymmetries of power and influence between cities. By comparison, King's rhetoric of exaggeration seems programmatically useful, since it forces one to acknowledge the effects of globalization on all cities of the world, thus expanding the field of debate and suggesting further research into the varieties of the urban condition today.

CITY CULTURES AND MODERNITY

Invaluable as much of this earlier globalization and urban-theory discourse was, it was often tone-deaf to questions about culture. The cultural dimensions of globalization remained poorly understood, either because theoretical and disciplinary frames marginalized culture as epiphenomenon or for the simple reason that "authentic" culture was seen as that which is subjectively shared by a given community and therefore local, whereas only economic processes and technological change were perceived as universal and global.[27] In this reductive account the local was either privileged as cultural tradition to be preserved as authentic and resistant, or it was held to be overcome as indigenous and obsolete. By contrast, the global functioned as "progress," seen either as panacea and promise or as a force of alienation, domination, and dissolution—another very traditional binary of modernity discourse. This global-local dichotomy prominent in the antiglobalization discourse, however, was as homogenizing as the alleged cultural homogenization of the global it opposed. It fell significantly behind the transnational understanding of modern cultural practices that was already achieved by segments of the modernist and avant-garde movements a hundred and more years ago. Rather than offering a new perspective on contemporary culture, it merely recycled an older sociological model for analyzing modernity (tradition or indigenous culture vs. modernity, Gemeinschaft vs. Gesellschaft, community vs. society), without any reflection on how the modernizing and globalizing processes of the twentieth century have made that nineteenth-century model obsolete.

Here one encounters a major weakness of the antiglobalization position in matters of culture. Such views typically posit the cultural dimension of globalization rather one-dimensionally as Americanization via Coca-Cola, McDonald's, and Nike. While the inevitable interaction between the local and the global in all matters is now widely acknowledged, glocalization should be considered a challenge rather than a solution. One must focus on differential histories and deep cultural knowledge as they shape the incorporation of the global in local or regional economies and cultures.[28] Indeed, the glocal will take different shapes in different cities. The methodological issues this raises are, however, not easy to solve. If globalization theorists suffer from presentism and easily lose historical specificity, the historical studies of cities are typically rich in empirical detail, but risk losing the global picture. The dialectical tension between the global and the local must be maintained. The often-heard argument that the persistence of strong local and historical specificities proves the weakness of globalization is not persuasive. One could easily argue the other way around by saying that the global proves its strength precisely in its ability to incorporate the local and to be transformed by and adapted to it. After all, incorporation will always be locally inflected and negotiated as the essays in this volume testify. The analysis of urban imaginaries and concrete ways of life may help one get beyond the methodological limitations of presentist model building and merely empirical historiography alike. Similarities *and* differences will emerge and remain in tension with each other as one studies different urban imaginaries side by side. Today's world cities in the broadest sense neither appear as intrinsically unique, nor can they serve as metaphor of some global whole. They are both part and whole at the same time.

If world-systems theory provided key arguments to study globalization historically, the more recent resurgence of debates about modernity after postmodernity offers another model to get at the cultural dimensions of globalization. It is no accident that ever since the waning of the debate about "postmodernism" and the rise of "globalization" as master signifier of our time the discourses of modernity and modernism have staged a remarkable comeback. Jean-François Lyotard's provocative quip that any work of art has to be postmodern before it can become genuinely modern has come true in ways he could hardly have foreseen.[29] There is much talk these days of modernity at large, second modernity, liquid modernity, alternative modernity, countermodernity, and what not.[30] Modernity and its complex and conflicted relationship to modernism across the world is being reassessed in architecture and urban studies today as it is in literature, the visual arts, music, anthropology, and postcolonial studies.

In a certain way, this is not so surprising. Modernity discourse has always been much more closely tied to issues of culture, history, philosophy, and the arts than has globalization discourse. The very history of the word in different languages points to the oscillation between the aesthetic and the social. Both *modernité* in French and *die Moderne* in German carry stronger artistic connotations than the English word *modernity*. As a result there is no immediate equivalent in French or in German for the English term *modernism*. Furthermore, modernity has been understood in its constitutive relationship with the European Enlightenment in its historical evolution and differentiation, a relationship that has been a bone of contention in Europe itself ever since the French Revolution and that has taken center stage in U.S. debates about postmodernity and postcoloniality. One of the most salutary developments in recent years has been the insight into the spread of modernity and modernism across the world, in their transnational, cosmopolitan dimension as much as in their colonial inscriptions.

Accordingly, one basic assumption underlying the essays of this volume is the fact that urban modernity is not limited to the West. The non-Western cultures of this world have all been deeply affected by globalization in an extension, acceleration, and transformation of processes that go back to the age of conquest and colonization. By the later twentieth century, modernity had pervaded all urban spaces, even if asymmetrically and to different degrees. As postcolonial and recent modernism studies have shown, colonial cities had their own very specific modernity distinct from the modernity of the Western metropolis.[31] Indeed, the contemporary phase of globalization must be understood as having emerged from earlier forms of modernity, their political economy, their urban and industrial forms, and their own coding of the international and the colonial, the cosmopolitan and the worldly. After all, many of today's world cities are formerly colonial cities and carry colonial legacies within them. Urban developments in the colonies were clearly affected by practices in the metropole and vice versa. The colonial or postcolonial city cannot be had without the metropole, but then the metropole wouldn't have become metropole without the colonial city. This dialectic deserves further comparative study.

It is my belief that the major sites of cultural globalization in the twenty-first century are the emerging megacities of what used to be called the Third World rather than the ever more musealized cities of Europe or the overanalyzed cities of New York (as modernist space) and Los Angeles (as postmodernist space). Both New York and Los Angeles continue to feed the frenzy of cultural globalization, especially in their function as nodes for globally operating media enterprises, but the focus of urban research is shifting away from such older Western cities. The aim of this book is to open up architectural, urban, and cultural studies to the imaginative geographies of alternative or different modernities that are usually sidelined by the still-dominant focus on the northern transatlantic in much of the Western academy. Such an approach is all the more urgent since the giddy utopianism of the 1990s, with its celebration of global flows and limitless markets and its catchwords of glocalization and cultural hybridities, received a double blow with the market meltdown of 2000 and the attacks of 9/11 and their worldwide political effects. The world remains much less global than even moderate globalization discourse suggests. Even at its highpoint in the 1990s and apart from certain globally disseminated brand names such as Nike, globalization operated in transnational, overlapping, but geographically limited clusters, rather than evenly across the world. Globalization is thus not just a question of inclusion versus exclusion, but involves an ever-changing process of geographically bound and distinct intensities. Rather than opposing the global and the local in a vertical and hierarchical relationship, it may be more appropriate to think in terms of shifting horizontal zones of regional relations such as customs unions or security alliances, for instance between Western and Eastern Europe, a South Asian cluster, the Mercosur in Latin America, the Central American economies with their relation to the United States, and so forth. Rather than producing connectivities and flows equally between all regions of the planet, globalization functions in horizontal clusters through and among which global, local, and regional dimensions are ricocheting with varying intensities and breadth. Analyzing the role of specific cities and their imaginaries in relationship to other cities in such geographic clusters remains a desideratum for further research.

NOTES ON THE ESSAYS

The essays in this volume do not embrace the imagination of the emperor in Italo Calvino's *Invisible Cities*. They are closer to sharing Marco Polo's perspective. Except—and here I take a step beyond the European traveler of Calvino's fiction—these Marco Polos, the contributors to this volume, bring a deep knowledge from the cities they are bound to in their lives and their work. The confluence of their visions gives a better understanding of the complexities at stake as one tries to imagine other cities and other worlds under the spell of globalization.

Issues of history and thus the history of globalization itself loom large in this book. Most of the essays share the assumption that in order to understand present-day urban imaginaries one must be attuned to the imaginaries which cities remember as their past. Here the utopian promise of modernity has shaped, in however different forms, the earlier histories of Buenos Aires and Bombay, São Paulo and Mexico City, Istanbul and Johannesburg. There is a consensus among the contributors that this modernist city, characterized by urban planning, developed infrastructure, public services and institutions, and the leading role of the national state, has been dismantled and transformed in recent decades by neoliberal economics and privatization as much as by new waves of migration from country to city and by transnational migrations.

Indeed, urban transformations of recent decades across the world are by and large the local results of the influx of transnational corporations and investments, world-trade agreements and disagreements, the weakening of the state and its sovereignty, increasing poverty worldwide, and the growth of privatization in the relation between public and private domains. The urban effects of such processes are described in detail by Teresa Caldeira for São Paulo, Beatriz Sarlo for Buenos Aires, Néstor Canclini for Mexico City, Farha Ghannam for Cairo, Gyan Prakash for Mumbai, Yingjin Zhang for Beijing, and, though in a more theoretical mode, by Ackbar Abbas for the Chinese city more generally.

The global megalopolis of today—Canclini in his essay on Mexico City speaks tellingly of the "monstropolis"—is indeed significantly different from Third World modernist cities of the twentieth century. With ever-increasing frequency, entirely new, sprawling, urban regions (Shenzhen, the Pearl River Delta) replace the slowly grown colonial or postcolonial cities that developed indigenously and in relation to the West over centuries. But traditional cities, too, have lost much of the bounded nature that made them nodes of national identity, centers of production, and sites of classical political discourse. As Caldeira argues, new forms of governmentality are emerging in what Appadurai has called "disjunctive democracy."[32] Canclini laments the inevitable belatedness, if not collapse of all urban planning under such conditions of uncontrolled growth and immiseration. Yet, as Gyan Prakash points out, the narrative of the rise and fall of the modern city tends to forget the problematic layering of the older modernist city itself. The tensions between the modern and its powerful traditional others (Bombay), traditional elites and fear of new immigrants (Buenos Aires), conflictual racial imaginaries and fear of urban violence (differently in São Paulo and in Johannesburg), the complex and changing relation of country to city (Mumbai, Johannesburg)—all of this suggests that the conflicts and tensions that characterize contemporary urban cultures have their predecessors in earlier decades. Nothing is new, but everything is changed.

The same is true for Enwezor's essay on the proliferation of biennales of contemporary art in African, Asian, and Latin American cities (Johannesburg, Seoul, Istanbul, São Paulo) and for Abbas's essay on the rise of the commodity production of fakes in the emergent capitalist power of the People's Republic of China. Both essays deal with the transformation, to put it in Brechtian terms, of the good old into the bad new. Different as their topics are, both authors discuss the multiple ways in which biennales and the fake are related to the image and representation of cities. Both deal with appropriations of cultural forms from the West—the art biennale and commodity design—in what used to be called the periphery. Fakes and forgeries are normally thought of as a threat to the domain of authentic art. In Abbas's essay, however, the fake is discussed as a phenomenon of commodity production made possible in East Asia at a time when cities such as Beijing, Shanghai, Guangzhou, and Shenzhen have become exposed to media and advertising representations of Western-designed commodities and when a basic split has emerged in the world economy between urban regions focused on manufacture and those specializing in service and design. The fake commodity is thus a significantly new cultural phenomenon of a globalizing economy that not only brings new challenges to prevailing patent and copyright law but also deterritorializes traditional notions of authenticity and originality in the world of urban commodities. Analogously, the appropriation of the biennale in the postcolonial world as a cultural form of expression is not just a fake imitation of its Western model—mere spectacle, all of it, as some art theorists would claim—but a conscious strategy of challenging the Western-art markets by posing fundamental problems of cultural translation between Western art and its others and by creating new forms of spectatorship in which spectators are able to encounter other experimental cultures without wholly possessing them, thus being trained in a new kind of cosmopolitanism.

Several essays focus on the relation of country to city, thus pointing to another dimension of globalization's historical depth.[33] What emerges in the essays by Judin, Prakash, and, in a different way, Mehrotra is a tale of two cities in one—the rural in the urban, the poor in the rich, the amorphous in the structured—but again the local conditions and histories make for significant variations. The conflict of country and city is of course a deeply nineteenth-century phenomenon, and it is carried forth in contemporary processes of urbanization, though in significantly different forms that can hardly be compared to the nineteenth-century constellations in Europe.

Thus, in Johannesburg the spatial and racial threads binding country and city have fundamentally changed direction since the end of apartheid. With the end of urban-rural segregation, the rural is now invading the city while the devastations of apartheid continue to haunt country life. Judin asks whether any future racial unity in Johannesburg can be forged out of such lasting divisions, whether the rural in the urban holds any possibilities for architecture and settlement, and whether it can be a seed of the future, rather than festering only as a symptom of the past. If Judin describes the country in the city, Prakash in addition focuses on the reverse development, arguing that in the megacities of the global South, urban form has imposed itself on much of the countryside, thus making obsolete the classical bounded city as space of civil society and political discourse. Prakash's reflections on today's Mumbai thus resonate strongly with Caldeira's discussion of politics in São Paulo. But even within choking and sprawling urbanization, there emerge new structures of mobility, provisionality, and entrepreneurship, as Mehrotra suggests in his analysis of what he calls the kinetic or bazaar city in India, which enters into an always transitory and improvisational relationship with the static city of colonial and postcolonial architecture and institutions. Mehrotra speaks of a "pirate modernity," while Abdou Maliq Simone, in his essay on Douala, a postcolonial city very different from Mumbai, sees African counter-urbanism at work in the displacement and de-anchoring of traditional structures of conviviality. What Simone sees emerging is a new urbanism of fragmentation, risk, and a radical living in the present moment. And yet there are multiple resonances between Mehrotra and Simone as both focus on people's creative use of social space. People and their resources of action, talk, look, and gesture are, after all, in Simone's felicitous expression, the infrastructure of lived urban space. Of course, there is always the double danger of either romanticizing the past of the modernist city and condemning the present or of uncritically celebrating the newly emergent city at the expense of past forms of urban life. While placing different emphases on past or present, the essays of this volume locate themselves in that tension and subtly refuse to make one-dimensional choices of assessment. The future of cities is neither panacea nor apocalypse.

Thus even where the negative effects of economic globalization loom large, as described in the essays on Latin American cities, there are moments of hope. Caldeira and Canclini attempt to draw on cultural and political change that might make the city a place of civic identification and refuge against the vertigo of globalization (Canclini) or a space of new forms of grassroots organization in which the current inequalities of access to media and culture can be overcome. The case of urban Latin America is especially interesting in that its colonial days and thus its postcoloniality date much further back than those of African or South Asian cities. As a result, much of Latin America, certainly Mexico and the countries of the Southern Cone, participated fully in the utopian and revolutionary promises of twentieth-century Western modernity. However, the current developments toward privatization, initiated in several Latin American countries by the military dictatorships of the 1970s and 1980s, have dismantled the structures of the modern state and its national and urban mission of providing public services and public architecture, general education and civic institutions. Cities such as Buenos Aires, São Paulo, and Mexico City have moved inexorably from modernism and its utopian promise for all to the postmodernism of gated communities and favelas, conspicuous consumerism for some and dire poverty for others.

A surprising resonance appears between the Bombay in Prakash's essay, a dynamic modern cosmopolitan city that emerged as both secular and national from colonial rule, and the Buenos Aires in Sarlo's essay, whose emphatically embraced European legacies made it unique in Latin America. The difference between Buenos Aires and Bombay/Mumbai is located primarily in their divergent histories of colonization. Modernist Buenos Aires developed in the twentieth century as a postcolonial city of immigration in which the Hispanic-criollo elites lost clout over time to a rising middle class and to populist political leaders. Sarlo places great emphasis on the early development of the advanced urban infrastructure in Buenos Aires and its social and political implications, something not immediately grasped and valued by visitors from abroad such as Katherine Dreier or Marcel Duchamp. The self-projection of Buenos Aires as the most European of Latin American cities reigned supreme, and given the absence of an indigenous population and the lack of visible architectural signs of colonization, there was also no subalternity to contend with. Bombay, on the other hand, always lived the double life of modernity and its others within. In its mix of ethnicities, religions, and castes Bombay could not evade the presence of subalternity, but even so it successfully established itself as a genuinely cosmopolitan city. In the Mumbai of today by contrast, globalization and provincialization through Hindu fundamentalism have de-cosmopolitanized the city, such that Prakash speaks of a city in ruins. Mumbai is indeed an industrial ruin, comparable in some ways to the Rust Belts of Europe and the United States, but—and this is Prakash's point—in its embrace of an exclusivist regionalism, it has also become a political ruin. Buenos Aires, a city whose culture was from the beginning deeply embedded in translations from Europe that created its vitality and allure, found its "Third World destiny"—or, if you will, its Southern subalternity in relation to the North—when it was simply abandoned by the International Monetary Fund and other institutions of the global economy in 2001 and left to its own devices. Hannah Arendt once philosophized about stateless people as superfluous. Despite Argentina's moderate rebound, its recent history looms as large as that of a whole country declared superfluous: worldless, as it were, in a most immediate, material sense. In the age of neoliberal globalization, it may be only one step from a city in ruins to a country in ruins.

The most radical transformation of urban landscapes today is no doubt found in Chinese cities such as Beijing and Shanghai. Zhang's essay on global, local, and translocal imaginaries in the frenzy of Beijing's reconstruction as reflected in the recent cinema gives a vivid account of how everyday lives are deterritorialized and thrown into drift by a pace of urban change that for many is beyond the imagination. The cinema becomes an essential medium to work through a great leap in urban change that happens faster and on a larger scale than anywhere ever before.

This volume concludes on a strong literary note with an essay by the Turkish novelist Orhan Pamuk, an essay that is also a central chapter in his marvelous, recently translated book *Istanbul: Memories and the City*. Many of the threads of *Other Cities, Other Worlds* come together in Pamuk's work, which is as much memory of the Istanbul of his childhood as it is urban sociology, intellectual history, and travel essay. As Sarlo does for Buenos Aires, Pamuk describes the imaginary of Istanbul through the prism of its writers and of visitors from abroad. Central to Pamuk's mental map of Istanbul, however, is *hüzün*, the melancholy of a formerly cosmopolitan city in ruins, the tristesse and black mood that is shared among Istanbul's residents since the dismembering of the Ottoman Empire and the loss of past glories. In the urban scenes and tableaux Pamuk conjures, hüzün becomes palpable almost as a material reality. In the linguistic play between the Sufi mystics' hüzün, which acknowledges hope within loss, Robert Burton's melancholy, and Claude Lévi-Strauss's tristesse, Pamuk suggests an urban imaginary that is determined in the minds of Istanbul's residents both by Turkish history and by the literary imagination of Western visitors from Gérard de Nerval and Gustave Flaubert to Théophile Gautier and André Gide. These travelers of the nineteenth century and early twentieth created an Istanbul under Western eyes that Pamuk, like other Turkish writers before him, has incorporated into his own memories of the city. The local and the global, the present and the past remain in productive tension in Pamuk's imaginary of Istanbul. The result of hüzün, however, is not the frozen paralysis of melancholy, nor is it the sense of historical decadence so prominent in Lévi-Strauss's account of São Paulo and of Indian cities in *Tristes Tropiques*. It is, rather, the creative tension between the Western gaze and his own Turkish formation that has made Pamuk into a genuinely cosmopolitan writer with strong Istanbulian roots. In a way, he is Marco Polo as resident explorer. In his book on Istanbul he never speaks of an urban imaginary, but he has offered one of the best definitions of its core elements: "What gives the city its special character is not just its topography or its buildings but rather the sum total of every chance encounter, every memory, letter, color, and image jostling in its inhabitants' crowded memories after they've been living, like me, on the same streets for fifty years."[34] In order to arrive at such a view one has to know the city intimately and at the same time be able to get lost in it in the way Walter Benjamin suggested in his *Berlin Childhood around 1900*.

As much as one needs the broad variety of social-scientific urban studies, one also needs and cherishes accounts of urban imaginaries such as Benjamin's or Pamuk's, as they conjure up and embody a certain place at a certain time, thus encouraging reflections about other cities, other worlds.

NOTES

1. For a superb critical summary of the field of global cities research see the editors' introduction to Brenner and Keil 2006 (1–16). For a sustained critique of and alternative to the binarism, economism, and functionalism of the earlier global or world-cities research by David Harvey and Manuel Castells, John Friedman and Saskia Sassen, see Smith 2001.
2. Chakrabarty 2000.
3. Calvino 1983.
4. The "production of locality" is one of the most useful concepts developed in Appadurai 1996.
5. Spivak 2003, 9.
6. See, for instance, Appadurai 1996; Hannerz 1996; Pieterse 2004; Smith 2001.
7. See, most recently, Taylor 2004; also Lefebvre 1991b.
8. Michael Peter Smith (2001) is most interesting in his attempt to reconstruct urban theory under the rubric of the transnational.
9. Leslie Sklair (1998) offers one of the most influential descriptions of the transnational capitalist class.
10. Robertson 1994.
11. Rydell 1984 and Rydell 1993 are two of the best guides to the history of World's Fairs.
12. Paul Hirst and Grahame Thompson (1996) develop their economic analysis in order to dispute the prevalence of a presentist globalization discourse.
13. David Harvey's (1989) notion of time-space compression, once freed from its technological and economic determinism, is especially useful for literary and cultural analysis.
14. Said 1978, 68, 71.
15. This dialectic has been emphasized well in Bennett 1988. See also Mitchell 1989.
16. McLuhan 1964.
17. Wallerstein 1979; Arrighi 1994.
18. Lefebvre 1991a, 1991b; Castells 1996; Harvey 1989; Soja 1989. For an excellent critique of their work see Smith 2001.
19. Hopkins 2002.
20. Koolhaas 1978. Koolhaas's own work has significantly expanded, from the Western metropolis to cities like Lagos and urban regions such as the Pearl River Delta.
21. Friedman 1986.
22. Sassen 1991.
23. King 2004, 3–22. King's book is a sophisticated theoretical and historical treatment of modernity and global culture in a postcolonial world. Together with Smith 2001 and Pieterse 2004, it counts among the very best of recent urban and global studies.
24. Robinson 2006.

25. King 1990, 82.

26. Marcuse and van Kempen 2000; During 2005, 94; Robinson 2006.

27. Culture as epiphenomenon of capital prevails in David Harvey's (1989) Marxist approach, whereas the identification of culture with place has deep roots in anthropology. For an excellent critique of the conflation of place and culture, see Gupta and Ferguson 1997, 1–29.

28. Jan Nederveen Pieterse, for instance, shows how wrong the McDonaldization thesis is both empirically and theoretically (2004, 49–52).

29. Lyotard 1983, 71–82.

30. Especially influential was Arjun Appadurai (1996) with his model of ethnoscapes, ideoscapes, mediascapes, finance-scapes, and technoscapes. For the new vital discourse about modernity in a global key, see also Gaonkar 1999; "Multiple Modernities," special issue, *Daedalus* 128.1 (winter 2000); Mitchell 2000; and Knauft 2002. For a critical view of this new modernity discourse, see Jameson 2002. For the analogous discussion in research on aesthetic modernism, see Huyssen 2005, 6–18.

31. Good examples of such work are Lee 1999, on modernism in Shanghai, and Hosagrahar 2005, on indigenous modernities in Indian architecture and urbanism.

32. Holston and Appadurai 1999.

33. For a classic study of this relationship, see Williams 1973.

34. Pamuk 2005, 110.

LATIN AMERICA

Beatriz Sarlo
....

CULTURAL LANDSCAPES

BUENOS AIRES FROM INTEGRATION TO FRACTURE

The occupation of the plains along the coastline of the Río de la Plata took three centuries. But after the civil wars, after the genocide that deprived the last of the pre-Hispanic inhabitants of their lands or slaughtered them in the 1880s, and after the defeat of traditional social fractions in the provinces followed by the violent unification of national territory in the last third of the nineteenth century, Buenos Aires entered into an original process of growth and consolidation. In the first year of the twentieth century a popular magazine, *Caras y Caretas*, stated that the city had dramatically changed over the course of five years. The remark was accurate: a wide, mile-long avenue had been layed out leading from the government house to the House of Congress. In a city that had been but a village in the nineteenth century this amounted to a decisive urban intervention. In less than a century Buenos Aires had not only emerged as a built city but had also decided what form it would take: a grid of identical blocks, regular quadrangles of a hundred meters on each side. It was a city plan that homogenized all urban space.

Buenos Aires was an international city from the very beginning of this modernization process, which had begun during the

Cupolas along
Avenida de Mayo,
downtown. Photo
by Facundo de
Zuviría.

last three decades of the nineteenth century. The projects for the modern
Buenos Aires combined models from different European sources. Paris was
never the only ideal of the elites, though they did design their hôtels de ville
in the Beaux Arts style. For the most part, public buildings did not present the
imprint of a dominant French style; their façades showed the aesthetic consequences of neoclassicism, Italian style, art deco, and even expressionism
and modernism. Erected in the 1930s, the Obelisk, a symbol of the city, is a
discreet modernist object, white, squared, innocent of the imperial grandeur
of the French obelisks. Against the commonplace many times repeated, Paris
was not the only European model. It was, certainly, an urban myth: a system
of images and a dream that in twentieth-century popular culture resonates
with the modern myth that is New York. An American imaginary developed
in Buenos Aires under the European imaginary and the boastful claims of
the Argentine elites.

When Le Corbusier visited Buenos Aires in 1929, he was struck by the originality of the small homes built by immigrant Italian maestros, modest houses that combined simple geometric forms. He admired their classical and at the same time modern image, which resulted from the local application of pure forms simplified by poverty and a lack of craftsmanship. He also pointed out that, unlike many European cities with an emblematic river (Rome, London, Florence, Paris, Budapest, Prague), Buenos Aires had turned its back to the river so that it could neither be seen nor reached by its inhabitants. Both traits, for Le Corbusier, pointed toward the local inflection of the imported projects.

What Le Corbusier pointed out is true. Without reflecting the image of any European city in particular, Buenos Aires is composed of fragments taken from many of them and distorted or recomposed in the Río de la Plata. The wide avenues remind one of Madrid, Barcelona's *ensanche*, and Parisian boulevards; the Teatro Colón was built *alla italiana*, as was the national government palace; the first skyscraper reminds one of Chicago, and the second and third bear the traits of modernism; the railway stations were built in an "English" cottage style, and the central station of Retiro resonates with the main forms of steel-and-glass industrial architecture. The city zoo combines a mixture of styles that mirror the city's eclectic quotations: Norman pavilions, pagodas, hothouses that copy those of the Universal Exhibitions, Japanese bird cages, and Roman temples.

Argentine culture is deeply embedded in translation, but the idioms it translates derive from almost every point of Western Europe. Its cultural mixture has diverse origins. The comparison between Buenos Aires and Paris (a comparison that does not come to the mind of a Parisian) reflects the desire that moved the cultural will of the elites. Were these men asked about it, they would have said that Paris was the city they most admired. But this rather inevitable choice—Paris was the city most admired around the world—met natural limits and economic conditions that modified the initiatives and prevented the modernization project from copying a single ideal model. The elites wanted a city that could provide a metropolitan pole and a modern townscape, and they pursued this to the greatest extent possible given the limits of their ideology, the principles of contemporary urbanism, and the money they had available for public investment.

Street in the proletarian suburb Villa Soldati. Photo by Facundo de Zuviría.

The originality of the city imagined and, partly, built by the elites is rooted in a combination of different technological, urban, and aesthetic models. As with Argentine culture as a whole, the originality of Buenos Aires lies in the individual elements that form the mixture, captured, transformed, and deformed by a huge system of translation. Buenos Aires is a translation from many languages and urban texts in conflict, a translation that bears the distortions of American space and social reality. It results from imitation as much as it does from bricolage and recycling.

Buenos Aires was built according to European models that, paradoxically, solved non-European problems, because modern Buenos Aires, unlike cities in the Old World, began almost from scratch. The immense Río de la Plata washes the low coast of the immense plains, which are monotonous and not very attractive as a natural landscape. Along the river there once stood a bunch of old colonial buildings, with little aesthetic value and no character, which were demolished during the first decade of modernization; some old criollo mansions that, with their patios and open galleries, were more charming than refined; and two or three colonial churches that were among the humblest of those built by the Spaniards in Latin American capital cities. In the Río de la Plata region the Spanish colony was poor and did not flour-

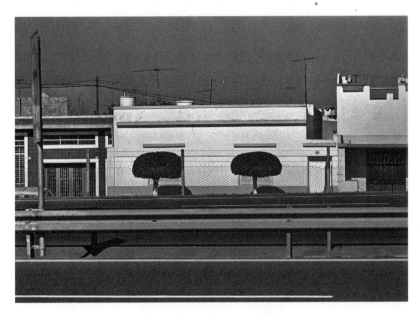

Working-class home across the highway. Photo by Facundo de Zuviría.

ish in the style of baroque artifice of the great viceroyal capitals of the New World such as Lima, Bogotá, or México. The colonial buildings that survive in Buenos Aires are modest examples of neoclassicism or very simple baroque churches. There was no court architecture or mestizo art because there were no flourishing native cultures in the territories south of the Alto Perú.

On this ground, deprived of the rich documents of colonial history, Buenos Aires invented itself from scratch. To this historical vacuum (a sort of original sin of the city), the wide plain added a symbolic and material emptiness that could be sublime even though it was never seen as picturesque and only rarely as beautiful. As late as 1930, when Buenos Aires was the most important city in Latin America, an Italian visitor wrote, "Buenos Aires is a slice of pampa translated into a city."[1] He was right, because the plain had been overlaid by the geometric principle of the regular urban grid.

The regularity of this grid was often remarked on by European travelers and Argentine intellectuals, all of whom shared the opinion that Buenos Aires was monotonous to a degree. Returning from Europe in the second decade of the twentieth century, the novelist Manuel Gálvez fell into despair at finding a city that avoided all picturesque beauty and lacked the local color of the

Spanish villages he had visited. Buenos Aires's modernity had been achieved through the regularity of a project deprived of cultural spontaneity and popular character. By comparing Buenos Aires with European cities, Gálvez was unable to recognize that, from a technical point of view, the monotony of the city grid embodied a trait of modernity absent from many of the Spanish and Italian towns he had visited.

At that time, Buenos Aires was a state-of-the-art city. It had the first line of subway trains in Latin America (built in 1913), up-to-date port facilities, paved streets, public parks designed by landscape architects, huge public buildings, sewers, telephones, and electricity. Unique to the city was the fact that these services were evenly distributed according to a socially balanced pattern that reached the poor as well as the wealthy neighborhoods. The street grid was a rational solution for disciplining urban growth, not only as an instrument of control but also as a symbolically unifying ideal. It also served as a pattern for the extension of services and technologies. But it seemed to have no picturesque potential or the ability to produce majestic perspectives.

Jorge Luis Borges was perhaps the only Argentine writer who grasped the quality of the modern in this city, with its geometrical expansion of streets extending toward the horizon. In 1921 he returned from Europe, where he had spent seven years, and before 1930 he had published his first three books of poems and his first three books of essays. In many of these early pieces he saw in the long straight streets the platonic form of the modern city. In 1923 he wrote,

> The poor neighborhood is a reflection of our weariness.
> My steps weakened
> Trying to reach the horizon;
> And I remained among the houses,
> The square blocks,
> Different and all alike
> As if they were repeated remembrances
> Of a single city-block.[2]

A tedious linear sameness of streets intersecting at right angles defines the physiognomy of Buenos Aires. A "single block," writes Borges, offers the essential image of the city. Vis-à-vis the surrounding plain, the grid is an adequate response to the simple coordinates of the pampas. Buenos Aires is the geometric border of the plain.

> And the chance of the pampas in the horizon
> and the wasteland that flows in grass and hedges;
> and the pulpería, so clear as yesterday's moon,
> looks familiar as a remembrance of the street corner.[3]

Borges, cleverly, understood that even if Buenos Aires was not surrounded by a picturesque landscape, the city should not aim to overcompensate for this imperfection with an architectural search for a character that would contradict its milieu and destiny. In that same decade of the 1920s Borges produced one of the basic ideologemes of his literature; he coined an image—"las orillas" (the border, the edge)—that represents Buenos Aires's geographical situation and also the Argentine writer's place in reference to European culture. Buenos Aires is a border to the plains, the limit and margin where the pampas touch the city and the city establishes its relation with its hinterland. This marginal condition (in Spanish the adjective could be *orillero,* which also conveys boldness, even criminality) can be thought of as characteristic of a city built in the nineteenth century at the most remote point of America, *finis terrae.* Buenos Aires, the border, the last limit in front of the vacuum of the ocean that severs it from Europe while allowing it to communicate with Europe.

At the end of the 1940s, another writer, Héctor Murena, published a book, *America's Original Sin,* in which he developed the idea of a city as *finis terrae.* The main thesis is as simple as the plot of a tragedy. In Europe men live on a territory over which history has deposited its layers. Working his field, the plowman cuts furrows into the layers of soil, which carry the memories of centuries. The earth has been humanized because it has been occupied by generation upon generation. As immigrants arrived in Argentina, they used to repeat, "In my homeland, I was raised in a house where there stood the bed and the table used by my forefathers."[4] Murena felt that the American difference consisted of being deprived of the density of the past. The Europeans that came to America abandoned places where it was possible to find meaning and established themselves in a wasteland empty of civilization and devoid of temporality. They could not and did not desire to construct com-

El ciudadano: Alemania
Avenue at Viamonte Street
downtown. Photo by
Facundo de Zuviría.

munities where the experiences could count as history and memory. They
built cities and societies overnight, cities that were completely turned toward
the future, societies that had no link to tradition. The American condition
was, thus, to be expelled from a world of meaning that had accumulated
through the centuries. Certainly, Murena had read some Heidegger.

Borges's idea of Buenos Aires is not as pessimistic as Murena's. He is less
tragic and more conflictive. He understands the contradiction between different cultures, a contradiction that has not been resolved, but that does not
amount solely to a fault, an imperfection, or a loss. For Borges, Buenos Aires
is geographically and symbolically an edge, that is to say, a space that does
not resolve itself on one side or the other, a line that folds and unfolds differences, but that also puts those differences into contact and communicates
with them. In other words, it is a frontier in the margin.

It was a peripheral modernity, brutal, reckless toward its inheritance, as all modernity was at some point. Above all, it was peripheral, claiming a recognition to which it was not fully entitled. But in the 1930s the development of the city was an impulse that promised not to be stopped. The construction of the city had something beautiful in its disorder. As Robert Arlt observed in 1929, "As on a stage, when lights are out and the props are left to themselves, there are houses cut in two, halls and rooms where the city-works have been left untouched, as by a miracle, a rectangle of wall-paper or a tableau from 'La vie Parisienne.' Steel and concrete structures seem more beautiful than a woman. Sewers. City-lights titillating in basements of yellow mud; the crunching and mumbling of an electric machine."[5] Arlt was describing a city in the making.

That Arlt compared Buenos Aires with a stage was quite meaningful. The city was being built at a frenetic pace that paradoxically responded also to an urban project, as if it should be ready for the next day's rehearsal. Buenos Aires was changing almost overnight: its streets were widened, and whole blocks of ancient buildings were torn down, becoming modern ruins; the new diagonal avenues introduced an almost expressionist perspective. The stage of a modern metropolis stems from an act of urban will and cultural improvisation. Buenos Aires was an explosion of history.

Writers like Roberto Arlt and Oliverio Girondo presented this new city through the techniques of collage. As for the European avant-garde, the city was not a continuum of time and space, but a montage of fragmentary images. In the 1920s and 1930s modernity's technical and communicational effects provoked a broken temporal experience and produced the impression that the city had no usable past: everything could be torn down and novelty was the only worthwhile quality to be sought. Buenos Aires had changed so fast that there had been no time to erase the scars of what it had been. As in a theater, the city-works went on night and day, finding only weak obstacles in the city grid.

Buenos Aires's simple geometricity impressed many visiting foreigners. In 1888 a Frenchman, Émile Daireaux, wrote, "Completely straight, the streets extend limitless. . . . I was taken by a sort of melancholy feeling walking along rows of houses that produce the effect of having been already seen."[6] Daireaux came from a country that had reformed its capital, Paris, according to the modern urban principles espoused by Baron Haussmann. But Haussmann's intervention took place on a built city, carrying the marks of a very long history. Parisian boulevards gave some regularity to a city that by and large did not lose its historical landmarks. Buenos Aires, on the contrary, lacked historical style: its style was to be found not in the past, but in the future.

In 1918, thirty years after the visit of Daireaux, an American woman, Katherine Dreier, a friend of Marcel Duchamp, discovered that in Buenos Aires even the best hotels did not admit women traveling by themselves. The city and the condition of women seemed to Dreier the product of a Hispanic culture, reactionary and anchored in a strong tradition. Buenos Aires did not strike her as a Southern metropolis, the Latin American Paris she had heard about, but as an imitation of, of all places, Brooklyn. She pointed, on one hand, to the monotony of the grid and, on the other, to the lack of a rich and dynamic society occupying public space: "One beautiful avenue, called the Avenida de Mayo, which stretches a little more than a mile might easily recall a Parisian boulevard, with its avenues of trees and its many cafes with small tables and chairs on the sidewalk. But how unlike Paris in reality! Here one rarely sees a woman, and, unlike Paris, only men frequent the cafes. Buenos Aires was constantly reminding me of Brooklyn. There was only a small section which was interesting and amusing, and the rest was endless, endless vistas of streets. Sometimes with good pavement, sometimes with bad, but just streets, streets, streets."[7]

In that same year Marcel Duchamp, well-known in the artistic milieu of New York and Paris, arrived in Buenos Aires in the hopes of settling down for a while. He had no friends in the city, and his visit went unacknowledged. Bored by a city that he considered only a small town, Duchamp returned to the United States several months later. In a couple of letters he wrote from Buenos Aires he judged that city severely and with condescension as a provincial and plain hollow, where nothing was known about contemporary art and the elites were rustic and ignorant. Dreier had the same impression regarding the taste of the elite that decorated its hôtels de ville with pompier art and had no idea about modern architecture.

These opinions on Buenos Aires adequately describe a society that had undergone a swift process of economic modernization, but whose habits were provincial, its morals catholic, and its refinements dated. However, the elites had led the process of modernization. They had instituted the demographic policies that, through immigration, had changed forever the cultural and social profile of the country.

Neither Dreier nor Duchamp were able (or cared) to see what was behind the rectangular grid of the straight streets. Those streets, "just streets," were the geometrical machine of modern Buenos Aires, which made possible its sweeping growth and dramatically multiplied its suburbs. Under those straight streets there were the sewers and the tunnels of the subway; on and above them, the rails of trams, the electric cables, and the telephone posts. While this functionality did not catch the attention of travelers coming from New York, it made all the difference when Buenos Aires was compared to the rest of Latin America. As a result of this technical structure, cultural change was taking place.

The web of services and transportation that Dreier and Duchamp failed to see was the most dynamic layer of the real city. These distinguished travelers overlooked the technical construction that moved the urban will in the design of a modern, regular, socially balanced city offering public services, schools, parks, and commercial centers, evenly distributed through the extension of its territory. Facing obstacles and debates, contradicting at times the interests of their own social group and of land speculators, the elites tried to avoid a city fractured along the lines of poverty and affluence. This endeavor produced a sort of mesocratic monotony which disgusted the intellectual travelers. However, less-well-known travelers who settled in the city, the European immigrants, would find material conditions which they had never experienced in the villages of their homeland.

Buenos Aires resulted from immigration. Certainly, all American cities received, through their history, people coming from other, and often very distant, parts of the world; America belongs to a civilization produced by drastic demographic changes. During the era of Spanish colonization, millions of Spaniards, using very cruel methods, established themselves in the lands that belonged to people of American origin. A Hispanic-criollo society was born with different grades of racial mixture. By the beginning of the nineteenth century, the cattle-breeding economy of the Río de la Plata was loosely organized in a predominantly rural society, formed by landowners and their gau-

chos, who were forced to work in the estancias by police edicts and the menace of military enrollment. Buenos Aires was a muddy and flooded village,
with neither parks nor public works, desolated, precarious, and ill-smelling
due to the slaughterhouses located close to the downtown area. Only after
1870 did Buenos Aires begin to consider herself as a future cosmopolitan
city. The formula that made this possible was an urban modernization project
combined with immigration.

The centrality of the city and the need for demographic policies appeared
together as early as the presidency of Domingo F. Sarmiento, where the wide
and wild plains and its cattle-breeding culture offered the perfect theater for
his despotism. Sarmiento trusted the civilizing power of the city, where civil
virtues could defeat the resistance of colonial tradition and civilize the pampas. His motto was: American-style farmers on the plains, schools for everybody, and a rich city to be the seat of a strong government. For Sarmiento,
the city was in itself a teaching machine for the formation of citizen-workers
(first of all in the formation of literate workers who could then achieve the
category of citizens). Immigrants were the central piece in this project, and
Argentina, he suggested, should obey the impulse of cultural internationalization.

Between 1880 and World War I, hundreds of thousands of immigrants
arrived in Buenos Aires. They were basically Spaniards and Italians, but also
Russians, Jews from Central and Eastern Europe, and Syrians. The Spanish
and Italian majority did not match the immigrant ideals defined by the elites,
who had imagined workers and artisans from Northern Europe—but those
immigrants, with good sense, preferred the United States.

However, at the beginning of the twentieth century, half of the inhabitants in Buenos Aires were foreigners, most of whom did not speak Spanish. Journals in Italian, German, or Yiddish were published by literate ethnic
minorities. In 1910, while the elites celebrated the centenary of Argentine
independence from Spain and rehearsed the brand-new rites of nationality,
one could hear on the streets of Buenos Aires exotic languages or a Spanish
pronounced with a peninsular accent very different from the criollo phonetic
version.

Over the Hispanic-criollo base, a population of foreigners established
itself whose members were younger and whose women were more fertile

than the native women. In a few decades, the immigrants and their children born in Argentina were more numerous than the Hispanic-criollos. These Europeans were not cosmopolitans; they were simply foreigners with international origins, coming from small villages, rural establishments, and picturesque landscapes. In their native lands the stones of churches and houses had been polished by the work of centuries. Their European villages were nothing when compared with the neutral extension of Buenos Aires; they were no bigger than any of the new neighborhoods where the immigrants settled. Such aspects of Buenos Aires did not impress Dreier and Duchamp, the travelers from New York, but they were overwhelming for the peasants who arrived from Extremadura, Galicia, or Calabria.

The immigrants were the protagonists of a process of identity, rebuilding what can be described as the cultural internationalization of a Latin American country. The overlapping cultural identities brought misunderstandings, disillusions, and conflicts. The Hispanic-criollo city did not recognize itself as a migratory city. The elites perceived that their Buenos Aires was increasingly occupied by foreigners, whom they had invited to come but whose impact they had not anticipated.

In 1910 a historian and literary critic of relevance, Ricardo Rojas, advanced an alarming diagnosis regarding urban transformation. He felt challenged by the journals, written in Yiddish, in Polish, in Italian, that communicated news about the Socialist Party or the trade unions; he had been told that immigrant clubs and schools, on whose walls hung pictures of foreign leaders, protected foreign languages and habits; he had seen foreign flags carried along the streets on the occasion of international anniversaries; he had noticed the Jews, with their hats and long coats, occupying traditional neighborhoods and raising temples. While Rojas did not wish to reject these recently arrived men and women, he worried about the methods through which they could be incorporated into a national culture. Education, in his opinion, was the privileged instrument for national acculturation. And, in fact, it was. The children of these immigrants were compulsively incorporated into public schools, where every cultural difference was repressed by the imposition of an Argentine credo. At the same time, the schools were enormously successful in providing immigrants access to literacy and enabling them to claim political and working rights.

The Jews fascinated (in every sense of the word), and their radical exoticism produced the first antisemitic phobias. But even those writers and intellectuals who could not be labeled antisemitic described the Jews as exotic children, as did Arlt: "Men speak a language more coarse and dry than the desert sand. The words echo like whips or drag as incomprehensible mutterings. For a moment, these men play like children, they push and hug each other, they run in the middle of the street, shouting as dogs; then, once more, they become rhythmically quiet and go on talking."[8]

The ethnic mixture changed the colors and the languages of Buenos Aires. Twenty years after Rojas's scared remarks, the process had drastically reconfigured the symbolic dimension, cultural and everyday life, and politics. With the immigrants also arrived trade-unionism, socialism, and anarchism. Political ideologies as well as labor organizations and new strategies of mobilization (strikes and street demonstrations) gave supplementary motives to the alarmed elites. Intellectuals of immigratory origins were considered as a threat, by dissolution, to national cultural unity. The process of internationalization ran parallel to the process of compulsory nationalization: both were faces of the same reality.

During the first three decades of the twentieth century, the debates returned to the same obsessive topics: racial and linguistic mixture; loss of identity due to unwanted internationalization; an endangered intellectual leadership that could not cope with the immigration problem. What does it mean to be an Argentine? Who is entitled to define the limits of a cultural field where everything is under the pressure of contamination? The once despised gaucho had disappeared, and the foreigners could offer no base of identification except their own varied forms of internationalism. This real and imagined faultline would define Argentina's future.

The heirs of the Hispanic-criollo elite sensed that their racial, cultural, and linguistic authenticity was threatened. "Our city is Babel," wrote Borges. Others, like Oliverio Girondo, a comrade of Borges in the avant-gardist trench, turned this loss of authenticity into a style. In the 1920s Girondo traveled through Europe preparing a book of poems about the cities on his itinerary. To these European postcards (Venice, Seville, Douarnez) he added other postcards representing Buenos Aires, where no lament over the loss of an organic culture or a tradition is to be found. Instead, he tried to present a new configuration of the poetic subject under metropolitan conditions.

It was the same with Arlt, who was a son of immigrants. He wrote, "Buenos Aires has four roofed streets, four roofed streets that offer refuge to the deprived: they are the shop-window of vagrancy, the museum of poverty; four roofed streets that represent the four cardinal points of human misery; four roofed streets that are the cauldron of filth, the sidewalk of illness, the sordid sidewalk of the beggars, the court de miracles of the petty adventurers in cosmopolis; four roofed streets and only one sadness: the sadness of empty pockets, women and immigrants with no hope, beaten men that find no shelter."[9]

Arlt perceived the contradictions of the international city, the ruin of every illusion of an organic community, the impossibility of translating experience into a common idiom. The city was full of people as never before, but it not only offered a shop window to the idle, a refuge to the distinguished solitary individual; it was also a desert where abstract capitalist relations destroyed the more archaic forms of community.

In the 1930s the idle walker was not always a flâneur, a dandy, or an artist. In Buenos Aires, after the world economic crisis, the vagabonds were also the unemployed, men whose immigratory dream had revealed itself to be a failure, their children, and the new migrants that were then arriving not from Europe but from the Argentine provinces. With a beating pulse, the labor market incorporated and expelled workers; in the process it produced new cultural configurations.

In the 1930s three factors proved fundamental to modern urban popular culture: soccer became a national mass sport; radio quickly developed commercial broadcasting while journals, illustrated tabloids, and magazines produced the habits of a new public; and tango gave the city not only its trademark music but also ideas for film and theater pieces. New masses and their tastes occupied the symbolic urban space and were the public of the local culture industry that flourished in the 1940s and 1950s. Mass culture, mass society: a new obsession.

The masses: José Ortega y Gasset inaugurated this topic in Spain and transferred it to Argentina with instantaneous success. Ezequiel Martínez Estrada, a writer of the same generation as Borges, wrote about the masses in the new city. He found that Buenos Aires was a sick excrescence of the pampas; even its skyscrapers were made of layers and layers of mud, masking a fake progress which he perceived as an undesirable disorder produced by the ambition and rootlessness of immigrants. In his view, the masses were especially weak and succumbed to the lure of false richness, false values, and a carnivalesque culture. In a city that did not honor its past, with no traditional patterns and no principles, the masses were a menacing shadow. They were formed not only by the children of immigrants (which began to constitute their better part) but by the new immigrants, coming from the backward regions of Andean Argentina. These new masses invaded the city and lived in *villas miseria* near it. They had no cultural pattern. They resisted all order because they were ignorant and blind to reason, inclined to follow their desires as recognized and articulated by demagogues; they were going to be the mob mobilized by Juan Perón in the 1940s and 1950s. This racist idiom shaped the terms of the debate.

The city that offered its stage to Peronist massive mobilization exhibited the traits of its metropolitan modernity. It was a predominantly white city even though it was occupied daily by workers of mestizo origin, who lived in the outskirts. It was surrounded by a belt of rich suburbia, modest neighborhoods, and *villas miseria*. Peronism extended the rights of citizenship to everybody: the intense use of the city by everybody and the new social rights came together and would stay together for two decades despite political instability and different military governments.

The end of the cycle arrived in 1976, with the military dictatorship. A word should be said about the debt that the City of Buenos Aires has yet to pay to this chapter of its past. The defense of human rights has been, since the very beginning, a global issue, perhaps the most positive face of cultural and political globalization because it produced immediate solidarity in many countries that also received thousands of exiles. During the Soccer World Cup in 1978, while a vast majority of Argentines chose to forget everything in the name of a repulsive nationalism, human-rights organizations were backed by little more than their own local militants and international opinion. Thus a small group of militants benefited from widespread international opinion, although their local echo was audible only when the dictatorship approached its end.

There were two Buenos Aireses living side by side during those terrible years: an underground city with a net of repression, death, and kidnapping, and an above-ground, wholly controlled city where expressions of resistance were isolated and, at the beginning, very rare. The visibility of the human-rights movement in the Plaza de Mayo during the weekly ceremony of the Madres was a sort of paradox: very few wanted to see what was going on there every Thursday. This blindness, due to fear and in many cases to the conviction that nothing could be done and that what had happened was irreversible, contributed to the most famous of Buenos Aires's images—the women with their white handkerchiefs in the plaza—which had wide international circulation.

The democratic transition made it possible for these images to illuminate the deeds denounced by the human-rights organizations, including the Madres de la Plaza de Mayo. But, unlike in Berlin, there is no evident symbolic place in Buenos Aires: no traces left by any structure metaphorically comparable to the Wall, and no political will in the government to obtain the sites occupied during the dictatorship by the Centros de Desaparición de Personas. The scars of this history have not healed, and may never heal. A *veduta* on this past must remain open forever. The question is what should be seen and how. There is no final answer to this question, as every monument should be thought of as a blueprint of a history that may not have a definitive version.

During those terrible years, the military imposed technocratic policies that led to a new chapter of authoritarian modernization in Buenos Aires: they expelled the poor from the city, moving them, through compulsory relocations, to the worst suburban zones; they consolidated material differences that divided the rich from the poor; they technologized the city grid and services, abandoning, at the same time, what had been a balanced pattern of distribution of facilities distribution, transportation, and access; they sorted out the traits of a new communications and urban profile that responded to economic globalization and followed, without interference, the interests of concentrated capital.

Today Buenos Aires is the center of a metropolitan region inhabited by seven million people, most of whom commute every day for work or leisure. During the first part of the twentieth century, government and civil society strove to create a city where the urban infrastructure, the parks, schools, hospitals, and banks, the transportation and commercial centers, would be evenly distributed around its territory. As a result, Buenos Aires was a relatively successful and democratic city.

Things have changed in the last three decades and especially in the last few

Industrial iron bridge in ruins, La Boca. Photo by Facundo de Zuviría.

years. Buenos Aires is now a broken city: radiant in the northern neighborhoods, where tourists find a replica of globalized services and shops in an environment beautified by parks built in the early twentieth century; filthy and deteriorated in the southern areas, where no important public investments have compensated for the indifference of global capitalism toward the city as a social and urban totality.

Globalization is an internationalization that is not responsive to local, fragmented pressures. It remains above the destiny of the captured area precisely because it can be abandoned. Unlike the elites who thought their hegemony belonged to the national space and unlike the popular mass movements that came to replace that hegemony, globalization is free of national ties and, because occupation is always temporary, feels no particular relation to the spaces it occupies. Globalization produces a world of fleeing capital.

Coffee shop in San Telmo. Photo by Facundo de Zuviría.

Concentrated capital does not defend cities; it defends business done in and with cities. Market forces, unfettered by public control and indifferent to the material landscape they temporarily occupy, consider the city only as an opportunity for development projects that, in the long run, will prove unsustainable. They have no local cultural conscience, and as globalized actors, they lack a total vision of the city they are transforming. At the city scale, globalization amounts to spatial fragmentation. Buenos Aires is now entirely defined by lines of poverty and affluence, except where the state still preserves something public like a park or a cultural center. Other "public" spaces, like the new developments in Puerto Madero, are really restaurants and corporate-office clusters where noncorporate users find little hospitality or leisure facilities. The use of such space is consistently offered to the affluent; its public quality is quite nominal, because although there is no interdiction, there is no reason to go there either.

Argentina's economic crisis (a typical globalized cul-de-sac) is to be held responsible for the darker accents of the city. Hundreds of homeless people roam the streets of Buenos Aires; hundreds work in the re-collection of garbage, and special wagons had to be reserved in the suburban trains for the movement of this informal commerce in a city that does not recycle and has no plans to do so. Most of the homeless have lost their jobs and homes in recent years. At least two thousand children, whose families live in the villas miseria around the city, sleep in the streets, in the halls of subway or railway stations, under the trees in the parks, beneath bridges or street crossings. In the evenings they inspect the garbage for food, or they wait for leftovers from the restaurants at midnight. During the day, they beg in subway entrances, in the bars from which the waiters chase them. They open car doors or commit petty crimes. They also lie doped with glue, and many of them are forced or lured into child prostitution.

Terrible conditions like these exist all over the world. What is new is that they are taking place in Buenos Aires, where for so long beggars were few and orphaned children a minority taken care of by institutions, most of them run by the state. Now, the church is the primary organization with efficient policies for these victims. During the day, poor people from the villas miseria or those who live in shabby downtown hotels cover the sidewalks with their merchandise. An irregular commerce of clothes, food, vegetables, small gadgets, and false *artesanías* occurs in whole regions of the city. The occupation of the sidewalks is a symbol: the poor and the less poor sell or buy junk in downtown streets that decline as a result of these activities. They are forced to live or work in a public space that is degraded and contaminated. They need to use that space as a marketplace because they have no other choice of job or occupation. In doing so they affect the rights of the other poor inhabitants who live or work in these decaying zones of the city. This junk commerce should not be compared to the ethnic markets found in other Latin American cities, for it has no roots in tradition and does not trade artisan produce. It is only the last resource of the unemployed.

Poverty privatizes public space. Only tourists can allow themselves a romantic view of this process. Poverty deteriorates precisely the same spaces that the government has overlooked and failed to integrate into the actual trends of private investment by millionaires. The poor suffer from a double segregation: not only do they get the worst and most depreciated places, but they also, being forced to live there, contribute to their decadence. A proud city that had managed to develop its style through a combination of European influences has found its Latin American destiny: an unexpected consequence of globalization.

In the old downtown many streets have changed dramatically. The more affluent dwellers tend to move out, and the buildings are turned into hotels for the poor. This takes place in "el centro," two or three blocks from what were once the most important theaters and best restaurants, and near the Plaza del Congreso and the government house. The concept of public space is losing its grip on the collective imaginary. Developers are redesigning the city against a republican tradition that ascribed positive values to public spaces. The new enterprises amount to a "losangelization" of the suburbs of Buenos Aires, dividing great extensions of land into private neighborhoods, country clubs surrounded by electrified fences, and massive shopping malls. The children that live in these enclosures may never have the opportunity to meet children of different cultural and social origins. No general perspective, neither from the government of the city nor from its citizens, is strong enough to control the impetuosity of market forces, whose impact is translated into cultural cleavages.

Big international business uses the city's historic buildings as a stage for shopping malls and restaurants. George Soros, for example, bought the Abasto Market, a magnificent building occupying a whole city block; his renovation resulted in a banal shopping center, hiding, behind the banners of international trademarks, the majestic, three-vaulted ceiling that Soros had promised to preserve. Small sectors in old neighborhoods are renovated as museums of the urban past. Ironically, one of these suburbs, la Boca, shows a modest public intervention along the river, which is lined by squatter houses and villas miseria. La Boca is but two blocks away from one of the city's most expensive restaurants, which was located there because the picturesque character of the neighborhood was popular with tourists. Tourists (and many affluent Argentines, as well) might not perceive that these blocks of open-air museum stand side by side with urban poverty. But what is more serious is that the government seems not to acknowledge this either.

Very near la Boca, corporate late capitalism has built its fortresses: Catalinas and Puerto Madero. They need no description because any globalized inhabitant of the world could recognize them. Their features are common, including corporate-landmark architecture, chain hotels, and leisure resources that are swarmed by hundreds during the daytime and almost desolate at night, when many of their users return to the gated barrios decorated with kitschy designs that include the false-English-cottage, false-criollo, false-colonial, or false-minimalist styles. Between the affluent kitsch, the post-international or postmodern style of the corporate buildings, and the global nature of the shopping malls, Buenos Aires has been deeply and dramatically transformed.

However, from a cultural point of view, the most spectacular change could be defined as the fall of the idea of the city as a common space where people of different social classes use the same facilities. Globalized entertainment has made its investments in movie theaters and shopping malls in the suburbs. As a consequence, the once very active and transsocial downtown is a wasteland, devastated from an architectural point of view, with traditional movie theaters having been turned into third-class restaurants or shops or merely having been left to decay.

It is said that globalization has also created a generational cleavage. Cultural tribes more apt and prepared for transnational consumption coexist with more classical cultural configurations. But if examined in detail, this cleavage, which could be thought as affecting the young and the very young of all classes, reveals that the poor and very poor have a pattern of cultural consumption that, although distributed through television, responds to habits that are well known: "tropical" music (*cumbia* and *cumbia villera*) is consumed by the young in the villas miseria as if the international pop idols did not appeal to them. Thus, the hypotheses that a globalized culture finds willing and well-prepared sustainers and consumers in the younger generations should be examined according to the profile of cultural goods offered to them, sometimes through globalized business but with a very strong local profile. If the hypothesis that there is no such thing as a transsocial juvenile culture is right, globalization is something that has a cultural impact on only 20 percent of the population who have access to the Internet, CDs, and international films. It leaves aside the cultural habits of another 20 percent of the population which receives cable television (which gets almost into every house), but uses it only for locally based programming.

Thus it is clear that a culturally globalized market attracts only those sectors that can access it as buyers; the rest are receiving, through globalized enterprises, a very locally based menu of options. Again, on this issue, the city is grossly divided.

Finally, there is a trend that evokes the international Buenos Aires of the beginning of the twentieth century, but with a twist. New immigrants have arrived in the last fifteen years, this time from the Far East: China and Korea. Unlike other cities in America, Buenos Aires never had a Chinatown. In fact, there were not, properly speaking, ethnic ghettos, although Jews or Italians tended to cluster more than other minorities. Although it would be an exaggeration to state that the city has finally arrived at its Chinatown or Koreatown, it would be a mistake not to acknowledge strong Chinese or Korean concentrations in traditional neighborhoods and to recognize their typical presence as owners of small shops all around town. This is new: Chinese or Koreans have set their quarters in Floresta or near Belgrano station, and the city, in very few years, has gotten used to their mostly friendly presence. New experiences will necessarily occur because of the influx of these minorities, whose cultural qualifications are higher than those of the immigrants who arrived at the beginning of the last century. I would not dare to make a prediction, but only to register a trend: Asian migrants are received more positively than the Latin Americans, especially Peruvians and Bolivians, who continue to arrive and settle very near the city center. There is a complicated line of racial prejudice against poor Latin Americans that does not seem to operate with the same strength against immigrants from the Far East, whose language immediately marks them as foreigners. The profile of these city ghettos (although, again, *ghetto* is a strong word) has yet to be considered. But this cultural image that brings history into the present can enable an Argentine living in Buenos Aires to remember what the city was like when, being the proud queen of the Río de la Plata, it attracted European masses with the promise of work and abundance that today is not guaranteed to their descendents.

NOTES

1. Massimo Bontempelli, *Noi, gli Aria: Interpretazioni sudamericane* (1933), 29, quoted in Gorelik 1998, 30.
2. "Arrabal," *Fervor de Buenos Aires* (1923), in Borges 1943, 33.
3. "Calle con almacén rosado," *Luna de enfrente* (1925), in Borges 1943, 78.
4. See Sarlo 1999.
5. Arlt 1993, 33.
6. Daireaux 1988, 119.
7. Dreier 1920, 40.
8. Arlt 1993, 85.
9. Ibid., 12.

Teresa P. R. Caldeira

FROM MODERNISM TO NEOLIBERALISM IN SÃO PAULO

RECONFIGURING THE CITY AND ITS CITIZENS

In the last twenty years the city of São Paulo and its large metropolitan region have experienced deep transformations. Some may argue that this is no news, for Paulistanos have proclaimed since the 1950s that theirs is the city in the world that grows the most, and they have adopted as its slogan "São Paulo cannot stop!" However, although the city and its residents may have been accustomed to constant change, to dismiss the past, to reconstruct the urban environment in a matter of each generation, and to play with images of the ephemeral and the transient to describe their modern city, they seem to be perplexed by the current transformations. In fact, one of the crucial changes affecting São Paulo is that its previous imaginary is no longer credible. The era of developmentalism and belief in progress has come to an end and with it the credibility of the frameworks in terms of which change used to be understood, explained, and criticized. No longer able to conceive of its transformations in terms of the optimistic imaginary anchored in notions of progress, development, growth, and incorporation, the citizens, administrators, and social scientists of São Paulo frequently find themselves ill-prepared to address the present configurations of the city. Moreover, since to abandon the thrill and the excitement of constant growth and of imagining the future in terms of progress seems to be difficult and frustrating, nostalgia becomes an almost irresistible impulse.

In this essay I analyze some of the processes that are transforming contemporary São Paulo. They affect almost all aspects of its life, from the polity to the urban infrastructure, from the organization of production to that of urban spaces, from the dynamics of everyday life to notions of public and private and of center and periphery. However, it would be hard to say that there is a master narrative articulating the new configuration and offering a blueprint for the future, something equivalent to the belief in progress and development. There are, though, some widely shared experiences and imaginaries, two of which I focus on in this essay. First, what is probably the main reference shaping the residents' engagement with their city is the fear of violence and anxiety about security. Old marks and symbols of ascension and dynamism—such as growth statistics, the ascending spiral that was the logo for the celebration of the fourth centennial of the city in 1954, industrial landscapes, modernist architecture, and open streets—have given place to high walls, homicide and unemployment statistics, gated parks and streets, private guards at building entrances, a local branch of postmodern architecture, and a new generation of streets without sidewalks or with empty ones. Second, there has been a sharp transformation in the way in which the role of the state is conceived. The developmentalist state was centralized, interventionist, and basically authoritarian. Currently, the state is supposed to withdraw from most of its previous attributions, to shrink, to manage private interests instead of intervening directly, to act as mediator instead of as a promoter of change. The state is supposed to remain in the wings, while the stage is occupied by civil society and its organized groups. If there is one dominant value in this configuration, it is privatization. This conception of the role of the state is usually labeled neoliberalism.

These two new narratives—that of fear and that of the reduced role of the state and enlarged space for nongovernmental organizations (NGOs)—took shape during the process of Brazilian democratization, and they coexist in tense ways with the new democratic institutions. In fact, they contribute to qualify and re-signify what democracy and some of its main attributes—especially participation, equality, and social justice—mean in the new context. I will look at the city of São Paulo and its transformations to retrace the transition from the era of progress to the neoliberal configuration, to indicate how the new conceptions intertwine in complex and frequently contradictory ways with the process of democratic consolidation, and to highlight how nowadays social and spatial inequalities become even more acute than they have been in the past.

THE MODERNIST INDUSTRIAL CITY:
PROGRESS WITH AUTHORITARIANISM

Modern São Paulo took form under the influence of a nationalist ideology of modernization known as developmentalism. Briefly, the idea was to promote, in a concentrated period of time, industrialization based on import substitution and directed at national markets. Its main instrument was decisive state intervention in order to promote accelerated industrialization and modern subjects, that is, rational and docile consumers. The slogan of President Jucelino Kubitscheck's plan of development in the late 1950s was "50 years in 5" and sustained not only São Paulo's industrial development but also the construction of Brasília and other state-sponsored projects aimed at generating the modern nation.[1] To promote progress through leaps in history, the Brazilian state took upon itself a wide range of tasks that ranged from building cities, roads, and electric plants to expanding the welfare state and modernizing television programs. From steel factories to hospital networks, from mines to television stations, from telephone companies to universities—all were materialized under the control and usually under the ownership of the state.

These projects happened under either authoritarian governments, such as the military dictatorship, or under the administration of populist leaders. In other words, modernization took place either without popular participation or with reduced and elite-controlled popular participation: to produce a modern political citizen who participates in political decisions at least at minimal level (i.e., electoral) was not among the elite's plan, especially during the military regime. As with the polity, so with society: social inclusion was not one of the parameters of the modernization project. It was necessary "to grow first to divide the cake later on," proclaimed the military regime, unashamed of its exclusionary policies.

São Paulo has always been at the core of Brazilian modernization. In a couple of decades in the twentieth century an unimportant provincial town was transformed into the center of the industrial production of the country and therefore of its promises of modernization. The slogans describing the city's growth were unabashedly modernist. From the 1950s on, Paulistanos believed that São Paulo "could not stop," that the city had become "the locomotive of the country," and that it was the "city that grows the most in the world." The belief in progress seemed to face no obstacles. City residents of all classes, from the traditional elites to the poor migrants from the northeast, who arrived by the millions in the 1950s, 1960s, and 1970s, shared the same faith that hard work was an infallible tool for betterment. With hard work, they would in time be individually better off, and the city would become the most important of Brazil, leading the progress of the country, making it modern. As did most Brazilians, Paulistanos believed that Brazil was "the country of the future." The inequalities separating social groups were obscene, but progress was for all, they thought.

Faith in progress helped to cement a peculiar social contract that generated, among other things, the urban pattern of segregation that shaped the city between the 1940s and the 1980s. São Paulo and its metropolitan region were structured on the basis of the separation of a sophisticated and well-equipped center for the rich and a precarious periphery for the poor working classes, a legal center of high-rises and an illegal periphery of auto-constructed houses. The center housed the most obvious symbols of modernity. It was dominated by skyscrapers that multiplied in a matter of a few years and gave the city its contemporary identity. The architecture was modernist. Modernism first became the official architectural style in São Paulo in 1954, when the city celebrated its fourth centennial, inaugurating a complex of administrative and cultural buildings in Parque do Ibirapuera. They were designed by Oscar Niemeyer and prefigured in some ways what was going to be crystallized in Brasília a few years later. Niemeyer also designed the spiral of progress that became the logo of the fourth centennial. In the following decades the elites adopted modernist architecture for residences, business, and cultural spaces, remaking the landscape of old downtown and configuring the new incarnation of Avenida Paulista. In the 1970s, during the peak of the era of development under the military regime, this avenue, first occupied by

Avenida Ipiranga, with Edifício Copan (right) and Edifício Italia (tower in background) in the 1960s. Photo by Marcel Gautherot. © Acervo Instituto Moreira Salles.

the palaces of the coffee elite and the early industrialists, became the address for the most powerful banks, enterprises, and museums of the city.

In the periphery the rhythm of construction was no less intense than in the center, but the lack of any kind of state support, investment, and planning resulted in a much less structured and ostentatious space. On the outskirts of the city, workers bought cheap lots of land sold either illegally or with some kind of irregularity by investors who failed to follow the city legislation regarding infrastructure and registration of developments. In spite of their illegal or irregular activities, these developers were never disturbed by the city administrators, who preferred to close their eyes to what was happening in the periphery. Workers always understood that illegality associated with dis-

Periphery of São Paulo in 1980. Photo by the author.

tance and precariousness was the condition under which they could become property owners and inhabit the modern city. Along streets without pavement or infrastructure, workers built by themselves and without financing their own houses. This could only happen in a slow and long-term process of transformation known as autoconstruction, a process that symbolizes perfectly progress, growth, and social mobility: step by step, day after day, the house is improved and people are reassured that sacrifice and hard work pay off. So workers moved to the middle of nowhere to build their houses and thus became the true agents of urbanization. It was essentially because of the expansion of the periphery that the urbanized area more than tripled in size between 1930 and 1954, and doubled again by the 1990s, to reach its current size of 850 square kilometers. In spite of remarkable population growth the population density of the city decreased by half between the beginning of the twentieth century and the 1960s.[2]

From the 1940s to the 1980s, everything separated rich and poor in the metropolitan region of São Paulo and contrasted the quality of the spaces where they built their dreams of success. But both in the center and in the periphery optimism in relation to the future ruled. While the economy was growing at rates of up to 12 percent per year, and while the authoritarian regime guaranteed that protest was not going to happen, people from different classes grew more unequal and lived farther away from each other, but shared some common efforts, beliefs, and some common public spaces.

In sum, belief in progress and in social mobility shared by residents of all social classes cemented the national project of modernization. Although the project was authoritarian and social inequality rampant, it was sustained by this collective engagement with the building of the future anchored in the belief in progress. This widely shared imaginary of modernization combined with a strong and highly centralized state to articulate the dominant notion of the public, a notion that conveyed a sense that the national (public) interest had priority over individual fulfillment and was a condition for it ("first the cake, then its parts"). The (modernist) notion that the whole had primacy over the parts was also shared by most opponents of the military dictatorship. Usually influenced by various shades of Marxism, the diverse opposition movements tended to repeat that it was necessary to overthrow the regime first and then address specific struggles. To put it in their language: first the revolution, then feminism. During the modernist period, the main imaginary shaping social and political theories and praxis of various tendencies established that the totality had priority over the parts (the state over the different sectors of society, the public over the private, the class over the individual, and so on). Although the elites were pursuing their private interests and enacting exclusionary policies, their discourse was inclusive (national). To emphasize publicly specific projects—whether feminism, regionalism, trade unionism, or any other group-specific interest—was to betray the possibilities of national progress, or of revolution, depending on the version. The main slogan of the military regime in the years of the highest rates of economic growth was: "Brazil: Love it or leave it."

This national-developmentalist project of modernization started to crumble in the early 1980s and was slowly put aside. It exploded under the influence of contradictory forces. Economic crisis and reform and political democratization combined to push to its limits the modernist model of the nation and of the city and its public. In the new city that has been developing since the 1980s, the whole has lost its primacy as organizing principle, the public is under attack, privatization rules, inequality is a value, and violence, fear, and crime offer the language in terms of which social life is interpreted and organized.

To contextualize the changes, it is helpful to consider the transition moment in which they started to become apparent, that is, the 1980s. One of the main elements of this transition was democratization. The transition to democracy was the last act of the old project of modernization: the act that forced its limits and by doing so helped to propel its implosion. Democracy in fact took roots in Brazilian society in the last twenty years. However, in the process it was also re-signified and transformed. The discourses that support it and the practices that it enables in the 2000s are not the same as those of the beginning of the 1980s and not even those that enabled the new constitution. In São Paulo many of the signs of this resignification are crystallized in the urban space and its conception of the public.

THE TRANSITION

Transition to democratic rule in Brazil was a lengthy process. The so-called political opening started in the mid-1970s; the first state governors were elected in 1982; and the first election for president took place in 1989. The main mark of democratization, however, was not electoral politics—something the military regime was always careful to maintain, albeit in restricted ways, and something the elites had long experience in manipulating. The main ingredient was an explosion of popular political participation and citizens' engagement in debating the future of the country that was synthesized in what is called in Brazil the "rebirth of civil society." Two forms of political organization were especially important in the transition process: independent trade unions and urban social movements. São Paulo was the core of the organization of both. On the one hand, in the late 1970s a new type of trade union movement emerged in ABCD, that is, the area of the metropolitan region of São Paulo with the greatest industrial concentration and which symbolizes the model of modernist development. The novelty of this movement was its rejection of the trade-union structure organized by Getúlio Vargas under a corporatist model and the generation of a new leadership that the state and the elite were not able either to co-opt or to repress. This movement organized numerous strikes, which had been prohibited by the military regime, and created new instruments of labor negotiation, from factory commissions to the *câmaras setoriais* (sector chambers).[3]

On the other hand, numerous neighborhood-based social movements appeared in the poor urban peripheries, frequently with the help of the Catholic Church, gaining legitimacy for the idea that they had the "right to have rights." Movement participants, a majority of them women, were new property owners who realized that political organization was the only way to force city authorities to extend urban infrastructure and services to their neighborhoods. They discovered that being taxpayers legitimated their "rights to the city," that is, rights to its legal order and to the types of urbanization available in the center. At the root of their political mobilization was the illegal or irregular status of their properties and the precarious situations of their neighborhoods, which the public authorities had failed to provide with services and infrastructure, alleging exactly their irregular status. Thus, a central inspiration for these movements was an urban and collective experience of marginalization and abandonment in spite of individual efforts of integration through work and consumption.

The urban social movements of the 1970s and 1980s were movements for inclusion; they were movements for the expansion of citizenship rights and of the legal city. Since the imaginary of development and modernization was expansive, it allowed the articulation of the struggle of the social movements with the same imaginary of developmentalism. The social movements were locally based and had specific demands, but they addressed the state using the language of universal rights to demand services that in principle should be for all and the expansion of the scope of citizenship.

The first state administrators in São Paulo to receive the demands of social movements were mayors directly appointed by the military government, but they still responded to these demands according to the modernist/state-interventionist model. The City of São Paulo (and many others in Brazil) borrowed heavily to invest in urban infrastructure, especially in sanitation, to the point that Brazil became the World Bank's largest borrower in the area of urban development.[4] As a result, the periphery of São Paulo (and of other metropolitan regions) improved substantially in terms of urban infrastructure and some social indicators, such as infant mortality. City administrators also responded to the demands of the social movements for legalization of urban land and offered various amnesties to illegal developments, enlarging substantially the amount of legal property on the periphery. This combination of legalization and improvement in infrastructure radically changed the status of the periphery in the cityscape, a transformation analogous to that of the political status that city residents obtained through the organization of social movements.

Still, from another perspective, the democratization process represented an extension of the modernist model: the emphasis on the rule of law (*estado de direito*). For the opposition movement that helped to overthrow the military dictatorship, democracy in Brazil was supposed to bring about the rule of law, rights, justice, and equality—all things that both populist regimes and the military dictatorship had denied the citizens. The demands of the political movement that provoked the end of the military regime included direct elections (*Diretas Já!*), amnesty for political prisoners and respect for their human rights, revocation of all "laws of exception" imposed by the military regime, and the convening of a constitutional assembly to write a new democratic constitution. In a word, a whole liberal-democratic creed. Several of these demands were met in the first years of the democratic transition, including the promulgation of a new constitution in 1988. It was written on the basis of ample consultation with organized movements and contemplated every possible demand for rights, from the right to four months of paid maternity leave and to family planning to the more traditional list of rights to life, to freedom of expression, and to justice.

It is easier to write a democratic constitution than to build a democracy, especially in an obscenely unequal country and one in which modernity starts to be reinterpreted in neoliberal terms. In the 1990s two tendencies revealing paradoxical aspects of the democratization process became apparent. On the one hand, there were antidemocratic discourses and practices, which usually came in indirect ways, that is, in ways that did not challenge democracy as the principle that should organize the political system. In São Paulo those discourses were articulated in relation to civil rights, the justice system, and the urban environment and are mostly formulated in relation to the issue of urban violence. On the other hand, there were re-significations of some of the main concepts that anchor a liberal democracy, especially those of participation, civil society, the public, and a redefinition of the role of the state. This reinterpretation has occurred as a neoliberal rationality of government has become dominant.

Brazil seems to be a nation that deals comfortably with contradictions—or, at least, a nation that is used to enacting what from the point of view of European and American patterns of modernity and liberal-democracy would be contradictory. In the same way that modernization was proudly achieved without democracy, the undermining of the modern public is being diligently enacted under a political democratic regime. In what follows I analyze some of the dimensions of this disjunctive democracy, of the new rationality of government that is shaping urban policies, and of the type of public and of urban space they create.

THE NEOLIBERAL CITY: PRIVATIZATION AND WALLS

The mythology of progress started to collapse in the 1980s, in São Paulo as elsewhere in Brazil, with what is called the "lost decade," the deep economic recession associated with changes that deeply transformed Brazilian society and many others in Latin America and all around the world. They continued to change as a result of the adoption of "structural-adjustment" policies. Although this is not the place to analyze these changes in more detail, it is necessary to mention the most important of them as they affected the metropolitan region of São Paulo in the 1980s and 1990s. They included a sharp decrease in population growth; a significant decline in immigration and increase in emigration, especially of upper- and middle-class residents; a sharp drop in the Gross National Product (GNP) and rates of economic growth; a drop in per capita income; a deep reorganization of industrial production associated with large unemployment and weakening of the formal sector of employment; a redefinition of the role of government in the production and management of urban space; and a significant increase in violent crime associated in part with the restructuring of urban segregation.[5] São Paulo of the 1990s was still responsible for a significant share of Brazilian industrial production—an impressive amount considering that Brazil is the eighth-largest economy in the world—but the optimism that lasted from the 1950s to the 1970s has given way to skepticism. As a result of the economic crisis and related changes, the distribution of wealth—already bad—worsened and perspectives of social mobility shrank considerably. In the periphery important aspects of the urban inclusion achieved by the social movements eroded. Many people could no longer afford a house of their own, and the reduced horizons of life-chances seemed to preclude even the dream of auto-constructing one. The number of people living in favelas in the city increased from 4.4 percent in 1980 to 9.2 percent in 1991 and 11.2 percent in 2000.[6]

One of the most important consequences of this combination of economic and social crisis was that the state abandoned the model of govern-mentality based on protectionism, nationalism, and direct participation in production—the main elements of the modernization project. The policies adopted to deal with the economic crisis—usually indicated by agencies such as the International Monetary Fund and labeled "neoliberal" or "structural adjustment"—resulted in the opening of the domestic market to imported products and in the withdrawal of the state from various areas in which it had traditionally played a central role as producer. These areas included urban services, infrastructure, telecommunications, steel manufacture, and oil pro-duction. As a result, the largest part of the state-owned productive sector was privatized, and numerous national industries were internationalized through fusions and acquisitions.[7]

Privatization became the order of the day, the dominant value of the new logic of government that replaced the modernization project. Privatization signifies various things and affects various aspects of social life. It means selling off most of the state-owned enterprises (including those offering basic services such as telephone and electricity) to private interests. It entails cut-ting state subsidies to national production. It signifies unmaking preroga-tives and social rights created both in the corporatist labor legislation of the 1930s and 1940s and in the 1988 Constitution.[8] It also means that the state "contracts out" to private enterprise and privately funded NGOs social ser-vices that it used to provide (from the delivery of milk to schools to prison management). Moreover, the state now hires NGOs with public funds to de-velop policy that government agencies used to produce. In sum, privatization undermines various pillars of the developmentalist-modernist project and its type of state. In effect, it subverts the idea that the state governs the nation, and indeed creates a nation in its image, by being a direct producer of its pub-lic through state-owned and -managed industry, state-directed public works and planning, and state-provided welfare.[9]

Privatization also affects in decisive ways the space of the city and its everyday practices. Pressured by funding cuts and new laws requiring bal-anced budgets, municipal governments throughout Brazil limited their range of intervention and level of investment in the urban environment. Simul-taneously, they called on private citizens to invest in their own space in ex-change for fiscal incentives and a flexibilization of building codes. In the periphery citizens have always invested in their space, but as a result of minimal state investment. Now, however, private investment becomes a matter of state policy for the whole city. Some of the most important instruments of urban intervention to appear in the 1990s are the so-called urban operations (*operaçãos urbanas*) and partnerships (*parcerias*). The former are somewhat similar to the business-improvement districts that exist in the United States. They are mechanisms through which the state coordinates private investment in urban infrastructure in combination with its own investment in exchange for some benefits, especially the possibility that investors build real estate above zoning regulations in delimited areas of the city to achieve certain urbanization purposes. The *operaçãos urbanas* that have taken place in São Paulo thus far have improved central areas and had the effect of increasing inequality and spatial segregation. *Parceria* is a very fashionable term that designates a wide range of activities undertaken by an association of state agencies and private organizations. In the most different sectors of society and branches of administration, it has come to be expected that policies be developed through a combination of private and public efforts. Accordingly, there has been a deep transformation in the way in which urban policies are undertaken. The emphasis on partnerships empowers NGOs of all types, as it is assumed that partnerships are established with formally organized private groups. As this type of organization grew in the 1990s, the type of social movements organized by residents of poor neighborhoods—those based on voluntary work, operating with little infrastructure—which were widespread in the 1980s, tended to disappear. Additionally, private enterprises have developed a new approach to their intervention in urban space and society. The new trend among Brazilian enterprises is to be "socially responsible" and use "social investment" as marketing policy.[10] The wave of partnerships has been broad and has had mixed results. Although they can be very creative and produce important results, as in the case of programs for improving literacy and retraining workers, partnerships can result in more, rather than less, inequality and have been used to directly deepen segregation.

Probably some of the most important forms of privatization affecting the urban environment and its pattern of segregation relate to the fear of crime. Crime and violence have become the most important factors for the articulation of a new pattern of segregation and a new way of imagining city life, as they offered the language in terms of which all the other processes were evaluated and expressed.

Rates of violent crime have escalated in São Paulo in the last fifteen years. Today, the annual murder rate of more than 60 per 100,000 inhabitants makes it one of the most violent cities of the world. Moreover, São Paulo has a violent police force that killed between 200 and 1,500 people a year during the democratic consolidation, that is, between 5 percent and 20 percent of the homicides of the metropolitan region in a year. In São Paulo fear of crime and violence is well grounded.

Fear is productive. One of the most important things it generates is what I call the talk of crime: conversations, narratives, rumors, jokes, stories that have experiences of crime as their subject and are reiterated many times. The talk of crime is repetitive and feeds a circle in which fear is both dealt with and reproduced, and in which violence is both counteracted and magnified. The fear and the talk of crime not only produce certain types of interpretations and explanations (usually simplistic and stereotypical) but also organize everyday strategies of protection and reaction that restrict people's movements and shrink their universe of interactions. Moreover, the talk of crime also helps violence to proliferate by legitimating private or illegal reactions—like hiring guards or supporting death squads and vigilantism—when institutions of order seem to fail.

The fear of crime helps to legitimate the expansion of a booming industry of security services that, under the guise of offering protection from violence, also enforces a new regime of distances and boundaries in city space. Increasingly, citizens in Brazil and in many other countries depend on private security not only for protection from crime but also for identification, screening, surveillance, and isolation of undesired people, exactly those whose stereotypes the talk of crime elaborates. In São Paulo not only is the privatization of security escalating, but it has also assumed a perverse and worrisome character.[11] The population does not trust the institutions of order—the police forces and the justice system—primarily because, even under democratic rule, the police frequently act outside the boundaries of the law, abusing, torturing, and executing suspects. As a result of this distrust and discredit, an increasing number of residents of São Paulo opt for private security and even private justice (either vigilantism or extralegal police actions) through services that are mostly unregulated and often explicitly illegal. These privatized services frequently contest, if not violate, the rights of citizens. Yet such violations are tolerated by a population that in many instances considers certain rights of citizenship unimportant and even reprehensible, as evident in various campaigns attacking the notion of human rights and those who support them. Thus, the universe of crime not only reveals a widespread disrespect for rights and lives but also directly delegitimates citizenship and indicates the limits of democratic consolidation and of the rule of law in Brazil. The universe of crime is a central element of what James Holston and I call disjunctive democracy, a contradictory democracy marked by the expansion of political citizenship and delegitimation of civil citizenship.[12]

Fear and the talk of crime also help to organize the urban landscape and public space, generating new forms of spatial segregation and social discrimination and shaping the scenario for social interactions. Central among the instruments creating a new pattern of urban segregation are the fortified enclaves, which are privatized, enclosed, and monitored spaces for residence, consumption, leisure, and work. They can be shopping malls, office complexes, or residential gated communities and depend on private guards and high-tech security for protection and for enforcing exclusionary practices that guarantee their social exclusivity. They reproduce inequality both as a value and as a social fact. They treat what is enclosed and private as a form of distinction, as expressed in an ad for the closed condominium Place des Vosges, a gated theme park that imitates the plan of the original square and announces its advantages: "The only difference is that the one in Paris is public. Yours is private."

Fortified enclaves require large spaces and are located primarily in what used to be peripheral areas either of the city or of the metropolitan region. Using the fear of crime as justification, the elites have migrated by the hundreds of thousands from the center of the city to areas of what used to be the periphery. As the new islands of distinction are placed in sites where only the poor used to live, walls, suspicion, and displays of wealth generate a landscape of social inequality that can easily be described as outrageous. Upper-class detached houses become fortresses. They disappear behind high-security façades in which the only openings in the walls, covered by bulletproof glass, indicate the presence of private guards.

Fences, bars, and walls are essential in the city today not only for security and segregation but also for aesthetic and status reasons. All the elements associated with security become part of a new code for the expression of distinction that I call the "aesthetics of security." This code encapsulates elements of security in a discourse of taste and transforms them into symbols of status. In contemporary São Paulo fences and bars become elements of decoration and of the expression of personality and invention. They have to be sophisticated not only to protect residents from crime but also to indicate their social status and guarantee differentiation. They are investments in public appearance and must enable comparisons between neighbors, to demonstrate both who is doing better and who has more sophisticated taste.

As the elites retreat to their new private and fortified enclaves, these spaces become the most prestigious expressions of status and distinction. Inevitably, this new language of distinction has reached other areas of the city, including the periphery of São Paulo where poor people live and where the material conditions of the buildings are obviously much more precarious. However, as the aesthetic of security reigns, the builders of autoconstructed houses in São Paulo now transform their façades, representing their personalities through designs of fences and gates and elaborate discourses despising other poor people, those who do not have the means to become homeowners. Fences have become additional categories circulating to distinguish the proper from the improper, houses of respect from spaces of crime, and they are to be found around both the poorest and the richest houses of every neighborhood.

All aspects of privatization and the disappearance of projects in terms of which different social groups could be brought together create a city in which separateness comes to the forefront and in which the quality of public space and of the social encounters possible in it have changed considerably. Many new spaces and practices in the city attest to the new pattern of segregation and the power of the imaginary of separation. Probably the most emblematic space is the region around Avenida Luís Carlos Berrini and Marginal Pinheiros Expressway in the southwest of the city. This region houses not only the new type of fortified and monumental office complexes and services but also the largest share of closed condominiums (in Morumbi and Vila Andrade) and the largest sample of what is considered in the city to

Security façade of upper-class house. Photo by the author.

Fence protecting a working-class house. Photo by the author.

be postmodern architecture. It has been the site of new urban experiments such as the *operação urbana* Águas Espraiadas and the forced removal of a large number of *favelados* by a partnership between private investors and city administration. This partnership joined city agencies of social work with a pool of corporate enterprises, the offices of which were located in the area of Avenida Luís Carlos Berrini. The objective of the association was to remove a favela near the offices. Berrini had become one of the most fashionable addresses for business in the city during the 1990s, and the poor neighbors were certainly an inconvenience. Although many favelas had been displaced before, this was the first time in which representatives of the private sector participated directly in the operation.[13] In the past the city had expelled poor people, but had justified such operations with discourses of public responsibility (hygiene, need to enlarge avenues for development) or of social responsibility. However, in the case of the Berrini-area favelas, although the enterprises involved tried to present their participation as an exercise of "social responsibility," the true goal of getting rid of the favelados to increase real-estate value was rarely disguised. Moreover, "social responsibility" and "concern" ended with the clearance of the area.

After the removal, the only remaining presence of the favelados in the lives and minds of the people of the region may well be Bar Favela, a club that opened, in 2001, on a street near Berrini. Its patrons are from the upper classes. Its attraction is a décor that imitates the details of a favela's shacks: a "kitsch style," saints and religious objects, clothes hanging on lines, and imitations of improvised and often illegal electricity connections. Bar Favela's proud owners announced that they learned this style by studying the most famous favela of Morumbi, Paraisópolis. They also learned a "spirit of solidarity and relaxation" that they try to recreate in the bar's atmosphere and in the slang that they use to name the menu items. In the previous decade, when there was a common project of development, poverty was most often an embarrassment for the upper classes, who tried to keep silent about it. At that moment the poor and their demands of incorporation represented a threat and were therefore forcibly silenced by authoritarian regimes. The aestheticization of the favelados' lifestyle and its consumption by the upper classes depends on clear separations and on the breakdown of a common project. They depend on distantiation: the favelados are out of the way physically

Favelas and upper-class residential building. Photo by Gal Oppido.

and socially and therefore may be incorporated aesthetically. But since this distantiation is precarious, favelados are always present as phantasmagoria: they are the most recurrent imagined criminals in the talk of crime and in the fears it helps to circulate and that pervade the everyday life of Paulistanos.[14]

Fear of violence and the city of distances and separations it generates do not allow the same kind of social contract among different social groups that progress made possible. While progress, nationalism, and development offered opportunities for social differences and inequalities to be put in the background, fear and privatization bring them to the forefront. The new public fostered by fear and violence is articulated and fragmented by inequalities and prejudices. It is exclusionary, not inclusive. It is not democratic. However, these tendencies do not prevent other rearticulations that are democratic. The new rationality of government based on a certain pattern of intervention of the so-called third sector assumes that organized social groups must have a role in the creation and implementation of urban policies. This assumption certainly also represents a departure from national-developmentalist rationality, as it breaks the omnipotent role of the state in formulating policies. Nevertheless, the inclusion of democratic popular participation and of partnerships in the formulation of policies is not necessarily a guarantee of the production of social equality and social justice, especially when distances and separations structure the city and its public, as the Berrini case demonstrates. Therefore, current tendencies suggest the development of a new configuration in which technologies and practices of inclusion and of exclusion are intertwined and simultaneously take part in the constitution of a new type of rationality of government that one may call neoliberal democracy.

NEOLIBERAL DEMOCRACY

Recent urban plans and legislation passed at both the federal and the municipal levels in Brazil offer a privileged way of analyzing the intertwining of the different tendencies. On the one hand, the plans and legislation clearly demonstrate the substitution of the modernist-developmentalist paradigm by a democratic one. On the other hand, they indicate how neoliberal assumptions are embedded in the way in which democratic participation has been conceived. Finally, they demonstrate how when citizens democratically take part in the making of urban policies, social justice is not a guaranteed outcome. Although this is not the place to present a detailed analysis of these plans, it is important to take them into consideration to highlight the directions of the changes transforming São Paulo, its space, and its polity.[15]

Pressed by organized social movements, the Constitutional Assembly introduced in the 1988 Constitution an innovative chapter on urban policy. This chapter was complemented by the remarkable Estatuto da Cidade (City Statute), federal law 10,257, of 10 July 2001, which institutes a new frame for urban legislation.[16] Incorporating the language and concepts developed by urban social movements and various local administrations since the 1970s, the City Statute establishes that the city and urban property must fulfill a "social function." It frames the directives for urban policy from the point of view of the poor, creates mechanisms to revert patterns of irregularity and inequality, and determines that urban policy must "guarantee the right to sustainable cities, understood as the right to urban land, housing, sanitation, urban infrastructure, transportation and public services, work, and leisure for present and future generations" (Art. 2, par. 1). The City Statute clearly establishes the production of social equality in urban space as a fundamental objective of urban planning and policy and, reciprocally, turns planning into a basic instrument for equalizing social disparities and securing social equality. However, the statute is not framed as a total plan, but instead introduces a series of innovative legal instruments that allow local administrations to enforce the "social function."

Two powerful instruments created by the statute to enforce its directives regard management: one requires popular participation in the formulation and implementation of policies; the other considers that urbanization is to be obtained by cooperation between government and private organizations. On the one hand, the statute requires that local urban policies be conceived and implemented with popular participation.[17] Chapter 4 of the statute establishes that cities must implement a variety of mechanisms to ensure public participation in management; those mechanisms include debates, public audiences, conferences, popular amendments of plans and laws, and a participatory budget process. On the other hand, the statute also establishes that the government must no longer be solely responsible for the process of urbanization, which should instead entail a balanced cooperation, or partnership, between public and private interests.

The City Statute exemplifies how democracy has taken root in Brazilian society and how basic assumptions of the national-developmentalist project of modernization have been put aside. The statute not only establishes social justice as the goal of urban policy but also imagines a society of citizens who are active, organized, and well informed about their interests and their government's actions. This imaginary of a society of active citizens could not be more different from the one that inspired modernist-developmentalist policies, which assumed a backward society of silent and mostly ignorant citizens who needed to be brought into modernity by an illuminated and elite avant-garde, frequently quite authoritarian. Moreover, the language of modernist policies was one of development, not of citizen rights, and its principal target was underdevelopment, not social inequality.

The City Statute represents a transformation of the role of the state in the formulation of urban policies. By establishing that the government will no longer be solely responsible for the process of urbanization, the statute fractures another basic assumption of the developmentalist model. The latter supposed the state to be the main producer of urban space and public policies. However, the statute establishes that urban space should be produced through partnerships between public and private interests. Thus, the state not only relinquishes its dominant role in the production of space but also assumes that urban interventions will necessarily be fragmentary as they reflect different partnerships. This new role imagined for the state and its way of implementing public policies is not a matter of democracy alone. The idea of partnerships and the notion of a society of active citizens belong in the imaginary of neoliberalism or of advanced liberalism. Nikolas Rose asks what it means "to govern in an advanced liberal way": "advanced liberal" techniques of government "create a distance between the decisions of formal political institutions and other social actors, conceive of these actors in new ways as subjects of responsibility, autonomy and choice, and seek to act upon them through shaping and utilizing their freedom."[18] From this perspective, the so-called third sector (or civil society or "nongovernmental sector") is not exterior to the practices of government, but rather inherent and instrumental to the new rationality of government, a rationality whose most fundamental and generalizable characteristic is perhaps "the ethical *a priori* of the active citizenship in an active society."[19] It is this principle of active citizenship that both the City Statute and São Paulo's Plano Diretor Estratégico (Master Strategic Plan) of 2002, a municipal law and local application of the statute, seek to implement.

However, the ways in which citizens engage with participatory instruments in the construction of their cities do not necessarily correspond to the dreams of democratic legislators or to the best intentions of democratic governments. As in the case of Berrini Avenue, the actions of partnerships can result in the production of segregation and discrimination and therefore undermine the principles established by the City Statute. In a society marked by fear and suspicion, and in which inequalities and separations are valued, it is easier to imagine how partnerships may turn into instruments of inequality, rather than of social justice.

Nor does direct participation in the formulation of urban plans guarantee less inequality, as the elaboration of São Paulo's Master Strategic Plan demonstrates.[20] It strictly followed all the guidelines of the City Statute on how to incorporate popular participation. When its proposal was being considered by the city council, it was debated in twenty-five public audiences either at city-council headquarters or in different regions of the city. The city council also organized numerous thematic debates on housing, environment, transportation, macrozoning, and management of the planning system. These audiences and debates were in addition to those that had been organized by Sempla (the Municipal Department of Planning) before the plan was submitted to city council. Besides the criticisms, suggestions, and arguments offered at these audiences, the City Council Commission of Urban Planning received numerous written documents and petitions. While these contributions indicated the level of citizen engagement with the problems of the city and the democratic character of the production of the plan, they also made evident how difficult it is to break patterns of inequality.

The audiences and debates were attended by numerous organized groups. In general, it was three coalitions of associations that articulated and expressed the different positions about the proposal for the master plan. The Frente pela Cidadania (Front for Citizenship) represented thirty associations under the leadership of Secovi, the powerful organization of real-estate developers.[21] The Frente Popular pelo Plano Diretor (Popular Front for the Plano Diretor) put together popular movements, urbanists, consultants, university laboratories, and institutes, and was especially instrumental in establishing the limits of Zonas Especiais de Interesse Social (Special Zones of Social Interest), areas of popular housing for which the plan reserved specific instruments for promoting spatial improvement and regularization or legalization. Finally, the Movimento Defenda São Paulo (Movement to Defend São Paulo) represented the interests of residents of middle-class neighborhoods in maintaining the zoning code that preserved their areas as strictly residential. These three coalitions reunited the type of associations with which the city government expected to establish partnerships during the implementation of the Master Strategic Plan.

The participation of these associations certainly made the formulation of the Master Strategic Plan into a completely different enterprise than modernist-developmentalist planning, which was usually formulated in the offices of experts and later imposed by the government as decrees. It became clear, though, that the positions that ended up being known publicly and found space in the media were those of the powerful middle- and upper-class organizations, the Frente pela Cidadania and the Movimento Defenda São Paulo. In contrast, the Frente Popular was not especially visible in the media. Moreover, the democratic debates at city council were shaped by class differences. The middle- and upper-class coalitions and the working-class front basically intervened in different aspects of the debate, almost as if they were dealing with different cities. Additionally, the public intervention and lobbying of the upper-class coalitions forced significant revisions on the original proposal, thus reproducing the power of these groups to frame public debate, urban policy, and urban space. The final plan still puts forward principles of equality, but citizen engagement with it has translated into the reproduction of class differences and inequality.

Inequality has always been a structural feature of the city of São Paulo. Although spatial segregation has assumed various forms during the twentieth century, the distance separating social groups and their spaces has been constant. During the period in which developmentalism and the belief in progress were dominant, the deep social inequality was eclipsed by the belief in future incorporation and modernization. During the period of the transition to democratic rule, when social movements expanded the horizons of citizenship, when new legal and urban instruments addressed directly the question of social justice, and when the spaces occupied by the working classes improved, it seemed that there was a chance that the city would become not only more democratic but also more egalitarian. However, the democratic city is also the city dominated by violence, fear of crime, and fortified spaces, a city where distantiation and separation are materially and symbolically recreated everywhere. It is also a city in which neoliberal interpretations of popular participation and of the new role of the state have resulted in new forms of inequality, in spite of the intensified level of participation and apparent incorporation that they promote. It is a city in which democracy and the expansion of technologies of communication have in fact promoted some new forms of inclusion, but in which structural-adjustment policies and different types of privatization have led to new forms of exclusion. In this city in which inequalities have been enhanced instead of diminishing, there are also new and contradictory ways of dealing with them. Inequalities may be aestheticized. They may be put aside by walls that simultaneously emphasize them and create distance and separation. But in the São Paulo of the 2000s inequalities are also denounced by some artistic and cultural movements that address class difference, segregation, and racism with an explicitness and directness previously unheard of in Brazilian society. The most important of these movements is hip-hop. Situating themselves in a periphery conceived as a space of despair, hip-hop artists elaborate the imaginary of a city where differences, inequalities, and distances became unbridgeable and where demands for inclusion make little sense. Paradoxically, however, as hip-hop denounces these conditions and creates one of the strongest forms of class confrontation ever seen in Brazil, it also generates new kinds of separations and distantiation.

Democratization has never been a straightforward process in Brazil. Although disjunctions are clear, the process of democratization has generated remarkable institutions that have changed how various aspects of social life—including urban policy—are conceived. The renewed challenge for these institutions is to unmake processes of reproduction of inequality and to find ways to enforce principles of social justice.

NOTES

1. For an analysis of modernism and modernization in Brazil, as well as of the creation of Brasília and Kubitscheck's plan, see Holston 1989. For an analysis of the industrialization of São Paulo, see Dean 1969 and Singer 1984. For analyses of the transformations of the city during the developmentalist period, see Morse 1970 (part 4) and Meyer 1991.

2. The urban area of the city of São Paulo was 130 square kilometers in 1930 and 420 square kilometers in 1954. In 1980 it reached 733 square kilometers, and by 1994, it had grown to 826 square kilometers. The population of the city grew from 579,033 in 1920 to 3,781,446 in 1960, according to the census. In 2000 it was 10,405,867 in the city and around 18,000,000 in the metropolitan region (the conurbated area formed by the city and its thirty-eight surrounding municipalities). Population density in the city dropped from 11.000 inhabitants per square kilometer in 1914 to 5.300 in 1963. In 2000 it was 6.823 inhabitants per square kilometer. (Statistics on population density from Saia, cited by Meyer 1991, 241).

3. Under the corporatist model, all trade-union organization was regulated and frequently co-opted by the Ministry of Labor. Câmaras setoriais put together workers, entrepreneurs, and state representatives to discuss and implement new production targets, technological renewal, policies of employment and salary, and export policies. On the new labor movement, see Cardoso and Comin 1995.

4. Melo 1995, 343.

5. Rates of population growth that had been above 5 percent annually until the 1960s, dropped to 0.8 percent in the 1990s. Fertility rates decreased sharply (from 5.8 children per woman in 1970 to 2.9 in 1990) and the rich residents abandoned the city and its central quarters by the hundreds of thousands. Brazil's GNP dropped 5.5

percent and the real minimum wage dropped 46 percent during the period 1980–90. Between 1940 and 1980, the GNP had grown 6.9 percent annually (4 percent in per capita terms). Between 1980 and 1992, it grew only 1.25 percent annually and per capita income dropped 7.6 percent (PNUD-IPEA 1996, 73). Inflation rates scaled during the 1980s and 1990s and reached 2,500 percent a year in 1993, before they were controlled by the Plano Real of 1994. The GNP of the Metropolitan Region of São Paulo dropped from US$ 92 billion in 1980 to US$ 85 billion in 1990. The GNP per capita dropped 27 percent during the same period (Marques and Torres 2000, 155). The industrial sector that gives the region its identity has been especially affected by the crisis. Since the 1980s, São Paulo's share in the value of industrial transformation has dropped. It was 58.2 percent in 1970 and 41 percent in 1991 (Rolnik et al. n.d., 27; Leme and Biderman 1997). In 1990 São Paulo was still responsible for 26.3 percent of the industrial production of the country, but this was a much lower percentage than the 55 percent it had represented in 1960 (Brant et al. 1989, 19). Industrial employment in the metropolitan region dropped 32 percent between 1989 and 1999 while general employment dropped 10 percent. During this period, the service sector grew 38 percent (Marques and Torres 2000, 157). Unemployment grew from 9 percent in 1989 to 15 percent in 1996 and 20 percent in 1999, affecting two million people (Branco 1999, 5). Formal employment has dropped significantly more than the informal one. Interpretations about changes in the industrial sector vary. Although some talk about deindustrialization, it seems that what has been happening is, instead, industrial restructuring. Given the end of subsidies and protectionism and the opening to external markets that framed the abandonment of the interventionism-protectionism model of import substitution, most industries adopted new technologies, styles of management, and reorganization of production. The results were increases both in productivity and in unemployment. Moreover, it seems that there was an intense displacement of occupations from the industrial sector to various segments of the service sector (Comin and Amitrano 2003).

6. *Favela* refers to a set of shacks built on seized land. Although people own their shacks and may transport them, they do not own the land, since it was occupied illegally. Autoconstructed houses may sometimes look as precarious as favela shacks, but typically they are built on land bought by the residents. There have been various controversies about estimates of the number of people living in favelas in São Paulo. The above estimate is from Camila Saraiva and Eduardo Marques (2004). They argue against a famous study by the Fundação Instituto de Pesquisas Econômicas da Universidade de São Paulo (FIPE) that estimated the number of favela residents in 1993 as representing 19 percent of the city's population.

7. Comin and Amitrano 2003.

8. Paoli 1999.

9. See Caldeira and Holston 2005 for a fuller version of this argument.

10. Paoli 2001; Garcia 2004.

11. In the early 2000s in São Paulo the number of police officers was equivalent to that of private guards in the legal market. In the United States there are three private guards for each policeman (see Caldeira 2000, chap. 5). In Brazil, however, there is a nonregulated and illegal market of private security probably as large as the legal sector. Many people offering services in the illegal market are either policemen or former policemen, who are often involved with crime and excessive use of force.

12. Caldeira and Holston 1999.

13. The transformations of the Avenida Luís Carlos Berrini and the removal of the nearby favelas are analyzed in Fix 2001 and Frúgoli 2000.

14. Caldeira 2000, part 1.

15. See Caldeira and Holston 2005; Caldeira 2003.

16. The statute represents a clear departure from the modernist model of urban planning that was dominant in Brazil from the 1950s and that is best exemplified in the case of Brasília. For an analysis of this legislation and the transformation in the paradigm of urban planning, see Caldeira and Holston 2005.

17. Chapter 4 of the City Statute is entitled "On the Democratic Management of the City," and its Article 45 presents the boldest formulation of the principle of popular participation: "The management organizations of metropolitan regions and urban agglomerations will include mandatory and significant participation of the population and of associations representing the various segments of the community in order to guarantee the direct control of their activities and the full exercise of citizenship."

18. Rose 1996, 53–54.

19. Ibid., 60.

20. São Paulo's Master Strategic Plan has 308 articles, which deal not only with urban policies per se but also with issues ranging from the rights of minorities to employment. It is impossible to account for its many innovations and important aspects in this space. For more on this subject, see Caldeira 2003.

21. Sindicato das Empresas de Compra, Venda, Locação e Administração de Imóveis Residenciais e Comerciais em São Paulo.

Néstor García Canclini
....

MEXICO CITY, 2010

IMPROVISING GLOBALIZATION

It has become a matter of habit to think of cities in relation to one another. The globalization of travel, tourism, and economic exchange has accentuated this comparative tendency and elevated certain large- and medium-sized cities to model status. In the 1980s and 1990s Berlin and Barcelona, for example, became global capitals of urban-planning innovation and of a process capable of resituating the development of cities as the most dynamic sites for reaping the benefits of the drive toward global growth.

Other cities have become emblematic for their monstrosity and decadence, in particular, Mexico City, which has been singled out as the world's most populous and most polluted city, and among its most dangerous and chaotic. Moving beyond the data refuting these "distinctions" (the population of Tokyo-Yokohama is in fact greater, and several Latin American cities exceed Mexico City in terms of pollution and violence), I explore why the Mexican capital inspires such nefarious images and encounters such great difficulties in facing the challenges of globalization. Furthermore, I evaluate some of its potentialities as a global city in the horizon of the year 2010. My overall goal is to compare the actual city with the imagined city—and with the city that is impossible to imagine.

The exercise I conduct with Mexico City may prove useful for understanding and detecting risks in other cities, as well as examining critically some problems in the theory of globalization. Just as the debate over modernity provided innovative resources with which to analyze cities such as Paris, Berlin, and Vienna, the study of New York, London, and Tokyo today helps clarify the processes of globalization.

If writing about globalization is, in the words of Arjun Appadurai, "a moderate exercise in megalomania," Mexico City, because of its size, is an optimal stage on which to attempt to do so.[1] In fact, this megalopolis meets the four usual requirements for being a global city: a strong multinational corporate presence; the multicultural presence of peoples from different regions within the country and from other nations; a prestige based on the concentration of artistic and scientific elites; and significant international tourism.[2]

While the contradictory development of Mexico City does not allow one to place it among the global cities I have just mentioned, the potential of Mexico City within the regional and global economy is comparable to that of Barcelona, Brussels, Paris, and Hong Kong. Like those cities, the Mexican capital is notable for extending beyond the country's borders its activities in the realms of finance, consulting, design, and the development of audiovisual and computer industries.

Even before there was any talk of globalization, that is, at least from the mid-twentieth century, Mexico City captured the imaginations of thousands of artists and intellectuals, entrepreneurs and tourists, thanks to its powerful pre-Columbian, colonial, and modern history. These attractions were decisive in seducing the world until the end of the twentieth century—perhaps after the construction of the city's National Museum of Anthropology and its Museum of Modern Art, both of which opened in 1964, and for a couple of decades thereafter. But these attractions are not sufficient in the twenty-first century.

What are the other forms of economic and cultural capital of which Mexico can avail itself today? There are at least three: a vigorous industrial infrastructure for the production of books, radio, television, and, to a lesser degree, film and contemporary popular music; multicultural communities created by domestic migrations and by artists, intellectuals, and scientists in exile from

Spain, from Central and South America, and from Eastern Europe due to the world wars and, later, the fall of the Soviet bloc; and many years of experience in existing *in between* Europe, the United States, and South America, in between indigenous legacies and the heritage of modernity. Mexico City is not only the nation's capital but also a privileged site of such cultural capital. As a country and a city, however, Mexico is only beginning to make use of its resources, and then only at a low profile within global circuits.

There are more museums in Mexico City (92) than there are in New York (88), Buenos Aires (55), Madrid (47), and São Paulo (32). Mexico City also supports a greater number of outlets that deal in crafts than exist in all of those cities combined, as well as a repertoire of entertainment sites comparable to that of those metropolises. But to become global, a city must also be safe, boast modern and postmodern commercial and cultural attractions, and, above all, possess efficient services and agile electronic connections.

Studies which register the conditions demanded by five hundred Latin American executives to determine the cities in which they will conduct business and would be willing to live show that a premium is placed on cities that combine high educational standards with qualified personnel, security, efficiency, cultural life, and a good potential for international communication and conducting business. Mexico City is not in a bad position in terms of communications, cultural offerings, and the qualifications of its workforce. Nonetheless, its efficiency and safety are not of a quality in which its residents could pride themselves. Entrepreneurs and leaders have voiced their concern over the increase in crime and the decrease in productivity caused by the slow pace of traffic (each resident spends an average of three hours a day making commutes that should take only one hour). The chaotic disintegration of public life, which has grown more accentuated as the population of the Mexican capital has grown from 3 million to 19 million over the last fifty years, has led writers such as José Emilio Pacheco to say that the Mexican capital is a "post-city"—or in the words of Carlos Monsiváis, "a post-apocalyptic city, because the worst has already happened."[3]

AN IMAGINED CITY, ALWAYS A ROUGH DRAFT

The contradictions between Mexico City's potential and its deficient realization of its calling to globalization make one wonder what may be the consequences of the tension between the exuberant imaginaries that the city has

Ambulant vendors
on Mexico City's
periferico. Photo by
Paolo Gasparini.

generated and repeated many times over in its history as a result of envisioning itself as a shared, inhabitable space.

But I will not speak only of Mexico City. It is convenient to link these developments in the city with the shift exhibited in the last twenty years by international thinking in the field of urban studies, to note the contrast between the expansion of studies about urban imaginaries and the reduction of the prospective horizon in urban planning. There is a contradiction, observes the Argentine humanist Adrián Gorelik, between "the cultural (generally academic) reflection on the most diverse ways in which societies represent themselves within their cities and build their modes of communication and its codes for understanding urban life, and the dimension of political-technical reflection (generally concentrated within a handful of professions such as architecture, urban studies and planning) on the way a city ought to be."[4]

Since the nineteenth century, the creation of Latin American cities has engaged in a lively interaction with the representations produced about those cities. Three analysts of urban history and Latin American intellectual history—José Luis Romero, Ángel Rama, and Richard Morse—have shown that urban imaginaries and cultural imaginaries converged as projects propelling social development. There was no easy agreement between the imaginations of intellectuals, writers, and artists and the work of urban planners, but they nourished each other and together generated matrices of a social understanding and social transformation of modernity.

Today, on the other hand, there is "a symbolic inflation of interpretations of the city and society," says Gorelik, in contrast with a softness of projection and lack of perspective in the diagnoses of urban planners.[5] Or, following the Brazilian analyst Otilia Fiori Arantes, there occurs a different kind of complementation: "Among urbanists—usually from a progressive background—and entrepreneurs who have found in the city a new field for accumulation: the former have dedicated themselves, apparently following an epochal mandate, to making projections 'in provocatively explicit, managerial terms'; the latter do nothing more than celebrate the cultural values of the city, praising the 'heartbeat of every street, square, or urban fragment,' for which reason both parties end up speaking the same jargon of urban authenticity that can be termed a market-culturalism."[6]

How has this tension and contemplation between cultural and urban-planning imaginaries unfolded? Without a doubt, it has manifested itself in a formidable capacity to conceive of something that has not existed for centuries and to invent a city where once there was only a lake. It was necessary to channel the rivers, cover the canals, and imagine a dry city in which there was such an abundance of liquid. It would be possible, too, to list many other conflicts between imaginaries that are still being disputed today in the megalopolis: the fantasies of those who arrive from the provinces seeking work and a better quality of life; the fantasies of those who have come from abroad believing that they have arrived at the most populous and most polluted city in the world. Few megalopolises have been imagined as much as Mexico City, from the descriptions of Hernán Cortés to those of American journalists and Latin American exiles, from travel agencies to international television.

But if the Mexican capital today is more disorderly than baroque, it is because the imaginaries in conflict have worked to destroy or ignore one another, rather than to create a shared utopia—and because many of its catastrophes are tragic revelations of a lack of imagination about the future that was taking shape.

The architect Yoshinoba Ashisara wrote that urban space could be created in one of two ways: by addition or by subtraction. The majority of urban inhabitants and city managers in Mexico City have never felt it necessary to choose between these two strategies. The city expanded from the historic-downtown district into the distant mountains, cutting down forests, paving hillsides, tearing down houses to build highway loops and street axes to allow access to the invaded outskirts, adding to those allegedly rapid thoroughfares thousands of overlapping billboards, saturating the visual space with so many promises that no one manages to read, and no one manages to imagine much at all.

Let me examine from several different perspectives how the tension between the imagined city and the unimaginable city occurs today. A first perspective is that of the consumer, who must orient himself or herself within all that has been added to and subtracted from Mexico City. It is difficult for this person to understand where she lives and what spaces she traverses when she crosses this megalopolis, which at the beginning of the twentieth century occupied 9.1 square kilometers and today spills out over an area of 1,500 square kilometers.

Several years ago I and other scholars in the Urban Culture Program at the Universidad Autónoma Metropolitana researched photographic archives to document the changes in the means of travel within the city over the last half of the twentieth century. We then gathered ten groups of people who traverse the city daily—food-delivery personnel, street vendors, taxi drivers, students, transit police—and showed them fifty photographs from which they were to choose the most representative. The images unleashed stories of those things one suspects when traveling through unknown areas of the city. One of the findings of the study was that the majority of participants found it difficult to imagine the city in which they lived, to visualize where it began and ended, even the places they passed through every day. Facing enigmas and threats, they made assumptions, created myths, devised short-term tactics to avoid traffic jams, and made occasional agreements with strangers. None of them had a clear picture of the whole map of the megalopolis. None of them attempted to grasp all of it. They survived by imagining small environments within their reach. Given the difficulty in understanding macrosocial transformations and the structural causes of the city's disasters, they placed the blame on specific groups: immigrants who arrived unprepared for life in the big city, political demonstrations that slowed down traffic, the excess of automobiles (although no one mentioned specific parties at fault), police corruption, or the irresponsibility of car owners who triple-parked their vehicles. A casuistically constructed urban culture thus engenders a *pre-political culture*, in which isolated instances of guilt are identified instead of systematic causes.

A second perspective is that of people who are able to view the city *from the heights* of power and communication. While the dispersal of the city makes interaction between its neighborhoods difficult and dissolves the image of the city as a whole, the mass media distributes images that reconnect its scattered parts. Just as the visuality of the modern city was organized by means of the flâneur and the literary chronicle, in the current megalopolis the pretension of providing totalizing narratives is delegated to the helicopter that hovers over the city and every morning offers, by radio and television, the simulacrum of a vision of the whole. Manned by the police force that patrols the city and by journalists who provide citizens with information, this new panoptic power indicates where there has been a car accident, which streets are congested, and which alternate routes can be taken. The system exhibits a collaboration between control by the police and control by television. Insofar as this media vision does not offer reasoned information about "the uncontrollable," it keeps citizens watching this spectacle of insecurity from their living rooms, rather than help them to imagine their citizenship. One has gone from the "lettered city," as Ángel Rama described the city conceived and narrated by literary texts, to an audiovisual city, the city as "told" by the mass media.[7] One's ability to make any kind of sense of the city now depends not so much on long-form narratives (for example, the novels of Carlos Fuentes and José Emilio Pacheco), but on the information provided daily by the ephemeral discourse of Televisa.

This passing from long-form narratives to instant flashes corresponds to the predominance of "planners" who have abandoned their interest in the total city, or who have simply come too late. No sooner does one learn that

At the cathedral of Mexico City. Photo by Paolo Gasparini.

the first normative plan for Mexico City was drafted in 1979 than one begins to think that the people in government between the 1950s and 1970s, during which time the city's population grew from three to fifteen million inhabitants, lacked the imagination to foresee with each passing term the traffic jams and pollution, the indignation and impotence that would afflict the city in the next *sexenio*. They added thoroughfares and cars and buses, and waited until the 1980s to see what needed to be subtracted or reduced or built at a less-monumental scale in order to avoid the disintegration that would triumph over a sense of community.

In recent years, given the difficult task of solving these problems as a whole, a few of the city's zones were chosen to serve as ultramodern focal points, places where one can fantasize that one is tuning in to globalization. The most recent imaginary, proposed at the start of the twenty-first century, is that Mexico might be able to save itself as a global city. Some theorists of globalization validate this fantasy: Manuel Castells, Jordi Borja, and Saskia Sassen write that the Mexican capital, in fact, meets several of the requirements for being a global city. But these theorists, as well as some local scholars, draw attention to the abysmal contradictions between the city moving toward globalization and the city that is in the process of disintegrating. It's odd: the rapid growth of Mexico City (like that of São Paulo, Caracas, and Lima) in the last half-century is due to the millions of Mexicans who migrated to the capital imagining that the city's industrialization could be of benefit to all. Since the opening-up of Mexico's economy to the rest of the world in the early 1980s, the city has been deindustrializing, and it is believed that the most dynamic growth areas are linked to the arrival of corporate services. Mexico City and its metropolitan outskirts have become one of the twenty urban megacenters with the greatest concentration of devices for development, innovation, and commercialization at a global scale. This change is most apparent in the nearly 800 hectares in the Santa Fe area that are taken up by buildings housing Hewlett-Packard, Mercedes-Benz, Chubb Insurance, Televisa, and other companies, as well as by shopping centers and upscale residential neighborhoods. It is also visible in the architectural remodeling of the Paseo de la Reforma, Polanco, Insurgentes, and Periférico Sur areas, in the proliferation of mega–shopping centers, new corporate hotels, the modernization of the telecommunications industry and its satellite connections, and the expansion of computer services and cable and digital television. The wager is that the "monstropolis," as Emiliano Pérez Cruz has called it, will be rescued through its connection with global imaginaries.

I find it suggestive at this point to attempt a comparative hypothesis with Berlin. I cannot for the moment enter into the long and storied public debate, generated in Germany and in the fields of urban and cultural studies and politics, over the metamorphosis of the Potsdamer Platz. But it is significant that the current cluster of corporate buildings, stores, and high-tech entertainment outlets, built by world-renowned architects, was erected in one of the most emblematic, central areas of the German capital city as "an amnesiac space," in the words of Régine Robin, which eliminated all references to the history of modernization in the early decades of the twentieth century, to the Berlin Wall, and to the other historical moments concentrated in that square.[8] On the other hand, Santa Fe—the largest business and corporate center in Mexico and Latin America—was built by overlaying an "American-style" tracing and architectural image onto a marginal area of Mexico City inhabited only by recent migrants, almost all of them extremely poor. But at the same time one could ask whether this great respect for the historical centers of Mexico City and the location of Santa Fe at the edge of one of the city's most important urban projects, with which president Carlos Salinas chose to give space to the project of "placing Mexico within the first world," do not represent a disconnect between a globalist "utopia" and the historic city resigned to a deficient modernity. While Berlin globalizes its urban space by substitution, Mexico City does so by addition.

The creation of nodes of development for global services attempts to isolate this area from traditional sectors, from informal or marginal economic activities, from deficient urban centers, from the frustrated fantasies of unemployment and the fear of crime. The doubling of the global city and the local, marginal, and unsafe city may be the first obstacle for Mexico to overcome in order to be imagined as an attractive site for global corporations. As Borja and Castells have warned, one of the great risks of globalization is that it could occur only for an elite: "One part of the city is sold, while the rest is hidden and abandoned."[9]

PREDICTIONS AMID IMPROVISATION

It is often said in city and tourist magazines as well as in journals of art and history that Mexico City is the most important pre-Columbian and colonial city in America. At the same time, it is often discussed as a megalopolis that has grown in such a staggered, awkward manner that it seems to lack any sort of master plan, a city in which one can barely conceive one's day-to-day survival. One has no way of knowing whether tomorrow the city's plumbing will burst again and flood who knows how many neighborhoods, whether the Popocatépetl Volcano will cover the city in ash, or whether forty different political demonstrations with participants numbering in the thousands will paralyze a quarter of the city.

Who can predict what Mexico City will be like in the year 2010? Amid so many uncertainties, some tendencies in the city's sociocultural development show a certain consistency. Furthermore, today it is more viable to establish what these predominant lines of development are than it was fifteen years ago, when the first studies relating cultural politics, consumption, and citizenship were conducted. Without a doubt, this is one of the important changes that have taken place in Mexico: one can talk about the city, especially its sociocultural aspects, using data that one did not have two decades ago.

I will rely in particular on the research my colleagues and I conducted in

Urban flooding. Photo: Casasola.

the Urban Culture Program at the Universidad Autónoma Metropolitana (UAM), in Mexico City.[10] This set of studies provides some basic references to what remains, and what is changing, in Mexico City from the 1990s through the beginning of the twenty-first century. I will first mention some things that seem rather stable and predictable, then some of what is changing and might trigger innovation by 2010.

PREDICTABLE ELEMENTS

The first tendency that relies on the development of the city is the spread of the urban blot in all directions. This has reformulated the city's relationships with the environment, just as it has shaped the downtown area's links with the outskirts of the city, and the relationship of that which can be contained within the city to that which escapes governmental control. This experience of the uncontainable becomes more acute as the Mexican capital develops as a global city, a node of communications, services, and migrations that link it tightly with cities in many other regions in North, Central, and South America, in Europe and Asia.

A second characteristic is the demographic predominance of the city's

Photo by Paolo Gasparini.

outskirts over the Federal District and the creation of commercial and cultural centers, often interrelated, in the inner and outer peripheries of the capital. More and more one is living in a polycentric, multifocal, and multinodal city. Nonetheless, the predominance of the outer city over the historical city does not allow one to ignore the interactions between the two circles; three million people living in twenty-nine adjoining municipalities commute daily into the city for work, consumption, and entertainment.

Third, one must make note of the democratization of Mexico City and certain aspects of its citizen culture, which manifests itself most importantly in the election of city officials and now also of officials for each district. It is an incomplete democratization, which does not include all aspects of urban life—its cultural aspects, for example.

Fourth, one might also point out the leading role of the mass media as purveyor of information and entertainment, as articulator of the dispersed city and organizer of the public sphere. I will not address at length this internationally generalized process, which has created a new type of public field, managed at its core by the culture industries and by the mass media. The prevalence of the media over firsthand interactions, which began in the mid-twentieth century, will continue to grow as a result of greater access to cable television, computer services, and other modes of home entertainment and information delivery.

Last, I will mention as a unifying trait among urban experiences the increase in violence and crime. These have extended themselves to the entire metropolitan area, not only as constantly occurring, real-life events, but also in the central role they have come to play in the field of information and the re-ordering of the urban lifestyle. This generalized experience is associated with important material and symbolic effects such as the predominance of the private over the public, the prevalence of the imaginary of risk and refuge in closed neighborhoods, or in the home itself, over imaginaries of the shared city.

CHANGES IN COURSE

In analyzing the transformations in contemporary urban life, I will take into account what is visible in the cultural development of the city and also what one might conjecture will be accentuated as 2010 approaches. I would like to begin with a self-criticism. In the studies I and my colleagues conducted over the last ten years in the Urban Culture Program at UAM, we had to rectify several ideas that we had been constructing about transformations in the city. For instance, in the first half of the 1990s we recorded the closing of many movie theaters, which had started happening in the 1980s as a result of an abrupt decrease in the number of viewers. This decline in spectatorship, from 90 million a year to some 28 million in 1995, has been partially reversed with the explosion of multiplexes in many parts of the city. A more equitable distribution of cinematic offerings has made our 1994 book *Los nuevos espectadores* outdated.[11]

However, other trends in audiovisual consumption found during that period have been reinforced. One of these is the expansion of television offerings. What was an open television media controlled by a single monopoly has been replaced by a more extensive offering, which could reach several hundred channels in just a few years. These changes have more to do with quantity than variety; when the television industry first began to expand (with the emergence of Televisión Azteca), it was widely thought that "nothing could be worse than Televisa"—but it turned out that there was something worse. However, with the introduction of the Sky network, a portion of the viewership does enjoy cable or satellite TV, and further technological innovations are promised. The expansion in television offerings is, of course, primarily available to the elite and middle sectors.

Second, the construction of multiplex cinemas is modernizing the moviegoing experience and attracting a larger public, most notably young people. Cinema complexes and shopping malls, which appear to be associated, are the main reactivators of public life and of cultural consumption in open spaces or outside of domestic life. While in the first half of the 1990s one could perceive a concentration of entertainment in the home, today one can appreciate that a certain reversal has occurred. Without having increased to the former 90 million cinema attendees, the numbers have nevertheless reached some 48 million moviegoers per year. Clearly, some aspects of public social interaction are being revitalized.

A third change is the expansion of technologically advanced communications networks, which are differentiated from the mass media or the cinema: computers, the Internet, faxes, electronically linked banking services, even electronic purchases, the development of which appears to be slower in Mexico City than in other metropolitan areas. In any event, this growth in high-level technological networks, accessible only to certain sectors of the city, is recomposing the fabric of communications, as well as many habits of consumption, in the metropolis. It also restructures the role of the capital as the center of the country and its relationships with global markets and circuits.

Fourth, as a result of the preceding two processes, the public is living with a predominance of video culture and, more recently, of electronic communication over traditional information media (newspapers, magazines, or face-to-face exchanges of information in neighborhood life). One of the most stunning findings in recent memory is the result of a survey on cultural habits, conducted by the newspaper *Reforma* in January 2001, which showed that the number of people who read newspapers daily in Mexico City coincides with the number who are, or claim to be, daily computer users: 20 out of every 100 inhabitants. Mexico City's low readership index is matched by public fascination with computers.

Between what is left of written culture and the acceleration of a digital culture that reaches very few people, there is a predominant system, at once disseminated and highly concentrated, which, as Paul Virilio suggests, no longer works with discourses but with flashes and images. Just as the process of partially substituting direct interaction with media communications, concentrated in the home, creates a new kind of relationship with space, the predominance of present-tense experiences over the long-form narratives of the lettered city (and in the case of Mexico, of its folklore) engenders a new relationship with social time.

POSSIBLE FUTURES

Finally, I will essay a few considerations on the cultural changes foreseeable as the year 2010 approaches. To this end it is necessary to differentiate between predictable cultural changes—those changes that will occur because they appear objectively inevitable—and those that might come about were there a transformation in the management of public life. In the first place, there begins to be a more equitable distribution of cultural offerings in the metropolitan space, but this distribution is usually carried out by private initiative, seldom by public programs—that is, through television and the cinema, rather than through the decentralization of state-funded mechanisms. There is an advanced democratization in the political sphere, but it is accompanied neither by a redistribution of cultural mechanisms nor by agreements between the Federal District and its surrounding municipalities for the articulation of information and entertainment, or for any other services.

What kind of spatial infrastructure does the public need for its cultural mechanisms? More *casas de la cultura*, more libraries, more well-equipped theatres and concert halls, in the north and south of the city, in the east and west? Certainly, but the city also needs to develop media and computer policies oriented by and toward public services. It is necessary to democratize the relationship between local cultures and promote their own development with greater resources. At the same time, a city such as Mexico City must assume

Goodbye at the
airport. Photo by
Marco Antonio Cruz.

its role as a Latin American capital and global city through festivals, investments in tourism, and cultural and mass-media attractions. At the moment,
there can be no cultural policy of the majority, in the city or in any country, if
there is not a media policy with a sense of public service. It must be said that
the dearth of initiatives in this field on the part of the city and of the nation's
recent governments reveals the lack of a globalist vocation on the part of
public actors in our culture.

Of course, these modifications depend not solely on government but also
on new options created by civil associations and by new citizens' initiatives.
After all that the 1985 earthquake subtracted from Mexico City, the public
was beginning to activate a more cooperative imagination. It appeared determined to bring together the imaginaries of social movements and political
parties, of citizens and consumers. However, when such catastrophes recede
from memory, the imagination veers away from the sense of common cause,
and citizenship is reduced to the limited areas through which one moves:

work, the children's school, the safety of the block on which one lives.[12] Will this megalopolis be too vast for its citizens to imagine it as a unified whole? Or is it perhaps one of the long-term functions of imaginaries to placate social disturbances, to propose equilibriums and pacts between conflicting forces in their most immediate manifestations? It would appear that in this time, in which global communications promote comparisons and even imitations among cities, the public finds it difficult to experience the different parts of a single megalopolis as being related.

Perhaps one chooses to live in cities not only because of the richness of stimuli that excite our imagination; perhaps one does so also because cities in which precariousness and disorder triumph contain and give rest to our imaginary vertigos. That is why one organizes one's experience of the urban environment selectively. In the words of Luis García Montero, referring here to his own city, Granada, "Each person has a city which is the urbanized landscape of his or her feelings."[13] Perhaps in order to understand the fascination that living in a global city elicits, it is necessary at once to think of the city, one's most intimate and restricted metropolis, as a refuge against what one finds vertiginous in globalization. The question that remains is whether this protective function of urban life can be fulfilled when inequality and disconnection prevail over all the things that make people live together.

TRANSLATED BY EDGAR LOY FANKBONNER

NOTES

1. Appadurai 1996, 18.
2. Hannerz 1996.
3. Monsiváis 1995, 21.
4. Gorelik 2002.
5. Ibid.
6. Fiori Arantes 2000, 19.
7. Rama 1984.
8. Robin 2001.
9. Borja and Castells 1997.
10. García Canclini et al. 1998.
11. García Canclini 1994.
12. Zermeño 2001.
13. García Montero 1972, 71.

AFRICA

AbdouMaliq Simone

THE LAST SHALL BE FIRST

AFRICAN URBANITIES AND THE LARGER URBAN WORLD

What I want to do in this essay is to raise the possibility that the ways in which life has been experienced in the diverse cities of Middle Africa over the past several decades constitute a potential capacity on the part of many residents to resiliently and strategically engage new forms of urban regulation, primarily elaborated elsewhere.[1] In other words, urban Africans may know a great deal about how to live through and in the emerging and highly murky terrains of European and North American cities that are, on the surface, a long way from home. Home has become, for many Africans, an impossible location in which to anticipate a future and is thus constructed across a variety of sites, networks, and compositions. As a result, urban Africa increasingly intersects with a growing number of cities external to the region and with more heterogeneous complexes of urban politics, labor markets, and cultural expressions. This intersection is, of course, a means of extending urban Africa across new geographies, as it is an instrument that also informs, complicates, and contaminates conventional understandings of urban processes everywhere.

PEOPLING URBAN INFRASTRUCTURE

Yet in positing the capacity of urban Africa to produce sensibilities, practices, trajectories of movement, and economies particularly conversant with the new terms, with the "new school" of urban formation and control, it is important to emphasize a fundamental risk in the deployment of such capacity, for this capacity cannot simply be the strengthening of human capital or social tactical proficiency in a logic of consolidation or development. What I am pointing to, rather, is a reality of people as infrastructure and a reading of the city as if there were no difference between people and infrastructure. The implication is that the consolidation of individuals, institutions, sectors, or specializations is no longer a predominant urban operation and thus no longer an impediment to converting people into all kinds of uses. People from all walks of life can be assembled to have remarkable reach and efficiency. At the same time, people, regardless of what they are, can be arbitrarily wasted. This doubleness is certainly reflected in the translocal illicit economies, smuggling circuits, and the making of something out of nothing that are increasingly important to African urban economies.[2]

Of course one must situate this present capacity within a particular reading of urban colonial history. What was attained by Africans in terms of their engagement with cities—particularly in the areas of social cognition and social practice—could never be fully instantiated within the city. Even when substantial rearrangements in cultural life and social economy were precipitated by an urban presence, the potential interconnections among emerging networks of social practice, economic specialization, and cultural reformation were constrained. Clear vehicles of institutionalization were usually foreclosed, largely by the dearth of available public spheres that were not heavily scrutinized or repressed by existing regimes.

Therefore, these urban attainments were usually dispersed outside of the city, invested in transitional populations situated in-between the distinct forms of rural and urban rule or moving back and forth among them.[3] The city became a site of deferral, where locally honed aspirations, emergent institutions, and economies capable of extending and deepening African uses of urban space were, for the most part, readapted toward deflecting the impositions and segregation of colonial rule. Simultaneously, they were also applied to maximizing the potentials of under-regulated spaces of opera-

Motor-taxi drivers, Douala. Photo by Stefan Barbic.

tion at the peripheries of cities, but without the urban topological and social complexion necessary to really incubate and develop these nascent urban orientations and practices.

At the same time, colonial rule was always partial and heterogeneous, always rearranged or distorted through the ways in which it was implemented.[4] Therefore, urban Africans incessantly looked for openings to actively "partialize" and distort imposed rule, to make it work for self-conceived agendas. This was a process which often meant large measures of dissimulation, of enacting what on the surface may have looked to be highly traditional or parochial practices as covers for incipient urban styles.

Today, at a global level, urbanism as a technological instrument and the systematic infrastructural and planning biases it implies have come to play a significant role in recomposing territories. This recomposition occurs through a networked geography of highly capacitated spaces inducing cities to extend their reach and to consolidate economic proficiency and extensiveness regardless of the histories, livelihoods, and aspirations of the majority of residents who reside in these cities. High-tech enclaves arising either within existing urban territories or adjacent to them increasingly operate on the

Douala from the cemetery. Photo by Stefan Barbic.

platform of connectivity with similar spaces across the world and are thus conceptually disconnected from the physical geography of the city. Through the dismantling of public infrastructure into an assortment of varying grada- tions and privatized delivery systems, specific domains of the city become in- creasingly delinked from each other as new infrastructures, at times custom- made for the new economic and social requirements of highly capacitated domains, circumvent the existing grid.[5]

What is at stake in revalorizing the urbanities of Africa in part centers on "heretical" uses of infrastructure and the "counter-urbanisms" they generate. These stand in stark contrast to those high-tech and privileged enclaves of unbundled and disconnected infrastructures whose speculative construction is seen to be driving new economies and new social conditions in the era of globalization. There is an incessant push and pull of these two kinds of ur- banisms (or forms of city building), one engaged with making the most of re- pair, breakdowns, dereliction, and obsolescence, and the other with the wired and wireless universe, with cutting-edge, high-speed, high-connectivity in- formation transfer and continuous logistics.[6] As enclaves erect barriers to ensure the security of increasingly networked relations among discrete cities and to maximize the coherence and predictability of various dimensions of urban life, heretical uses of existing environments constantly compromise and breach these barriers, reconfiguring them and exposing them as forms of attack on heterogeneous lives and livelihoods. Conversely, the speculations associated with new urbanism strategies thrive on the reinforcement of the fragmentation of existing urban environments and often use infrastructural materials to enforce this fragmentation.

All cities remain the densities of stories, passions, hurts, revenge, aspiration, avoidance, deflection, and complicity. As such, residents must be able to conceive of a space sufficiently bounded to consolidate disparate energies in order to make things of scale happen, but at the same time conceive of a fractured space sufficiently large through which dangerous feelings can dissipate or be steered away. In middle Africa this is particularly important as institutions lack sufficient authority to instill any overarching matrix of definitions and spatial framework capable of holding residents in stable articulations with infrastructure, territory, and urban resources of all kinds.[7] State administrations and civil institutions have lacked the political and economic power to assign buying, selling, exchanging, collecting, dissembling, stealing, importing, fabricating, and residing to specific bounded spaces of deployment, codes of articulation, or the purview of designated actors.

So a major preoccupation of African urban actors is the concern with what kinds of games, instruments, languages, sight lines, constructions, and objects can be put in play in order to anticipate new alignments of social initiative and resources, and thus capacity—rather than to represent or embody a specific set of aspirations, values, or social formations.[8] How can people from different walks of life be engaged in each other's lives without necessarily obliging specific transactions and obligations?[9] The subsequent permutations resuscitate mutual interest in the game, even when the discernible benefits may not be clear or when participants are faced with inconclusive evidence of their own positions within them.

PROVIDING WITH THE PROVISIONAL

The constant litany regarding urban Africa centers largely on the need for more efficient planning, for the common assumption is that planning gen-

Zone Nylon, Douala. Photo by Stefan Barbic.

erates enhanced productivity and viable livelihoods. Yet for the most part African cities intensify their existence as places of speculation, something which is frequently misread as an overwhelming inertia. Indeed, individuals, groups, and institutions which minimize their commitment to trajectories set in advance and with clearly delineated stages and operational procedures, so as to maintain a certain opportunistic resilience and an ability to change gears, can often appear to be doing nothing. And, certainly, nothing is often what takes place, as any cursory look at urban landscapes with their rusted cars, collapsed buildings, and overgrown public spaces will testify to. While it is clear that the pursuit of structured plans, development agendas, and rational decision making require economic supports and political will often lacking in impoverished societies, the apparent provisionality of African urban life also masks the degree to which residents capitalize on some of the most elemental facets of "cityness" itself.

What are people paying attention to in the highly public scenarios of trade, exchange, domestic management, and transport which characterize everyday African urban life? Attaining even the minimum livelihood often requires complex styles of staying attuned to the shifting intersections of gestures, excitements, languages, anxieties, determinations, and comportments enacted across markets, streets, and other venues. The city is a field of affect where specific dispositions and attainments are contingent on the ways actors' bodies, histories, and capacities are mobilized and enacted. With so much going on, what will people pay attention to and how? What are they prepared to do? What configurations of words, movement, and sound affect particular inclinations? For many, the job of urban life has been to maintain a heightened sense of engagement with all that could ensue from applying a barely indiscernible gaze, from overhearing a conversation, from securing an almost invisible yet strategic proximity to others, from interrupting the flow of events ever so slightly but powerfully enough to move something in another direction.

Like in any game of speculation, it is not always clear what is gained or lost. In all the work that market touts, cart drivers, bar girls, store clerks, and street phone vendors do to quickly scrutinize the scenes unfolding in front of them and with actors in various states of consumption, the evidence needed to feel confident that one has done a good job at seizing some unanticipated opportunities and rewards is rarely sufficient in itself to keep the game going. Yet as long as those actors believe that something has been set in motion, that someone has been affected in such a way that at some point in the future there will be rewards to be collected, they will continue to make sure that something will have been inserted — a few words, a glance, a small talisman, anything that attempts to steer the scene and its contents in a direction that they believe they can follow. In classical economics the transaction costs in these microeconomies are enormous, yet these peculiarities that can be supplemented to any transaction, however routine and mundane, are exactly the only things that many have to work with.

When reference is made to the art of making do, of getting by, too often it concerns that which is weakly guarded, underplanned, or overly vulnerable, rather than the cognitive and affective efforts that go into maneuvering the relations between social spaces, visual fields, symbolic resources, concrete objects, and linguistic materials. Whereas planning discourses center largely on defining, consolidating, and articulating a given position in relationship to others, the urban game for many Africans is to become nodes of gravity that

The new public square, Le Village, Douala. Photo by Stefan Barbic.

draw attention not by standing still and defending a niche, but by an ability to "show up," make oneself present, no matter the circumstances, in a kind of social promiscuity. Just when one thought that the hustler in the market would be content to ply his or her trade in the narrow side alleys, he or she would show up at a high-school fair selling cakes, or at a seminar at the university, at a press conference for the minister of finance, or at the wedding of a dignitary of a distant neighborhood.

The idea is to try to insert oneself in many walks of life so that the sense is created that many walks of life are coming to you. This is why much attention is paid to how people are eating and drinking, how they are having sex, how they are talking to different people—in other words, how they are being open to the world, how they are enacting their aliveness, how they are trying to secure a connection with the larger world. And as these tasks are accomplished with particular tools and materials—linguistic, behavioral, symbolic—they are available to interventions, rearrangements, and simulations. In cities where nearly everyone is trying to sell something which many others are also selling, the key is how to become a source of attraction, how to get people to pay attention, how many people with different needs can come to see them being fulfilled by you.

In scores of conversations I have had with various "entrepreneurs" over the years in the city of Douala, Cameroon, seemingly peculiar, often obsessive decisions are attributed to be at the core of certain unanticipated advantages or opportunities. A young girl waits for hours in the rain for weeks, convinced that some passing car will eventually feel sympathetic and carry her away to a different life; a bartender plays the same song over and over, knowing that eventually a white expatriate will pass the place and, hearing his "favorite song," stop by the bar and begin a conversation that could change the bartender's life; a motorbike taxi driver stops to eat at a different roadside restaurant everyday so as to surreptitiously sprinkle a powder he is convinced will compel the diners to dream of him; a university graduate leaves designs for new wastewater systems behind the wipers of parked cars; another has a friend in the home-affairs department check the birthdates and addresses of every Chinese female storekeeper in the city so that he can deliver a bouquet of flowers on each of their birthdays. In each case, the individuals professed that something extraordinary did happen as a result.

Although generalizations are both difficult and dangerous when it comes to characterizing the complexities of contemporary African urban life, many youth clearly indicate that they live in an incessant present. Sometimes different "scores" can provide enough money to live months down the line or simply until the next day—there is no predicting. How this prolonged present is lived in and operated by various individual and collective actors can vary widely across a given city. Often the apparent dysfunction of transactions is a product of highly circumscribed views of the complex relations existing among residents from varying walks of life. Particularly important to this discussion is evidence of the concrete ways in which particular neighborhoods either attempt to erode differences among who people are and what they are doing or, alternately, to emphasize the singularities of people's actions and find ways to make use of most everything that is produced.

For example, the owners of an Internet cafe in the Douala neighborhood of New Deido have experimented with a text-messaging system that serves as a kind of catalog for the usually unpublicized and unofficial work being done by neighborhood residents in specific sites. As people pass a photocopy booth, or a cigarette stand, or a small bar, those with MTN messaging services will receive a text message indicating that the proprietor or worker at that site is also preparing elaborate business plans for the development of generators that run on cassava husks, or designing witchcraft-detection devices, or compiling lists of best truck routes from Chad to Libya. At the core of the project are the notions that the neighborhood cannot afford to dismiss any idea or project, no matter how seemingly absurd or unrealistic, and that there is a potential audience for any project, that someone can make some use of these efforts if only they know about them.

In part, this continuous revalorization of what exists drives the operations of increasingly dispersed markets, where more and more urban space is "turned over" to a kind of incessant marketing, where things and services are bought and sold, or seized and dispossessed. For the past several years the Central Market in Douala has been treated as the source of simple inputs for the parasitical lifestyles of large numbers of youth, most of whom live in the surrounding residential areas of New Bell. They get up early in the morning to intercept small items from those who are on their way to the market to sell or in the early stages of opening their stalls or shops. Those doing this prolific but gentle looting just take those items that can be immediately consumed for that day or that can be quickly sold. To do the minimum is what can be guaranteed and anticipated, in a merging of necessity and expectation that puts aside the ever-increasing gaps between what is viewed as possible and what is actually hoped for, gaps that have characterized so much of the urban mentality. After the looting, there is a ritualistic recitation of the items acquired, a roll call where the items are bartered for or matched to running lists of items that neighbors often actually request (e.g., "If you happen to come across a broom, would you let me know?"). Without wages or large bankrolls or scams behind them, the "minimalists" are forced to make every opportunity count.

In the scores of neighborhood markets that operate with small margins across the rest of the city, the indiscriminate valuation of goods that has emerged from the quotidian parasitism rampant in the Central Market has led to a practice whereby, in addition to the sale of the usual array of commodities, various items, services, and prospects are bundled together and sold as such. For example, boxes of pasta are bundled with reparations of household water taps as well as with opportunities to acquire aluminum roofing materials that are purportedly on their way to the area after "falling off a truck" at the Nigerian border. Different materials—commodities, information, services, commitments, affiliations—are converted into a single unit of sale, and markets are thereby opened up to the participation of a wider range of actors, seeking opportunities, proclaiming skills, offering insider information, or looking to be that extra person who is needed to complete transactions wherein some kind of labor is involved. By removing things from set privileged positions or from accustomed frameworks of use and regard, there is potentially greater latitude to get whatever exists in the market into more expansive and intensified circulation. Here, things and services try to "piggy-back" their way into wider dissemination through their often highly unconventional associations with other things.

While it defies economic common sense, both excess and scarcity are brought together so as to get what can be marketed—which is now nearly everything—to move. Hoarding and profit taking, of course, continue to exist, yet the dispersion of the parasitical enables a kind of mediation between two problematic tendencies: on the one hand, the tendency of urban residents to narrow the scope of their social worlds to the familiar tropes of ethnicity and family as the arenas through which some kind of trust can be guaranteed; on the other, the tendency to try and opportunistically seize chances to involve oneself in scenarios, deals, and networks that do not obligate any particular course of action or responsibility.

After all, Douala has long been a town of entrepreneurship, of keeping the deal going beyond the contingencies and institutions of politics, and of resisting stabilized meanings and anchored positions. As the past years of civil conflict demonstrate, urban politics has rarely been creative, but markets are still places where there is some experimentation with political comportment, a way of enacting individual need and skill that gives up immediate reward in anticipation that interweaving oneself with others might prove lucrative in the future. The development apparatuses of nongovernmental organizations and multilateral institutions tend to think that economic revitalization rests with a more systematic mobilization of underutilized social capital, with relations based on reciprocity and trust. Even if such remains the case in the everyday transactions of neighborhoods, something more ephemeral is taking place.

This is reflected in current popular understandings as to what makes a

The new middle class, Douala. Photo by Stefan Barbic.

successful man or woman. In the colonial era those of status were those able to effectively mimic the behaviors of the foreigner, that is, the psychological compensations of the classic *evolué*, which centered on cultivating highly inflated egos and appetites. Today, the act of inflating oneself largely centers on the ability to absorb whatever game needs to be played. Whose desire can the actor become an element of, what scheme can they become an accomplice to—again, always with the idea of converting something into something else. Conversion is everywhere in urban Africa: the conversion of the otherwise wasted or obsolete into instruments of repair; the conversion of individual aspirations for success into the exigencies of evangelical salvation; and the conversion of the autonomous self into a "superhighway" through which all kinds of traffic will flow. In the last, the fear that life will pass a person by is dealt with by "selling" his or her life to one or more "secret societies." These societies, popularly known in Douala as *femla*, guarantee that the lives of many others will pass through one and that all one has to do is to "skim" resources off the top in order to be secure for life—an opportunity obtained only by essentially giving up one's life to the dictates of others. In some respects these secret societies represent the institutionalization of accumulated knowledge of the city as zones of affect. In other words, what passes as mystique may simply be a consolidation of knowledge concerning how residents over many years have sensed the city, how they have consumed, where and what they have consumed, what traces they have left behind, the variances in intensity and passion that have characterized different acts of buying and selling, arguing and working together. These "maps" are thus offered to those willing to submit themselves to the demands of the group, demands which often center on giving up family members as labor to be sold to local plantations or trafficking rings, or as bodies to be "harvested" for their parts or specific energies.

While preoccupations with such social arrangements of mystique continue to persist, their limitations in Douala are clear. There is increasing evidence that the molar structures of the *femla* are no longer so adept at spawning new opportunities. Rather, it is a new breed of individuals who make few allegiances but are still capable of acknowledging who has been important to them and where—affiliates who might be satisfied with minimal gestures of support and reciprocity, and steered into some new direction; relations maintained through fleeting intersections that come and go and may come again at some undetermined time in the future—who are being acknowledged as the "successful ones." These are not adherents to a crystallized set of knowledges and procedures for, say, attracting customers, lovers, or associates, or for getting others to do one's bidding. Rather, they are those who are able to add something to every transaction. Those capable of adding themselves to an impending scenario in ways that do not attract too much attention are almost unnoticed in what they have to offer, yet are able to be recognized as somehow indispensable for reasons that are not really clear or talked about. Again, this is a plying of the city by using its vast quotidian resources of actions, talk, look, and gesture. Nothing is off limits and everything is potentially an open source of opportunity.

Of course the sense of an urban public sphere based on social conviviality would appear to be gone forever in such circumstances, and indeed most African cities have become substantially more insecure, violent, and unethical. Yet the critical question becomes whether urban Africa is thus less social, and to what extent the social itself—however ambiguous the concept may be—is an object of speculation. Hedging on everything that appears to be social may, as a byproduct, actually intensify the enactments of sociality.

THE NEW LOGICS OF URBAN CONTROL

Great effort is expended on the part of substantial numbers of city dwellers from middle Africa to get out. There are long waits in informal camps on the outskirts of Moroccan cities or in the decaying interiors of their Libyan counterparts; there are dangerous journeys on small boats; there are often enormous expenses associated with repeated attempts and failures, as well as the costs entailed in securing a variety of real and fake documents. Once Africans cross the Mediterranean or the Atlantic, what urban worlds must they adapt to? What kinds of logics and practices are being applied to shape those urban worlds?

Contemporary technologies and apparatuses appear to supercede systems of control based on confinement and subjectification—what one might call the changing of the guard from the "old school" to the "new school." This new school does not so much supplant or erase the former logics of urban regulation as much as it repositions them in terms of multiple countervailing powers.

In a highly oversimplified way, one might talk about the "old school" as based on practices of confinement and subjectification, confinement referring to the circumscription of bodies within designated territorial and cultural parameters. Within these parameters persons assumed responsibilities for social reproduction and a range of protections were availed that supported relatively stable frameworks for interpreting the world, as well as procedures of coercion and conformity. What place meant, what it could be used for and by whom remained points of contestation that generated a politics, a process of negotiating meaning, rights, stabilities.

Within the classic governmentality literature, subjectification referred to the cultivation and disciplining of persons performing specific assumptions about what it was possible for them to do.[10] Persons were trained to display a certain coherence and consistency of character and action across discrete contexts. They were to consider themselves as embodying specific understandings and rights, and the self became an object of autointervention directed toward enhanced efficiency and wisdom.

The "new school" operates through notions of openness and desocialization. To clarify what I mean by openness, I must say something more about confinement. If control based on confinement connotes a restriction on the freedom of movement and interpretation, it also implies some functional means for individuals to spatialize an assessment of their life chances.[11] In other words, it enhances the ability of individuals to have some sense that if they act in a specific way, those actions are likely to have a particular, limited set of consequences. After all, the ability to act is predicated on having some sense of what is likely to ensue if a person acts in a particular way. As a result, life trajectories could be pursued: education would likely mean a certain kind of employment, a certain kind of employment a specific habitat, and so forth. Thus the city's inherent volatility and persistent ungovernability could be "screened" in such a way as to enforce a constant, reproduced territorialization of everyday life.[12]

Increasingly these screening devices, these institutions of mediation have been displaced, in part through divestment in the city's public institutions and welfare systems, in part because discrete cities must manage the events relevant to their well-being across larger scales of consideration.[13] What is discernible to city residents—their everyday life situations, their livelihoods, the characteristics of their living spaces, security, and life prospects—is increasingly connected to unknown events, situations, and persons. Regimes tend to play on a basic fear incumbent in urban life, that is, that residents who navigate the city can never be sure how their own existence may be implicated in the narratives of others, can never be sure whether their immediate positions and actions inadvertently place them in some "line of fire." The possibilities to convert differences of intensity and disorder into clearly defined locations, corresponding entities, and fields of reliable interpretation diminish. As a result, the sense of potential harm increases. And so lives are increasingly open to potentially everything, which promotes an incessant wariness and preoccupation with security, as well as investment in various technologies of calculation and probability.[14]

In Africa, it is difficult to imagine such a politics, at least in a conventional sense. It is difficult to imagine a politics that attempts to engineer a consolidation of mutually recognizable interests and interpretations. Rather, the situation looks similar to that of managing refugees, where the right to place—

that is, the sheer ability to live in the city and survive—may be guaranteed, but not the right to the city—that is, the right to use the city as an arena to actualize and/or transform specific aspirations. Like refugees, greater numbers of urban residents are induced into a social and political nonexistence, a kind of endless present without the possibility of cultivating points of anchorage on which specific and reliable modes of habitation and institutional existence can be built.[15]

The other facet of new-school urban regulation entails the move toward desocialization. Increasingly, the nature of urban sociality and social control are being transformed. Control itself is less dependent on techniques of coercion and discipline. Rather, control aims to enhance the provision of opportunities and services by reducing the contingent elements associated with their consumption as much as possible. Instruments that precisely target specific commodities and services to specific demands and contexts generate conditions where the specific characteristics and performances of individual actors are increasingly irrelevant.

Profiling of prospective consumers and participants may still determine the eligibility of individuals to participate in specific domains, whether it is employment, health insurance, banking, shopping, or various forms of decision making. But once eligibility is granted, the tendency is for all consumers to be treated equivalently in terms of their rights and risks. A series of norms and procedures are established that align provision and consumption with minimal mediation.[16] As long as the individual follows the predetermined parameters of formal interaction set up by the institution, it is largely irrelevant what the individual thinks or feels.

Cities thus act as patchworks of impersonal and atomizing institutional controls applied to fragmented uses of particular places and services to enforce a sense of normative consumption. Urban sociality is remade as negotiation and evaluation is attenuated in favor of institutionalized codes of consensus. What ensues is a depreciation of social investments in creating impressions that inspire trust, respect, or confidence. At one time, mobility, opportunity, and interactions were guided by the tailoring of specific performances so as to appeal to specific sentiments and moral values. Now, social spaces appear increasingly dissipated.[17] The possibility of negotiation or of a culture of evaluation is thus reduced.

The further development of 3G technologies, while enhancing the potential productivity and coverage of various municipal services, also enhances the salience and scope of more latent collective actions that will increasingly respatialize urban investment and capacity in highly skewed ways. Recall the text-messaging catalogs of New Deido that sought to supplement the capacities of residents across the neighborhood. Now, in the major cities of the north, mobile technologies are combined with advances in geographical-information systems to provide thick, real-time assessments along multiple parameters about any location within the city. Information on property valuation, services, education profiles, crime, changing ownership rates, commercial planning, entrepreneurial-activity profiles, traffic and environmental conditions, as well as databases containing popular views and knowledge about any locale will soon potentially be available to urban operators able to afford and use these technologies. But instead of opening up possibilities to the widest number of people, these assessments tend to result in even more stringent hierarchies of what is considered useful or valuable. Therefore, trajectories of residence, movement, investment, and consumption will increasingly follow patterns that accord to where such operators discern relative advantage—an assessment increasingly dependent on rich information environments.[18]

RESPONSES FROM URBAN AFRICA

What has happened to African urban residents that has enabled their potential to generate important and viable ways of negotiating the new schools of urban regulation?

In part, this potential may simply rest in the fact that many different kinds of activities, modes of production, and institutional forms have intersected to provide provisional possibilities for how people live and make things, how they use the urban environment and collaborate with one another. The specific operations and scope of these intersections are constantly negotiated. They depend on the particular histories, understandings, networks, styles, and inclinations of the actors involved. As a result, highly specialized needs arise, requiring the application of specialized skills and sensitivities that can adapt to the unpredictable range of scenarios these needs bring to life. Regularities thus ensue from a process of incessant convertibility—turning commodities, found objects, resources, and bodies into uses previously unimaginable or constrained. Therefore, the more things urban actors are willing or able to do, the more adept they become at operating within these intersections. In theory, then, the experience of being urbanized in Africa enables them to perhaps make the most of a new urban world everywhere.

If such is the case, these abilities must be cross-referenced to the enormous difficulties that Africans face in simply accessing cities elsewhere. With protracted and tedious procedures established by foreign embassies, low percentages of visa-approval rates, and the capacities of new technical systems to "see through" albeit often highly creative efforts at fraud and dissimulation, the mobility of Africans is substantially curtailed. At the same time, once some measure of mobility is accomplished, Africans in Dubai, Singapore, Jakarta, Shenzhen, Istanbul, Jeddah, Brussels, and Dallas, for example, display an often incisive ability to adapt their economic aspirations, entrepreneurial practices, and styles of conduct to maximize points of intersection with a wide range of other actors and networks.

For example, in the historical commercial districts of Sukhumvit (Bangkok) and Deira (Dubai) a deteriorated yet still-functioning infrastructure of urban services and built environment is appropriated by a wide range of African actors often working in different forms of syndicated arrangements with others of the same and divergent nationalities. Entrepreneurial groupings can be both well-defined, with stable participants and sectors, and highly fluid and malleable, with different forms of collaboration and trade being constantly renegotiated. Each has to work out ways of operating in dense commercial spaces, forging and sharing sometimes competitive, but often complementary relationships with local retailers, landlords, transportation agents, commercial brokers, and local officials in order to support the transactions necessary to move goods, services, and people along specific trajectories of exchange. While structured commercial associations and companies have been established, the bulk of these transactions operates under the radar and moves opportunistically across different kinds of goods and markets.

In Deira I have seen Somalian residents working as janitors find unused and underregulated spaces for Senegalese money merchants to set up shop, in turn financing Nigerian electronics transactions, which bring in Nandi merchants from Bunia who do mineral concession deals with Malaysian holding companies that in turn bring in other Somalians to drive trucks from Mombassa to the Great Lakes. Actors come and go in these arrangements, rarely consolidating specific niches, but rather opening up any particular deal, negotiation, and setting onto others as a means of both maximizing opportunities and regulating visibility.

While this entrepreneurship is a long way from the laborious work of Africans in the agricultural fields of southern Europe and far from the daily grind of all of those who cannot go anywhere, it does point to how African actors are attempting to elaborate articulations between their cities and a larger urban world based on intricate experiments with how varying social arrangements and incessant negotiability can cut through the constraints governing formal residency, official trade, tax and customs regimes, transport regulations, and pricing mechanisms.

For the majority of Africans who make their way to Europe and elsewhere, these capacities still need a platform; they need ways to operate at larger scales. There are multiple vehicles through which the intersections of African urban actors and changing European cities are worked. Yet one must note the importance of constituting dynamic expressions and practices of Islam in Europe as just such a platform. There are far too many complexities entailed in the use of Islam as a platform to focus and concretize African capacities for engaging northern urban spaces to do any real justice to this process here. Rather, I simply wish to point to areas worth further examination. Islam as a framework of circulation may be particularly important as the goal of many African emigrants is to establish themselves both at home and abroad, to come and go, and to use the resources of stays in the north as a way to change conditions at home.

Living within precarious economic and social conditions, with highly constrained access to the conventional political instruments usually relied on to improve such conditions, African immigrant communities have relied on various forms of local associations and initiatives in order to consolidate their lives across European cities. Yet, increasingly for Muslim Africans, Islam is the vehicle through which multiple social engagements worked out at local levels seek to consolidate broader levels of solidarity and political mobilization that cut across ethnic and national levels.[19] Across Europe it is possible to witness the implantation of a wide range of religious, social, and entrepre-

La nouvelle libérté. Photo by Stefan Barbic.

neurial projects broadly connected to this engagement with constituting a European Islam in the peripheral suburbs, the increasingly vacated industrial districts, decaying inner-city neighborhoods, and small towns now part of larger urban systems.

Whatever Africans have experienced that prepares them to deal creatively with changing urban worlds is largely deployed through highly localized maneuvers to maximize opportunity and livelihood within the domains of usually informal work and under-resourced urban territories in northern cities. For example, it is hard to predict just what skills and performances will be necessary in order to eke some kind of advantage from territories that are both under more proficient surveillance and, at the same time, often off the maps of policymakers and developers. Yet, if long-term changes in lives and creative engagement are to be viable, these singular local operations must be articulated across platforms of mobilization and belonging that value these singularities and at the same time network them in coordinated actions and investments.[20] In this way, Islam operates as a gestational form of urban correspondence, relating the initiatives, styles, interpretations, and experiences of different kinds of Muslims, opening up circumscribed resource bases onto a wider range of opportunities, even under conditions of intense scrutiny and fear. Thus, Islam continues to re-offer urban Africa a form of belonging that exceeds the communitarian and the national and works toward a proficient, if yet and perhaps always incomplete capacity of collective social action.

NOTES

1. Particular reference is made here to areas of the continent conventionally including West, Central, and East Africa.
2. Gore and Pratten 2003; Hardin 2003; MacGaffey and Bazenguissa-Ganga 1999; Nordstrom 2003; Raeymaekers 2002; Roitman 1998.
3. Conklin 1997; Ferguson 1999; Raftopolous and Yoshikuni 1999; De Boeck 2000.
4. Thomas 1994.
5. Graham and Martin 2001.
6. Wark 2004.
7. Biaya 2001; De Boeck 2003; Fanthorpe 2001; Herbst 2000; Ribot 2000; Roitman 2003.
8. Latham and McCormack 2004.
9. Berry 1997.
10. Mitchell Dean 1999.
11. Shields 1991; Philo 2000.
12. Osborne and Rose 1999.
13. Amin 2002; Brenner 1999; Cox 2001.
14. Athanasiou 2003; Levin, Frohne, and Weibel 2002; Massumi 2002.
15. Agier 2002.
16. Urry 2002.
17. Feldman 2004; Macleod and Goodwin 1999; Nielsen, Albertsen, and Hemmersam 2004.
18. Galloway 2004; Ghose 2003; McCarthy and Miller 2003.
19. Cesari 1999; Cesari 2003; Mandaville 2000; Nielsen 1999.
20. Saint-Blancat 2002.

Hilton Judin
....

The loss of my father, and temporarily my profession as an architect, has brought me back to Johannesburg. It is not so much a
return home as another attempt at finding my way back into the
city which I am always on the verge of abandoning. I have still to
find there a less angry place to practice. The more I move away, the
more I seek to secure an understanding of what it is that makes
parts of this city impossible for me to reconcile, the intimate with
the estranged, the particular with the global, and the immediately
evident with what is hidden from my gaze. Over this last decade, I
have looked into archives and enclaves juggling threats of indifference. Yet Johannesburg still offers me a way to confront the promises of architecture with an ambiguous mix of fact and metaphor
through which a cultural space might be defined.

The complex spatial threads binding the rural with the urban
are not only a legacy of colonization and apartheid but also
central to questions of emerging national identities. Many of the
rapid shifts and associated senses of loss taking place in Johannesburg revolve as much around ruralization and the absence of public infrastructure as they do around suburbanization and decentralization. This involves both the social landscape (as formerly

segregated white spaces become black) and the cultural landscape (as informal settlements and trading relationships become established and exclusion takes on new forms). A city built in the image of modern Europe has had to accommodate a rural poor and periphery, which is suddenly moving freely across previously strict separations of functions, resulting in new urban scenarios such as a public park carved out of a private lot, a religious sect renting secular bypasses, and loosely delimited individual properties.

The black population's lack of access to the essential elements of the city has always been part of the struggle to produce innovative urban forms and relations. Rural homeland policies and influx control in South Africa under apartheid generated tensions between the rural and the urban that moved beyond interethnic political violence into cultural territorial claims. The images of lack and deprivation associated with the country need to be examined as much as the images of concentration and mobility evoked by the city. It is in their complex interrelationship, rather than through their contrast, that Johannesburg is emerging. Finding a place for the rural still imagined outside the urban is central to notions of national belonging and identity being formed in this period of exaggerated globalization and nonconfrontational politics.

Sometimes it seems as if the change with which the Greater Johannesburg Metropolitan Area is grappling is really a concentrated symptom of the conditions of South Africa as a whole. One has the reduction of a certain center, loose edges without boundaries, nature finding its way through crevices, the loss of familiar places, and newly formed communities, thrust up against each other. Frenetic social life and erratic urban spatial development is escalating at the expense of an abandoned countryside. It is no longer a matter of who originally left for the city and who stayed behind in the country, but why neither space affords a clear position for its inhabitants to accept as settlement. What uneasily happens in this city often runs through the country to make its appearance on the national landscape.

Johannesburg in this sense reproduces the tension and social reality of the nation at large. It embodies for some a spiral of despair that was broken momentarily by democratic elections, but followed immediately by a descent into a desperate period of reconciliation. Architects can continue to disparage these urban consequences without having to confront the larger social unravelling, or they can search out a place for the country in the city, a place for all the associated activities and desires the country represents, where it has never been easy for architects to find spaces in common.

South Africans' sense of the national has hardly allowed for self-definition, for any drawing up of a description that does more than contain our differences. Divided still by white racist constructions, real and imaginary, South Africans are unable to share the others' concerns and aspirations. Whites still refuse to step outside their moral vacuum and offer even a simple conciliatory gesture. In a land where people are grappling from opposite sides of a traumatic history, some architects search elements perhaps too ideal or too formal for those inherent to such a land. Such division, however, could be seen as offering a suspended space for critical engagement. For within that divide there is all that South Africans share, the terrible ordeal and unrequited promises of a struggle with apartheid.

COUNTRYSIDE

Johannesburg has, since its extraction out of a gold reef, been generated as a reaction to fears of the distant country. For white authorities, defending the city meant defending order and modernity, the values and ideas of a metropolitan center over those of an undeveloped rim. A certain comfortable style of life was produced for whites through the requisite urban-planning models of Europe and the Modern Movement. Both the apartheid state and urban professionals readily defended imported productive and consumptive spatial arrangements. This was especially so for those seeking to emulate living patterns and successful typologies from abroad. A thorough separation of functions and then of communities followed progressively: public from private, leisure from work, workers from managers, and as an extension of the colonial enterprise, natives from settlers, and blacks from whites.

There is a long history in Johannesburg of attempts to maintain order and prevent uncontrolled migration from the country and the establishment of squatting strongholds. As one part of the country appeared in the city, it was quickly torn down until the sanitation laws and the Prevention of Illegal Squatting Act could be adopted to provide legal mechanisms for continuous evictions. There was always a public policy to generate a sanitary or communal obligation that disallowed settlement. The rural poor remain excluded from urban economic-infrastructure planning yet never marginal to its consequences. Limitations to the spatial expansion of necessary settlements exaggerated the very conditions city authorities grappled with in emergency. The country in the city was even until recently being legislated at all scales: as restrictions on pavement traders, as limitations on newly arriving families, as rituals or customs without accommodation, as denial of all that the city could not contain. Imagined as natural, sparse, and wild, but in decline, the country and all that it encompassed was relatively easy for city authorities to reject.

Seen still today as backward or isolated, slow or bound by routine, the country acquires the requisite speed and connections to be marginally acceptable only once it has been transformed by the city. Holding these characterizations of development to their seeming opposite areas is a routine in urban planning that is most susceptible to challenge by the actual existence of a bit of each in the other. Neither is able to offer to planners a solution in itself, for there is no childlike, idyllic, communal past to which one can return. Nor is there an unbounded metropolitan hub that drives the future. Such ambiguity continues to influence the racial and spatial imaginary it inspires, with differing consequences. Under evolving historical realities, the country and the city take on new material meanings, expressing the diverging interests and imaginations of our social bodies. Johannesburg and its furthest reaches remain bound together today in a seamless spatial dependency, challenging notions of permanence and change.

For Raymond Williams, the contrast of the country and the city is one of the important ways in which we become conscious of the crises of our society. "But, when this is so, the temptation is to reduce the historical variety of the forms of interpretation to what are loosely called symbols or archetypes: to abstract even these most evidently social forms and to give them a primarily psychological or metaphysical status. This reduction often happens when we find certain major forms and images and ideas persisting through periods of great change."[1] Awareness of the coexistence of persistence with change, of the manner in which changing interpretations speak to permanent needs, is essential to grappling with this problem. The recurrence and subtle transformation of urban and rural, the way in which they have been turned upside down in this period of massive social change, is at work in an emerging Johannesburg. Why, then, do we despair about the loss of control, see breakdown in the spreading or sharing of services, or find only the rural in any display of tradition?

The country in the city is maybe just another way to both see and be in the city. Here is a conceptual as well as perceptual transformation that can be undertaken to see beyond narrow distinctions. Johannesburg has boundaries that extend beyond its municipal edge to reach deep into the country, with transport and kinship routes in the first instance, while back in the city, the country continues to form alternative living patterns to a planned or imported urbanity. If one is able to work openly with the parts these spaces have embedded in each other, then the planning conventions that hold these spaces apart might dissolve their mutual formal encapsulation.

Although migration from rural reserves has not produced most of the population growth of Johannesburg since the abolishment of influx control in the mid-1980s, interaction with the country is still being translated into urban disparity and spatial schisms. Conditions dividing ethnic groups and generations were originally exacerbated by the official controlled release of rural migrants into congested urban environments. The centrality of the country to current cultural and spatial interaction is today easily underestimated, as rural homelands and migration are at worst a conflicting but suppressed legacy of apartheid. Migrants to Johannesburg had under apartheid to return periodically to the country, making the customary a complex cultural constant of urban life. Mahmood Mamdani draws attention to this imposition by native authorities of land entitlement and attachment. "Both the right and the compulsion were customary. Even when this right was significantly emptied of content, as when migrants clung to no more than a customary but nominal patch, the notion of customary rights—as of customary patriarchal privilege—was key to understanding the ideological baggage a migrant brought from the rural to the urban context."[2] An overlapping of ethnic identity with the customary then further relegated this relationship to the urban-planning fringes.

The decentralization, growth, dispersal, and servicing of Johannesburg, however, demands that the complex of spaces be filled more by people displaced from the backyards of the townships than those drawn from the country. Yet the huge increase in informal urban dwellings has, significantly, been accompanied by a sharp drop in traditional rural homes. Data from a 1995–99 household survey that shows an absolute increase of 653,000 informal dwellings (of which 97 percent are in an urban environment) must be seen against an absolute loss of 191,000 dwellings in rural areas.[3] Without the income contribution of residents to the maintenance of service delivery in the country, there has been a rapid concurrent infrastructure decline. Growth in the city, on the other hand, continues to significantly outstrip growth in economic demand. So both the country and the city compound each other's deficiencies.

As an invisible line of mining concessions along an inclined reef, followed by a strip of mines with labour compounds, the landscape of Johannesburg was always more of a threat than a promise to those in the country. Migrant labour for the mines, and for the accompanying industrial belt, was drawn from rural reserves that were being developed primarily as recruitment areas during decades of destructive apartheid legislation. Ethnic enclaves were constructed in the compounds, hostels, and dormitory townships of the city in correspondence with these policies of separate development. But even these enclaves were never the controlled environments the state intended, and as Mamdani notes, they ended up unleashing other challenges: "Every effort was made to turn urban hostels in which migrants lived into enclaves shut off socially and physically from surrounding townships, just as an effort was made to subordinate migrants inside hostels to a regime of indirect rule; but the more migrant links with the reserve were kept alive, the more effectively they functioned as conveyor belts between urban activism and rural discontent."[4] With political influence running in both directions, it was hardly surprising that the state was never able to entirely enforce the spatial as a social division.

Some of the difficulties of distinguishing city from country are apparent in the vagueness of boundaries that came to be associated with the definition of the country as informal in its use in the urban context. Held at the margins of legality and set against modern technologies, the informal has emerged as a definite break in the notion of a dual economy, with a clear dividing line between the urban and the rural. Although the informal is no longer confined to employment on some periphery, it remains strictly characterized by a reliance on indigenous resources, family ownership, small-scale operation, unregulated markets, and labor intensity. But whatever else defines it, the country is for new arrivals part of a protective platform for entry into the city from the outside, whether legal or spatial. This country is not fixed and timeless, even though its pace is slower than the city. It beats, in fact, to the rhythm of its urban counterpart. Just as the city has always had organized communities operating in the urban chaos, so there is alienation in the countryside alongside village communities. Ultimately, there is no single country; there will at all times be many versions with distinct customs, beliefs, desires, stories, and organized environments that can never be traveling in any one direction.

What one can finally recognize is that many of the very structures that shape the city are in part built as a negation of this country, which is coming in from all sides. Attempts to limit, control, engage, and accommodate this country in the city have brought about many of the significant patterns and structures of settlement one sees in Johannesburg. So disturbances to rural social structures that appear as outbreaks within the city are not a simple transference, but both an actual residue and primary generator of these forms. Peripheral settlements not relegated to the fringes but accepted into the city can best be seen as making even greater cultural promises. The living strategies and arrangements they represent are there as well, to force actual spatial and formal changes into Johannesburg's urbanity. Architectural responses that follow from this can then be seen as attempts at building space out of what actually defines us, rather than what we are constantly attempting to define.

THE HAWKERS' TROLLEY PARKADE

David Madzivhandila is paid by hawkers in Johannesburg to look after their trolleys and bags each night when they leave the city center. He must check each morning that what the hawker takes out is the same as what he brings in the evening, which means sorting out more than 900 trolleys and bags without labels for the 400 or so hawkers. He can match a face to a stack of vegetables. Lizeka Mda reports that the majority of hawkers using this lot come from rural areas and across Africa, leaving their families behind and renting rooms in the city or shacks in settlements.[5] Together with seven assistants, Madzivhandila quickly locates the baggage and replaces any damaged produce. Although these goods may appear to be of little value, they are in fact worth hundreds of thousands of rands to their owners, who have to contribute only a small weekly sum, without receipt, for his services. Madzivhandila clearly lives for these trolleys: "I dream about the trolleys. Often I wake up in a cold sweat, fearing that the trolleys have been stolen. But that has not happened. That is why I say this is God's work."[6] Madzivhandila masterfully serves the community. He fetches the trolleys of those elderly persons who cannot push them. He cooks for his assistants so that they are not tempted from hunger to steal. And he stores trolleys for owners encountering problems in their distant homes or raising money for stock.

LOSS

Individuals in Johannesburg must ask how one is able to deal with loss living in the city if one is unable to confront it. What exactly does one see in the city? What is each of our dominant experiences? Estrangement, maybe, if one is white. Discomfort. Invasion. And fear. And if one is black, it might be access. Arrival. Also anxiety. All these are perceptual as much as social. Increasingly parts of Johannesburg are being less visited by those who feel they have no place there. No longer are blacks closed off, as they were under apartheid, from some or socially enclosed by others, with all in their proper places. Certainly, structures still abound to provide consistent friction and points of ignition. Each is afraid of the other, and in fear becomes for the other that anxiety, reflecting the traumas and prejudices anticipated in each other.

Memory is as selective as observation and is structured by conditions propagated through race. According to whites, there had always been, in the past, clearer water and cleaner streets, quieter strolls in the park on a Sunday and safer holidays by the sea—it is simple to invoke a happier past. For most black people, the city was traumatic. They were there not to be seen. Johannesburg was a built environment constructed entirely for the purpose of excluding the black majority; it had been assembled not just to meet the needs of its white citizens, but at the expense of those blacks living there.

Although they now share in a loss of purpose and meaning, both black and white residents of Johannesburg continue to project their conditioned selves, in equal measure protective of their own interests and threatening to each other. The self-interest of whites remains at the core of most private commercial enterprises and continues to dominate spatial development. Change has hardly been embraced, and this, together with less-formalized modes of white racism, stifles our ability to confront and deal with our losses. What has been lost is more than a way of life and doing things. It is as if the unimaginable longing under apartheid for home and belonging continues.

For Njabulo Ndebele, returning to Johannesburg without being able to return to his house represented more than the loss of a place associated with long memories: "Where so many homes have been demolished, people moved to strange places, home temporarily becomes the shared experience of homelessness, the fellow-feeling of loss and the desperate need to regain something."[7] Almost all the people of the country endured this form of internal exile. "At some point in their lives the roots of social memory [were] cut, and traumatic fresh beginnings had to be made and endured. Individual and social growth became a series of interrupted experiences."[8] Longing for home was as much for rest and safety as it was for shared moments or a personal ideal.

Our recent short-term memories likewise repeat concerns directly related to our divided circumstances. Fears of invading masses, loneliness, dirt, unemployment, crime, declining standards, lack of amenities, lack of sanitation, and overcrowding are recalled in panic. Johannesburg is no longer familiar to anyone. It is not that such feelings are merely reflective of real conditions, but rather that change is being absorbed as a larger, daunting, and undefined social process.

Our constructs have always followed the common dichotomy of progress and stagnation, with cities idealized as European being set against the chaos, disorder, and poverty of those caught outside civilization. Fears and complaints of Johannesburg in decline have been around for decades, so it is hard to say exactly when their most recent manifestations began. Our urban history is filled with ravings against the arrival of blacks in the city, ravings that have always provided an excuse for official action. Due to such public reporting during apartheid, attempts by blacks to move from one part of the city to another were immediately stopped. White communities collaborated enthusiastically with apartheid bureaucrats, and the problem of the need for urban surveillance across the city was reduced, as white citizens everywhere could more readily report infringements from police on patrol. While this watching and informing certainly damaged any sense of neighborliness, it served even more to reinforce consciousness of any differences that might give advantage or security.

We are sad today because our personal past is no longer with us in any but a massively altered form. It is not perceptible to us in the city that shifts and changes with the enormous social movements currently under way. We long for this past in direct proportion to its disappearance. Our yearning for lost and unspoiled places is especially strong, as we perceive ourselves caught in a present over which we have little control. Whether it is the neatly trimmed suburban pavement or the corner store, we no longer find them where they were. We continue to lock out, as we always have, aspects of the silent exclusion exerted under apartheid. For all of us who cannot make a return, we take flight in another distant manner, getting out of here rather than to somewhere else. Nostalgia for an irrecoverable place serves to hide an uncomfortable present for which we are responsible. This is nostalgia, however, for what is not really past; it is merely not present, as it has been taken away from us and not just eliminated by time. It is nostalgia for a present denied — all that we might have imagined, the very future from which we one day expected to look back, has not come to pass.

In Johannesburg, as the country moves back into the city, the focus falls not on the loss of the natural ideal, but on the threatened loss of the orderly center. Although the city landscape has been rapidly abandoned by white business and society for its outer urban reaches, it cannot easily be settled again as if vacant or barren. Much of the economic and legislative framework is still in place, and it is with these — only partially — spatial structures that new black arrivals have to contend.

The city has, in our time, become the haven from the natural, which seems to have broken through in revenge, rather than in rescue. We do not turn to nature, as we once might have, to balance or to provide a sanctuary from the threat of the city. The country is no retreat in South Africa, as it is reckoned to be from metropolitan centers. It is not the safe alternative to challenge the endless grids and blocks of urbanity. While cities are often seen in South Africa as sucking the resources of the country, the flooding and infiltration of the urban has come to be feared. Where previously, in the romantic interpretation of nature, we felt that the proper environment for a society was not the city but the country, we now turn to the ordered and concrete urban as a defense against the loose, invasive nature of the rural.

If we look again to Williams, we find the elements from which this reversal can be understood as an advancing of the counterpastoral. What is at work in Johannesburg is the negative identification Williams describes in relation to literary works: "That is to say, the exposure and suffering of the writer, in his own social situation, are identified with the facts of a social history that is beyond him. It is not that he cannot then see the real social history; he is often especially sensitive to it, as a present fact. But the identification between his suffering and that of a social group beyond him is inevitably negative, in the end. The present is accurately and powerfully seen, but its real relations, to past and future, are inaccessible, because the governing development is that of the writer himself: a feeling about the past, an idea about the future, into which, by what is truly an intersection, an observed present is arranged."[9] So the country has become, to the residents of Johannesburg, for example, emblematic of social decay rather than economic adjustment, and its consequences are neatly separated out of the urban system.

This is a personal loss of a particular past and place as change in the country accelerates, as services replace traditions, and as our individuality is detached from our surroundings as a result of our freedom of choice. Land is only a speculative commodity divided into abstract units for buying and selling, and it is not easily maintained as either sacred site or local venue. Whereas white indifference to the destruction of communities and settled ways was essential to forced removals under apartheid, these whites accepted the new communities and changing forms of urban settlement only grimly, as apartheid's urban demise.

Our anger is at the loss of our position. We cannot accept the real origins of change. We must idealize the past or explain the present by the absence of new conditions. All goodness and humanity is projected onto lost city conditions, and its opposite onto current changes in the form of retrospective regret.[10] City order and ambition are seen as under threat from the poverty and idleness of the country. A moral contrast is drawn, with little room for protest. Any actual disparity could hardly be recognized by those linked or dependent on it, and those able to recognize such differences are still without a voice to talk of their daily experience. Not much order can be put in question, as none is ever visible.

Williams warns of these displacements to simple fantasies of past and distance.

> Great confusion is caused if the real childhood memory is projected, unqualified, as history. Yet what we have finally to say is that we live in a world in which the dominant mode of production and social relation-

ships teaches, impresses, offers to make normal and even rigid, modes of detached, separated, external perception and action: modes of using and consuming rather than accepting and enjoying people and things. The structure of feeling of the memoirs is then significant and indispensable as a response to this specific social deformation. Yet this importance can only be recognised when we have made the historical judgement: not only that these are childhood views, which contemporary adult experience contradicts or qualifies; but that a process of human growth has in itself been deformed, by these deep internal directions of what an adult consciousness must be, in this kind of using, consuming, abstracting world."[11]

The country that comes to us does so in a form that cancels rural reality in the same stroke that it finds its place in the city, not as that which arrives from the country, but that which only refers back to the country as a caricature: the herbalist, the migrant, the *sangoma*, the hawker, the ancestor, and so on.

In confronting this loss, the task might then be not simply to realize or uncover the real, but to encourage already shared cultural figures as elements on the way to even more fantastic forms, and thus to recognize them not as less than or lacking, but as elements which another context is required to welcome. Their very surroundings should begin to take on the rhythms, timetables, and platforms through which they best operate. The market must not be legislated to take hawking off the street; instead, the street must be reconceived for marketing (signs and surfaces on which to bargain apply here). If spiritual communion requires temporary night sojourns, the paths of hawkers must be paved and their accoutrements given lock-up shelters; not merely the municipal bicycle stands but fiercely decorated shelves for books and mitres. So instead of the city making place for the country, the country could be remaking the city.

"POLICE FIND COWS SLAUGHTERED IN BEDROOM"

It is unclear whether it was the fact that the cows were stolen or that they were being reduced to carcasses in an inner-city bedroom that caught the attention of the reporter Rapule Tabane. Either way, he enthusiastically joined a police raid on the old military-headquarters building in central Johannesburg.[12] Since these barracks had been abandoned by the military shortly after elections, growing numbers of people recently arrived in the city had been

All eight photos by Jodi Bieber.

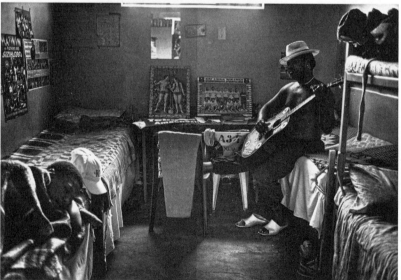

settling in them. It had quickly become a territory out of municipal control, and it was only in dire emergencies that an outsider could enter. In this case, police from the Stock Theft Unit found a makeshift slaughterhouse in a stinking room that appeared to also be used as a bedroom. Cowhides and various cuts of meat surrounded a man who, at the time of the raid, was in the process of cutting up one of two cows in the room. One official commented, "There is an increase of livestock-killing in suburban areas. The problem is that there is no law governing this practice." These cows had most likely been stolen from outlying areas of the city, before having been transported into this building in the city center for slaughtering and sale on the streets. Police reinforcements finally had to be called in to control a crowd of people living in the building who were demanding to be given the meat.

COMMON GROUND

In Johannesburg today it is easier to get to know more about people and places at a great distance — Los Angeles or London, for example — than those in the immediate vicinity. Trends, products, and characters bind South Africans together, or force us apart, as much as do our notions of a local community. Our social linkages to the global circuits of capital provide us with either the competitive edge or strategic partnerships to ensure continued urban growth. In the city, on the other hand, individual local communities are rapidly submerged within the greater metropolis. Both centripetal and centrifugal forces of urban colonization have been at work in Johannesburg from the earliest indications of its international tendencies in the modern era.

For this entire era, African men left the country to work in Johannesburg, and women mostly stayed behind. This is a legacy of apartheid that continues to weigh heavily on the difficult contemporary socioeconomic situation. Alienation in the modern Johannesburg extends far into the most intimate reaches of the country. Communal relations are able to expand in multiple directions: from a family on a farm to another in the town, between urban neighbourhoods, across manufacturing industries, and over disparate political parties. These are intricate interconnections that can, with effort, overcome spatial barriers, as well as the formidable obstacles once placed by the apartheid state in any path of liberation.

Notions of the communal in South Africa continue to retain the traditional element of a shared, uniform, and common foundation, which, in many respects, is a purely customary idea. It is as if the community that is transplanted into the city derives in its entirety from an imagined tribe. Left unaccounted for are the actual and various relationships of kin and organization that have withstood the alienation and isolation of the city, despite having been weakened by the dislocation of a mixed urban culture. We must also bear in mind that the customary notion of community was officially encouraged by authorities at the expense of the individual, as a form of indirect rule. As Mamdani remarks, "The African was containerised, not as a native, but as a tribesperson. Every colony had two legal systems: one modern, the other customary. Customary law was defined in the plural, as the laws of the tribe, and not in the singular as the law for all natives, but roughly as many sets of customary laws as there are said to be tribes. . . . More than anywhere else, there was in the African colonial experience a one-sided opposition between the individual and the group, civil society and community, rights and tradition."[13] Such a necessary notion of community could best be sustained as long as the struggle was directed against the city—as long as there were entry restrictions to be overcome, places to be fought for, authorities to be opposed, and rents to be boycotted. Communities could still draw on deep feelings of the political as resistance to an economy dependent on competing individuals. In this way, the stability demanded of a citizen and a laborer was constantly set against the mobility of those wandering in from the country.

The growth and maintenance of those social organizations displaced from the country hold simultaneously the threat of political instability and the promise of informal networks outside state control. While some organizations remain stagnant and paternalistic, others are continuously renewed, for example, savings associations such as *stokvels*, buying collectives, or women's housing groups. Such organizations are presently recognized and encouraged through the double-edged activism of self-help and sustainable development, and their own labor is discounted as swiftly as structural adjustment is demanded. Such advocacy arrives in the midst of a shared global crisis, that is, of a crisis shared by international agencies with their developing-world counterparts. Competition takes on nongovernmental forms as readily as political labels are shed. The country's rising rates of poverty and dependency on welfare are exacerbated by conflict within rural social organizations with communal responsibility. Chiefs, arguing that they are the traditional and legitimate custodians of communal land, are pitted against local government councils managing state-owned communal land. Without a renewal of roles, the regeneration of the country cannot be brought about independent of urban subordination and land abuse.

What planners of Johannesburg, in understanding their communities, must describe is the flaunting urbanism of public malls and casinos set against the invisible destructive emergence of the HIV/AIDS pandemic. While the legislated development of casinos blatantly compounds and diverts peripheral public sprawl along the northern, eastern, and southern coordinates of the city, deaths from AIDS, which are expected to rise to epidemic proportions in the next decade, appear only within the most private family realms and pulmonary wards. In a nation with few public forums, debates around these issues have traditionally been confined to municipal reports or media battles between press and government.

Yet it is precisely in our ability in Johannesburg to deal with disparate realms — while remaining vigilant to the divisive potential of ethnic thinking and racism — that we South Africans share the burdens and opportunities of other developing global cities. Our struggle is for incremental gains in the way we live and make our living, rather than open defiance of a concerned bureaucracy or benevolent state. Within our porous and diverse social body, mixed identities operate, strained and channeled, even though they are never without conflict. For us, there is not some vacuous and ethereal space of operation, but a highly contested terrain, one in which we have to go ahead and construct, rather than discuss and convene in anticipation of a response. So our pavements are overrun with enterprise, and a house appears long before its most public amenities of water, sanitation, and electricity. Deals are put together without storage space for a successful transaction. We become whomever we must, for enough time to complete the last set of negotiations. National longing is only ever temporarily able to congeal within such a loosely defended culture.

LACK AND DISPOSSESSION

One is obviously able to see the crowded, unsanitary, informal, and unbounded as if these elements of the country could not be kept out of Johannesburg. Without the strict confines of the urban grid and legislation, all order is seemingly unsettled, leaving us without the conventions we require to complete our urban transactions. As architects, we might ask whether this lack can be viable without the formal separations of public and private, without the associated delimitation of individual properties, and without the strict enclosures—sacred, secular, consumptive, and exchange—placed on social performance and civic permissibility.

If we remember that squatting settlements have always been the common edge of newly industrialized landscapes, even those of Europe in the last centuries, then we are forced to recognize that this is not just some recent phenomenon, but actually fundamental to our urbanization. This phenomenon must then be understood, as it changes into its newest capitalized form, as both the unintended result of technological modernization and its most visible manifestation, as both a desperate social environment and a significant and accomplished form of habitation, as both scourge and hope. There is finally no way to distinguish this informal structure from the complex urban economy. There is, in fact, no outside to which it could have been relegated, other perhaps than as that component of the economy functioning with fewer costs and more limited means. Paying rent and taxes is sometimes a matter of time and social consolidation for those in this region.

Country and city, in a larger sense, reflect conditions after colonization, in which the center is set against the periphery. Williams describes this contrast between advanced metropolitan states and under-industrialized agricultural societies: "Much of the real history of city and country, within England itself, is from an early date a history of the extension of a dominant model of capitalist development to include other regions of the world. And this was not, as it is now sometimes seen, a case of 'development' here, 'failure to develop' elsewhere. What was happening in the 'city,' the 'metropolitan' economy, determined and was determined by what was made to happen in the 'country'; first the local hinterland and then the vast regions beyond it, in other people's lands."[14] The economic and political model of the country and the city can be seen as a model of the dependent relationships of the larger world. What needs to be considered are the similarities between all these forces of development in the continuing reordering of the global economy.

It is easy in this quick shift to the global to underestimate the extent to which the sociospatial system of the country survives in a city such as Johannesburg. Unlike the growth by accretion of many European cities, which consumed villages over time by bringing them within city borders, Johannesburg's absorption of the country was accomplished by incorporating migrants uprooted from vastly distant locations without giving them a place in the city. This was done while only reluctantly acknowledging their accompanying social rituals, objects, and ways of doing things, and then only as a state-sanctioned means of social disruption. Rural dispossession was clearly fundamental to the urbanization of Johannesburg. The city could only grow and develop to the extent that it was able to draw on vast and cheap labour resources, which it never had to accommodate seriously. The impositions on the rural social and spatial environment were enormously destructive, even while they were being carefully controlled and calculated. Against this damage, political unity and momentum in resisting the apartheid bureaucracy was always going to be limited in its spatial challenge to the status quo.

While most significant growth in Johannesburg is not directly related to the migration of the rural population, the disparities between these urban and rural environments created under the bantustan separate-development policies of apartheid continue to disturb urbanization. There is still limited migration from one rural region to another, partly due to simmering ethnic tensions. Dispersed economic development zones are not proving to be sustainable. Transportation networks, originally set up to deliver labor, provide no more than the semblance of economic infrastructure. Education under the present government is only barely able to address the devastation that apartheid wrought with regard to skills development and innovation. This absolute failure to have adapted to economic realities or to have encouraged productive relationships under apartheid is apparent in the urban concentration without commercial application that initially followed the abolition of influx control. It remains a fundamental question, for us, how we bring into alignment the newly settled areas with the order long imposed on Johannesburg.

Lack was developed in all aspects of black social life in Johannesburg. Black people were without public buildings of any significance. They were without even the most basic cultural facilities. Infrastructure was there to support only the bare mechanisms for survival and movement. Public space was carefully eliminated. Common space was nonexistent. Separation was fundamental. Since the end of apartheid, none of this has been easily or aggressively challenged. The present government has prioritized the urgent provision of housing accommodation and the maintenance of basic communal facilities. While this is taking place within a fundamentally new and concerned bureaucracy, the broader society is little able to renegotiate an urban inheritance or to achieve the consensus necessary for any extensive reconstruction and development program. To restructure such a vast and singular undertaking as the apartheid city of Johannesburg is a task that would require all the planning and dictatorial legislation our current constitution and policy of reconciliation seeks to avoid.

MOURNING

Avalon—the main cemetery of Soweto—had seen its fair share of funerals for people who had been killed by violence. The funeral procession for one criminal who had been killed by police, however, could best be described as part carnival, part rodeo, and part shebeen. Since the criminal had died in a raid after officials were tipped off about a cash-in-transit robbery, many claimed that he had been lured into the crime by law-enforcement officials and been killed even as he tried to surrender. Others thought that he had made his choices and had no one but himself to blame. Such moral ambiguity and paranoia abounds in Johannesburg. For the journalist Antony Altbeker, the man's family sitting at the graveside provided a sharp and moving contrast to the young, intoxicated entourage; in their eyes, the criminal had been a moderate man of moderate style and taste, not the criminal of notorious reputation. Here were two different perceptions of one man: either a larger-than-life gangster or a model citizen. As Altbeker commented, "Whatever the reason for the family's attitude, this is a saddening story. Instead of encountering an unambiguous rejection of crime and criminals, there is almost nothing other than tolerance and rationalisation, or celebration and endorsement."[15] How can the socializing processes that discourage crime work in this situation? The difficulties are no less evident than the persistent violence surrounding apartheid's lost generation. For the family, the circumstances of the man's death were inexplicable in the context of the life they knew he had led.

As we in Johannesburg search desperately for common values and some kind of shared consciousness, we wonder if it is possible to forge unity out of such lasting division. Is it possible to find patterns with common purpose and sense in all this urban commotion? Njabulo Ndebele looks to cultural calendars to produce communal competencies such as social cohesion, security, and predictability.

> The kind of activity around death and burial, for example, tends to be restricted to specific events, which centre on individual families, and galvanise social, largely informal, support systems. They have yet to evolve effectively towards support for civic, impersonal events beyond the immediate personal dimension. We have yet to see a similar galvanising of social support, for example, for a functioning community school system, or for effective local governance. For these, a civic calendar has to emerge triggered by the need for a co-ordinated social response to a series of community-defined needs. For this to happen, the social support systems we have seen will have to evolve from a survivalist orientation towards the positive ownership of the entire social and civic landscape.[16]

For Ndebele, what is at stake is our ability to imagine and define ourselves, through more than the personal, by moving into a shared public space. This requires exposing the relationships between economic, civic, educational, and moral institutions in order to rediscover their implications. As our community boundaries are not easily crossed physically, Ndebele feels compelled to look to the curriculum, the world of work, and the celebration of public holidays in public places.

We have always had our social identities and places reproduced for us as if they are natural constructs. Such a naturalizing of human and spatial relationships was intended by the apartheid planning process, and we continue to live its brutal reverberations in Johannesburg. Yet we can also understand the customary as contested, and traditions as continuously emerging, never fixed or sufficiently stable to be grasped as more than a sample. So, as architects, we might wonder if the edge of the city is not the limit but the frontier. Can the rural we find in the urban be less a symptom than a seed? Can we perform as easily as we prescribe? Can we move past the building as an object to concentrate on the role it enacts in its daily use? Can our cities be made to give us the necessary room to improvise?

There is another important question about our urban landscape, which is addressed by Ndebele.

> Are we evolving a split personality which may generate its own forms of creativity? What does it mean to use the vacation house as a vantage point from which to look down on others, when we have yet to prove that the house belongs to us and that we are its rightful owners, when we still live in an environment in which we are the ones being viewed? As I write, the landscape of apartheid is reproducing itself with a vengeance. Townships are bursting with informal settlements, reinforcing old dichotomies on the landscape. The psychology of apartheid, the culture of the game lodge, would teach us to regard informal settlements as a potential threat to civilisation, menacing the Europe in our midst. While defending this European residue may allow us to keep the vacation house intact, it may also prevent the emergence of the recognition that what is going on in the townships carries the defining characteristics of our new society. The informal settlements and all the problems they present, are they not vital context in which we can define, plan and build for ourselves, not merely maintaining the vacation house but constructing a new home? Could the game lodge itself be transformed in the service of rural development?[17]

The rural is definitely able to place in question our inherited urban concepts, not merely as European constructs, but increasingly as timeless and preemptive ones, as if they will only continue to meet our worst expectations and match our bleakest statistics.

In our search for distinct architectural and urban forms in Johannesburg, we architects have to delve deeper into the complex landscape within which we work, not simply to define something regional, nor even for the city somehow to become more African—both of these are marketable elements, and neither implies that the other take the form of the country. Distinctions don't so readily apply, for reality is contradictory, giving us more than a little of the country in the city, and vice versa. These pieces of each in the other give us opportunities to overcome—for example, the isolation that threatens the overcrowding—and challenge the bureaucracy now hard at work with our independence.

Even while fulfilling urban projections of uncontrolled sprawl and infrastructure decline, the growth of the country in the city also promises planners elements thought to encompass an African metropolis. It offers exciting features contained within the parameters of urban paranoia and global indifference. As homogeneity grows globally apparent, so the last vestiges of urban difference are strained out, and the local survives mostly as that which enables a place to draw attention.

The difficulty is one of being able to thrive in an increasingly competitive global market of unique cultural localities. If we are the accumulation of images and symbols in our midst, then our version of the national, historically limited and narrowly defined, places us at a disadvantage globally. How distinct can it be? Perhaps, then, an idealized version of this city Johannesburg does not have to be set against the country, but could embrace it. What was initially defended and sterilized could now be adopted. The architectural problem is how to define the national at a time when we find the national so questionable, or whether a national is even desirable, given our more urgent need to be identified with significant trade blocs or regional markets.

The country has forced us to modify our boundaries. It has forced us to no longer confine spatial relationships to private enclaves or conventional descriptions. We need to look again at the room and street and neighbourhood and state and home; to take activities out of distinct zones and extend edges beyond their legal limitations; to make our gains quietly, rather than only in protest; to get elements in the city to actually do what they lay claim to—and so to string together households, open up vistas, heal the community, tend the cattle, invite the public inside, and address municipal concerns, loudly.

We need to not just build more, but to place building itself in question. If ritual could find a place literally within, as well as against some of the amenities of the city under apartheid, how might it continue to override architecture of good intentions?

What if culture were infrastructure and the market a library? If we were not just building and planning, then what more could we architects be doing? If movements of influence were encouraged in both directions, back and forth between country and city, past and present, formal and informal, could we not still be advancing? If the country and city were not just being defined in terms of each other's limits, might their mutual entanglement not offer us new conventions?

NOTES

1. Williams 1973, 289.
2. Mamdani 1996, 219.
3. South African Institute of Race Relations 1999.
4. Mamdani 1996, 220.
5. Lizeka Mda, "No Fines from the Trolley Traffic Cop," *Mail and Guardian*, 13–19 February 1998, 14.
6. Ibid.
7. Njabulo Ndebele, "The Intimacy of Home," *Mail and Guardian*, 26 April–2 May 1992, 28–29.
8. Ibid., 29.
9. Williams 1973, 78.
10. Ibid., 82.
11. Ibid., 298.
12. Rapule Tabane, "Police Find Cows Slaughtered in Bedroom," *Star*, 13 September 1998.
13. Mamdani 1996, 22.
14. Williams 1973, 279.
15. Anthony Altbeker, "The Unquiet End of a Gangster Life," *Sunday Times*, 6 May 2001.
16. Njabulo Ndebele, "Culture Can Redeem Where Politics Fails," *Sunday Independent*, 25 February 2001.
17. Ndebele 1998, 119.

Okwui Enwezor

....

MEGA-EXHIBITIONS

THE ANTINOMIES OF A TRANSNATIONAL GLOBAL FORM

> World exhibitions glorify the exchange value of the commodity.
> They create a framework in which its use value recedes into the
> background. They open a phantasmagoria which a person enters
> in order to be distracted. The entertainment industry makes this
> easier by elevating the person to the level of the commodity.
> —Walter Benjamin, *The Arcades Project*

In the last few years a new figure of discourse, one that seeks to analyze the impact of global capitalism and media technology on contemporary culture, has asserted that the conditions of globalization produce new maps, orientations, cultural economies, institutional networks, identities, and social formations, the scale of which not only delimits the distance between here and there, between West and non-West, but also, by the depth of its penetration, embodies a new vision of global totality and a concept of modernity that dissolves the old paradigms of the nation-state and the ideology of the "center," each giving way to a dispersed regime of rules based on networks, circuits, flows, interconnections. These rhizomatic movements are said to operate on the logic of horizontality, whose disciplinary, spatial, and temporal orders enable the mobility of knowledge, information, culture, capital, and exchange, and are no longer based on domination and control. In the short term, globalization was part of the maturation of a certain kind of liberal ideal, which in its combination of democratic regimes of governance and free-market capitalism was prematurely announced as the end of history. Underwriting this paradoxical culmination of a form of modern totalization embodied by the world-system was the fact that serious doubts about the equity of globalization were forestalled by one of the longest periods of sustained economic growth; by phenomenal technological accomplishments in cybernetics, communication, and genetic encoding—in short, in every facet of the scientific system; and by the cosmopolitanization of global society and identity, which in turn has assured the astounding growth of consumer culture and entertainment.

It seemed not so long ago that everything global was celebrated, although it should be added that globalization always had its opponents as well. Nonetheless, globalization was to become the final and full realization of the idea—since the European conquest of the new world, the circumnavigation of the globe, the expansion of trade into hitherto unpenetrated societies, the founding of colonies based on the then hyperpower of coercion and pacification—of a truly unified modern world-system whereby all systems of modern rationalization would finally be properly fused. Theorists of the benefits of globalization tended to see in the dispersed regimes of global governance and in the multilateralism that emerged after World War II with the creation of the United Nations, the Bretton Woods institutions, treaties on the protection of minorities, the International Court of Justice, and so on checks on the power of the state, on the forces of domination and control (whether of empire or multinationals), and the possibility of the developing world to finally become partners in a broader critical conversation on the equitable distribution of the global common good. Open borders of exchange were believed to not only protect cultures but also to enable backward cultures to innovate, to become modern. This was to be achieved through transparency and multilateral negotiations, be they in scientific, biotechnological, economic, political, juridical, or cultural matters. As could be expected, skeptics of globalization tended to see this picture through a completely different set of lenses. To them globalization was exploitative, disadvantageous to developing economies, and disproportionately concentrated in the hands of a very small number of states who exerted power and control over vast economic, natural, and human resources. Moreover, the skeptics believed that globalization was harmful to fragile ecosystems and shot through with bad examples of governance, inequality, and the like.

How wistful those halcyon days were, especially in light of the now emerging doctrine of American hyperpower. At least it was possible in the past to engage in productive debate (now perceived as mere illusion) on the merits and demerits of globalization, and this may well continue in isolated pockets. But today the world is facing a new kind of menace, namely the return of institutional power as the authorizing force of contemporary narratives of history, art, culture, and ideas. To say there has been a rupture in the belief that globalization adds positive content to new-paradigm formations in art, culture, and ideas is to be an optimist of a certain mien. However, the impressive performance of countries like India, China, South Korea, and Brazil gives pause to the sometimes derided benefits of globalization.

BIENNALE FEVER: CONTEMPORARY ART AND GLOBALIZATION

Perhaps it is premature to write the obituary of the global ideal, which throughout the 1990s brought the promise of greater connectivity and allowed for proximity between spaces of culture, sites of artistic production, and contexts around shared interests in new artistic formations that were taking place across different regions around the world. The vehicle for this critical pursuit was based first on the reconceptualization of the nineteenth-century model of the display of cultural heterogeneity and spectacle overseen throughout the great period of the industrial revolution by the world exhibition. Secondly, the expansion and extension of the world-exhibition model came about through its proliferation. Today the world-exhibition model—for better or worse—has been readapted in the form of mega-exhibitions such as biennales. What follows is an assessment of the rise in the mega-exhibition model in the last two decades and a generalized review of how the exhibition systems it gave rise to have financed a way of thinking about contemporary art and globalization at large.

I will also examine specifically two such exhibitions—the Dak'Art Biennial in Dakar, Senegal, and the Johannesburg Biennale in Johannesburg, South Africa—as representative of two distinct ideologies of globalization that have

Installation view, Second Johannesburg Biennale, 1997. Photo by Werner Maschmann.

emerged in the context of Africa. To do so, I shall analyze the assumptions that underlie each biennale, namely the notion of internationalism in the case of Johannesburg and Pan-Africanism in that of Dak'Art. For the moment, I wish to sketch a broader picture of mega-exhibitions and offer some theoretical and historical issues to consider in relation to their formation.

The putative discourse around globalization—particularly in relation to modern and contemporary art as they are embedded in museums, models of large-scale international exhibitions, and the culture industry—has increasingly come to articulate the notion that conditions of cultural and artistic practice today and the complexity of institutional discourses that mediate their circulation and insertion into broader global networks face the risk of homogenization and subject to ideological control.[1] On the other hand is the view which sees in the globalization of contemporary art a necessary development of late modernity into a sphere of greater inclusion of artistic practices that converge with and extend the historical discourse of modernism.

At the nexus of this convergence and extension is the negotiation between the classical aesthetic language of European high modernism and those other modernisms that offer differential interpretations of what is modern in modern art.

Yet what this discourse so far has not made clear is: to what end? Merely integrating the view of other modernisms into highly selective Western museological programs does not concretely address this question. All too often such programs of integration are based on expediency, rather than on conviction of real intellectual and historical purpose. While other modes and histories of modern and contemporary art are increasingly being seen within the frameworks of Western institutions, the incorporation of these modes and histories have been selective, perfunctory, and limited. Though a few selected contemporary works by, say, African or Asian artists may appear in recent museum collections, rarely do older historical works of modern art make it into the museological narratives. This is the area of scholarship and curatorial practice where globalization raises further issues. For even in historically grounded studies, Western modernism still remains uncomfortable with the modernisms of the South. In the past this discomfort has been addressed by the insistence that modernism is specific to the European experience. Which leads one to ask whether the exuberant celebration of the globalization of art, museums, exhibitions, academies, universities, and their various industries does not mask something more troubling, namely a return to the cynical absorption and integration of a range of counter-hegemonic contemporary practices that seek to highlight the crucial factors of difference, experimental cultures, and recalcitrant notions of art into an already well-honed system of differentiation, domestication, and homogenization, as most modernist ventures have attempted with non-Western societies in other areas. If one is to have any meaningful debate about the nature of globalization and art, one would do well, also, to remind oneself that the historical transformation currently under way must not be seen as merely a fanciful notion that impedes serious thinking about the very nature of art. Rather, one needs to consider it as a transformation whose potential for the dehistoricizing, delegitimizing, and dismantling of the norms of control and domination that inform many Western modernist claims of uniqueness is already meeting serious resistance.

Today antiglobalization has been derisively—often with ideological intentions—constructed as antimodern, nationalist, and anti-Western, or it has been described as the rage of an archaic subalternity unable to confront its failures. Conversely, any embrace of the potentialities of globalization as a means of broadening the space of international participation across a range of cultural, social, and political spheres has been decried as a neoliberal, capitalist attempt to assimilate into the West non-Western spaces and subjectivities. Even where the spaces of inclusion are mutually and dialectically embraced across the borders of ethnic, racial, cultural, gender, and sexual difference, the pull and pressure to hold on to the coordinates and demands of certain identifications—be they local, exclusionary, nationalist, fundamentalist, orthodox—remain strong. There are no easy answers to these oppositions. Still, it is possible to look at the issues from the perspective of a number of structural and philosophical differentiations within which one can understand the current discourse of modernity, contemporary art, and globalization. At least within the sphere of culture, the given doxa of artistic practice and the heterodoxy of forms of globalization (for example, in film, in world music, in the strong emergence of national literary traditions) have continuously called attention to the broader means through which to apprehend and appreciate the formidable forms of contemporary art currently being produced across many regions (as, for example, in Iranian and Chinese cinema, which are in full flower).

There are two ways to study the present situation. On the one hand, there is a vigorous expansion of museum and exhibition programs as well as of academic curricula directed toward extending standard art-historical views of modernism and contemporary art and integrating artistic contexts hitherto thought marginal to the intellectual economy of Western modernism. On the other hand, there remains staunch resistance to such a critical rapprochement between Western modernity and non-Western modernities in the so-called developing world. Such resistance has made its claims through recourse to what amounts to a theology of modernism propagated from the peculiar viewpoint of the Western avant-garde, but without situating that avant-garde within the larger, complex political, cultural, and economic determinations of colonialism and imperialism that made possible the great expansion of European economies in the first place. Increasingly, through recourse to notions such as medium specificity, post-mediumness, artistic autonomy, institutional critique, artistic particularity, and so on, a number of influential historians and journals have encouraged this Occidentalist re-iteration of modernity and art, with very little said about the historical conditions around which art was produced and practiced throughout the entire modern period.

Yet it would be futile in this debate (without necessarily making any easy concession as to the value of the global) not to recognize that much of what has been constituted as the fact of globalization and as a historical rupture par excellence has done little to explain those historical conditions under which the labor of art and culture is manifested outside the developed economies of advanced capitalism. However, the presumption that globalization and its alliance with market liberalism and politics brings one further along the road in the long, arduous march toward modernity is today kept in check by a number of oppositional activities and critical negotiations that have recently arisen to force new debates about globalization's disciplinary and institutional efficacy. There are two areas around which these debates are being waged: one is in the domain of cultural and social production of identity; the other is in the political and economic arena of democratic rights, national sovereignty, and economic self-determination.

For metropolitan audiences the most visible of the struggles around globalization is often seen in the mediated activities of a loose network of social movements, labor and environmental organizations, and nongovernmental organizations (what I shall call the Porto Allegre contingent) and in antiglobalization tussles such as those recently witnessed in Genoa, Seattle, Prague, and Montreal.[2] But there are yet other views of such struggles, "third worldist" in their perspective, only nominally antiglobal, more complex, and differentiated in that they are much more embedded in a historically determined analysis of global regimes.[3] More important, such struggles are concerned with questions of justice and sociopolitical-economic agency, none of which at face value contradict the positive theories of globalization. This second phalanx of struggle attacks globalization—in its present form—from the point of view of its attempt at hegemonic control over vast areas and systems of production and knowledge (whereby those Michel de Certeau calls everyday users are systemically disadvantaged and deprived of the means to assert their agency).[4]

In these debates, therefore, even a cursory probe reveals that the defining features of globalization, with its apotropaic promises, contain a range of antinomies. Some of these antinomies are historical, based on a disequilibrium of power and material resources, while others are built around careful cultural reflexes that manifest themselves in the form of resistance to the hegemonic influence of supranational global forums controlled by the forces of industrial and technological capitalism. One must also note the degree to which resistance within Western institutions to other forms of knowledge inscribes another level of antinomy. Likewise, the imagined community of global culture, seen from the point of view of new transnational artistic communities, global exhibition enterprises, and museums, and telegraphed through global-exchange networks and reception systems such as the media, is no less fraught with these antinomies, saturated as they are with institutional control of vast resources that constantly obviates the possibility of serious exchanges.[5]

But must contemporary culture and art, along with the discursive and market-oriented sites in which they are produced, reproduced, marketed or exhibited, and received, be subjected to and put into the service of enunciating the radical shift in paradigm increasingly apparent in the complex systemic delocalizations of capital, labor flows, markets, technologies of communication, and mediation (between the Net and the self) that globalization is said to have engendered?[6] How do institutions of art integrate the putatively slower, critical cultural shifts that arrive in the wake of these transnational, denationalized, global transformations? Where does the final arbitration about the status of the work of art occur today? What are the criteria for recognition, within the global mainstream, of artists producing outside the rich circuit of advanced institutions, media, and economic visibility? As for the preceding modernist period, who are the artists to be included in broader discussions of modernism that are yet to be properly developed among museums? The record of museums both in the United States and Europe is not particularly encouraging, especially in view of the bourgeoning and ever-diversifying range of available artistic and historical options that exist in quite prolix forms: in curatorial procedures; in museums and exhibition spaces; in the media, catalog historiography, academic journals, and art magazines; in commercial galleries and auction houses, private collections, and other economies of art.

These questions mark a tension in the formation of the global public sphere, of which mega-exhibitions are seen to be exemplary. Further, they reveal a space of instability as the contemporary art arena expands, tracing, as it mutates, the complex mechanisms of control and subordination that exist in the domains of various institutional forums of modern art. In the end, if the fact of globalization is, as often pronounced, the unhinging of the proscriptions of institutional modernism by mobilizing new artistic thoughts, histories, practices, and conditions of production from beyond the borders of the West, one sees levered into relief a number of issues that shadow and foreshadow the anxieties of the present artistic context, within which perform a range of actors: curators, exhibitions, museums, collectors, media, market. The awareness of the three-dimensionality of the space of artistic modernity as multifaceted, however incompletely grasped or acknowledged by dominant teleologies of museums or exhibitions, is at the heart of Stuart Hall's observation that because

> contemporary art practices locate themselves within an awareness of the slow decentering of the West, we see the constitution of lateral relations in which the West is an absolutely pivotal, powerful, hegemonic force, but is no longer the only force within which creative energies, cultural flows and new ideas can be concerted. The world is moving outwards and can no longer be structured in terms of the centre/periphery relation. It has to be defined in terms of a set of interesting centres, which are both different from and related to one another. . . . Any museum which thinks it can incorporate or grasp the best texts and productions of modern artistic practice, believing the world is still organised in centre/periphery model, simply does not understand the contradictory tensions that are in play.[7]

Rather than abolish the center-periphery opposition, globalization has sharpened and made visible its fault lines. Some of the underlying problems that arise at the juncture where global capitalism and culture intersect become evident in analyzing the nature of the museum and mega-exhibitions today, especially with regard to three broad areas—the market, institutions, and media—that affect a range of subsystems within the contemporary artistic framework, such as exhibition models, curatorship, artistic practice, and epistemes of contemporary art.

MEGA-EXHIBITIONS AND MUSEUMS
AS TRANSNATIONAL GLOBAL FORMS

In the summer of 1997 I was a participant in a three-day conference organized by the Rockefeller Foundation and Arts International (both institutions are headquartered in New York). The conference was devoted to the rise and proliferation of large-scale international exhibitions embodied in the phenomenon of biennales and other art festivals, with the tacit hope of understanding the critical shifts being initiated internationally by such large-scale exhibition structures and to gauge their global dimension and impact. The gathering was convened in a beautiful villa situated atop a cliff that overlooks the small northern Italian town of Bellagio, on Lake Como, with the Italian Alps hovering on the horizon—an edifying place to think and work through the travails of contemporary art and the alarmingly mutating map (as some would describe it) of the international art economy. The very notion of mutation is, however, highly suggestive of the kind of disorder that systems of knowledge that have been the bedrock of Western imperialism have been plunged into when confronted with the critical values of other forms of knowledge previously subordinated to imperial authority. Preferable to notions of mutation or disorder are those of the transnationalization, translocalization, and denationalization of the international contemporaryart world, insofar as biennales and other such exhibitions are concerned. By 1997, the popularity of these expositions had reached a peak, to the extent that every conceivable cultural context was host to some version of them. This multicultural context was most clear in the diversity of those present at the conference; there were speakers from São Paulo, Venice, Istanbul, Dakar, Perth, Pittsburgh, Costa Rica, Havana, Austin, Sydney, Bangkok, Johannesburg, and many other places.

Throughout the conference, participants raised questions about the pressures that accompanied the astronomical growth in exhibitions and the new demands they brought to bear on artists, as well as on specific cultural and artistic scenes as they became more and more unhinged from the stable ground of local sites (the nation-state) and transformed into increasingly transnational endeavors. In short, discussion focused on the contexts of power through which artists eager to enter the global scene were being pro cessed. Such contexts are not only artistic but political, social, and economic as well, for it is in the context of the global production of artistic identity that one witnesses the strategies deployed by artists hoping to leap outside under-funded contexts and into the resource-rich pastures of the global space. In other words, biennales are important proving grounds, since they offer opportunities to attract both institutional and curatorial attention. One adjustment strategy used by artists in biennales involves the scale of the work, what I would call the biennale scale; biennale works are often large, spatially distorted installations, cinemascope projections, and mural-size paintings and photographs. (A curator-colleague has described these huge works as the artistic version of genetically modified organisms.) But, for many artists, the anxiety of anonymity and failure in the face of stiff competition has led them to seek visibility by dramatically expanding the spatial relationship of the objects and images produced, thereby creating works that are commensurate with the global ambitions of the exhibitions themselves. In other words, mega-exhibitions require mega-objects.

Blind to the complex historical and psychological issues at stake, most critiques of biennales have vociferously condemned these expansions as the bane of serious art. However, the emerging formation of an itinerant phalanx of artistic strategies and curatorial concepts that respond directly to mega-exhibitions is far from naïve and really quite shrewd, because it is based on the realization that the space of the global is a Darwinian universe. While depicting the biennale as an agon of epic struggle may be slightly overstating the case, there is something in the destiny of all artists who join in the agonistic struggle for professional visibility that is well captured by Pierre Bourdieu when he states, "The literary or artistic field is a *field of forces*, but it is also a *field of struggles* tending to transform or conserve this field of forces. The network of objective relations between positions subtends and orients the strategies which the occupants of different positions implement in their struggles to defend or improve their positions (i.e., their position-takings), strategies which depend for their force and form on the position each agent occupies in the power relations [*rapports de force*]."[8]

Therefore, to reflect seriously on the problematic of the mega-exhibition requires forms of critical analysis that could properly assess the attempts biennales have made to recode the complex dialectics between globalization and the long process of modernization toward market-based economies, a course on which much of the developing world has been set since the early days of decolonization. What such an analysis would furthermore seek to comprehend is the impact felt by institutional practices, in both the West and non-West, as contemporary art has expanded into the global scene. In my own close observation, the circumstances within which biennales are made provides a remarkable filter through which to witness globalization at work, especially in the funding basis between the haves and have-nots, between the access available to artists from well-funded countries and from those without funding.

This last issue dominated the deliberations of the conference. It extended to the nature of the relationship between biennales and globalization and multiculturalism, to multiethnic metropolitan identities, to local cultures with few cosmopolitan attachments except in terms of relations of power and production in the circulatory logic of capital, and finally to the spatial and temporal disjunctures that lie at the heart of modernity, especially as expressed through the filters of different colonial and postcolonial discourses. There were diverse opinions and approaches to curating contemporary art, including those focused on heritage and the ethics of representing the art of fragile cultures such as First Nation peoples of the United States; those constituted specifically on bridging territorial, regional, and cultural worlds, such as the Asia Pacific Triennale in Queensland, Australia; those of institutions whose mandates concern the representation of the art of minorities in the United States (Asia Society and Studio Museum); and those representing seemingly independent organizations that organize biennales (the term is employed purely in the most generic sense) such as those in Istanbul, Venice, Johannesburg (for which I was the artistic director), Sydney, Carnegie International, Dakar, Havana, and São Paulo.

Two points emerged from this array of institutions defending, promoting, or historicizing contemporary art. First, almost without exception, these organizations were founded on considerations of ideology before those of art or artists; what form an organization would take was largely determined by local political, social, and economic issues. Even for museums, ideology preceded art, even if the latter was ultimately the main object in question. Museums, however, conveyed not just culture but civic pride and a sense of belonging in the great tradition of civilized cultures. Second, almost all the organizations (with the exception of the Venice Biennale and Carnegie International) imagined themselves as furthering an alternative view of internationalism, and each believed it possessed the historical outlook to bring this about. Of this camp the city of Istanbul had the most marketable image, billing itself as the bridge between East and West, between Europe and Asia. In the main, the imperative that drove the idealism to build museums and to invent and host biennales was an organization's connection to cosmopolitanism and, to the degree that it made sense, to globalism. Thus, cosmopolitanism and globalism both furnish a positive content in the image-making strategies of cities that believe in the capacity of art to bring economic benefits, cultural capital, civic pride, social cohesion, and global visibility. Note, for example, the phenomenal success of Guggenheim Bilbao (which also opened in 1997). In that structure, art, architecture, and tourism have been carefully fused and displayed in resplendent, shimmering titanium reflectors—a beacon for all cities looking to globalize. The success of Guggenheim Bilbao has led other cities to attempt to replicate its iconicity as a monument to cultural capitalization.

What I have thus far enumerated are the realities, beliefs, and hopes of those who see mega-exhibition spectacles and museums as transnational mediating systems, as well as forms of civic politics and subjectivity. The conference offered a rare opportunity to debate many subjects around which contemporary art, exhibitions, museums, and art academies were being defined. It also afforded a perspective to see contemporary art fully caught in a transitional and transnational nexus. There were no conclusions to be drawn, no decisions reached at the conference, but there was agreement on the enormous and growing cost of staging biennales and building more museums. The conference participants also agreed to find a better way for the dominant institutions to cooperate (a kind of G-something of biennales), in order to avoid further diluting the cachet of an incredibly ambiguous global brand. They also promised to meet again—as indeed they have, again and again, as new biennales and similar exhibits, running into the hundreds, have entered the global circuit in a wild spiral.

SPECTACLE CULTURE: BIENNALES, HISTORY, MODERNITY

In its expansionist mode, as well as in its insatiable propensity to absorb even the most arcane of artistic grammars and scales of production, the biennale has not only come to exemplify important scenes of cultural translation and transnational encounters between artists, art markets, institutions, and various professionals, but has also engendered a negative impression of its own form as an agora of spectacle that defines its relationship to art. While this tendency toward spectacularization and dispersion into the logic of what Theodor Adorno and Max Horkheimer defined as the culture industry may be true, it nonetheless requires further explication to make obvious the fact that not all biennales function along the logic of spectacle. Even if they wish to, economic and institutional limitations militate against their capacities to become purveyors of spectacle. In truth, most biennales—particularly those that function within and address specific artistic contexts—operate as low-budget, modest projects, the scale of the work usually being small, portable, and intimate, and the appearance of site-specific works and that of the exhibitions seeming rather improvisatory and often compensatory. Making such distinctions, however, still does not provide a full picture of the motivations behind the exponential growth in large-scale international exhibitions, whose chief attribute is the heterogeneity of strategies and objects they assemble.

Why has a global culture of biennales emerged at this historical juncture? While scholarly discussion depicts biennales as descendents of a genus known as world exhibitions and locates their pre-history in the accumulations of so-called *Wunderkammern*, my interest is in the present historical context.[9] Why biennales?

HISTORY AND TRAUMA

If one excludes the Venice Biennale and Carnegie International, in Pittsburgh, most, if not all, large-scale, cyclical exhibitions that currently exist within the international framework are primarily post–World War II activities.

To some degree, the desire to establish such exhibition forums has been informed by responses to traumatic historical events and to ruptures occasioned by dissolution of an old order, as exemplified by Documenta in Germany, the Kwangju Biennale in South Korea, and the Johannesburg Biennale in South Africa. The founding of these three institutions closely mirror the political and social transitions of their respective countries. In fact, such transitions are central to the identity of these exhibitions and the chief impetus behind their formation. So one could say that the exhibitions are, in a sense,

Documenta 11, Museum Friedericianum, Kassel, Germany, 2002. Photo by Werner Maschmann.

commemorative, much in the way that the building of the Crystal Palace for the great exhibition of 1857 in London was meant to commemorate both the rule of Queen Victoria and the international power of Britain during the Industrial Revolution. Carnegie International in Pittsburgh, for example, even with all of its international gloss, is nothing but a monument to the progressive and modern outlook of Andrew Carnegie. However, both the Crystal Palace and Carnegie International are constituted around a different sort of ideology, namely the ideology of progress and power.

Trauma looks into something darker, more ambivalent, perhaps melancholic. Therefore, in the postwar context the commemorative takes on the symbols of celebration from an entirely different outlook: as a set of instructions in history and the limits of power. Documenta's critical signpost is Germany's post–World War II attempt to rebuild its destroyed civil society, which had caused the exile and death of many important thinkers and leaders of the European avant-garde. The Kwangju and Johannesburg Biennales were both founded during historic political and social transitions in their respective countries. For South Korea, the critical moment was the return to democracy after years of repressive military dictatorship. For South Africa, it was the end of apartheid that provided the impetus to signify to the rest of the world that the ground for the work of the imagination, as a fundamental part of a society in transition toward democracy and of developing new concepts of global citizenship, was an important part of the transition.

MODERNITY AND MODERNIZATION

Recently, while waiting my turn at a barbershop in Brooklyn, New York, I happened to cast a glance at a publicity bill, pinned up on the salon wall, with the heading "Black Inventors." On the chart was listed every conceivable invention one could think of, from the toothpick and ironing board to stabilizing instruments for the space shuttle, airplane engines, computer hardware, software, and so on. But the entries that caught my attention were the first four on the list: "culture = African," "alphabet = African (Egypt)," "writing = African (Egypt)," and "paper = African." Having lived in the United States for twenty years, I was fairly familiar with the ways in which many African Americans assert a sense of cultural worth in response to cultural marginalization. From the days of slavery through the height of the civil rights movement to the era of the Black Power movement, the construction of African American cultural value and worth was a battle waged in part on the grounds of the fanciful ideology of origin. Given the basic historical schism between the United States and its black citizens, I was not surprised, though I was still struck, by the deft deployment of the entries on the poster, which sought to underline the precondition of social visibility for any knowledge-based society, namely that one must be not only a consumer of culture but also a producer and inventor of the norms of modern society. According to the well-told tale of the poster, civilization has its roots in a black cultural past, which continues today. And if Africa is the primal scene of civilization, having invented culture, the alphabet, writing, and paper, then it must also be the basis for the ontological construction of modernity as such, through a range of inventions which culture, the alphabet, writing, and paper have made possible. As bombastic as this list may seem, its presumptions are almost identical to those through which Western subjectivity conceives its own cultural self-understanding. Equally, Western epistemological thought constitutes the dimension of a knowledge-based society as essentially springing from the European imagination. Here, then, is an obvious example of one antinomy of global culture: the struggle over cultural legitimation.

It is striking to see in this ideological struggle to establish the prehistory and history of the modern world how the text of historical legitimation has been written out of the bitter imposition of indenture, marginalization, and opposition to it through counterhegemonic strategies. In fact, one consequence of Western imperialism and colonialism is the degree to which cultures and societies seen to be marginal to Western culture have written, out of their antagonism to European imperial conquest and hegemony, a complex narrative of other human life-worlds. Having started in the Brooklyn barbershop, let me stay in the contemporary and cosmopolitan Western realm and consider what this antagonism looks like from the perspective of someone like Jürgen Habermas. In the second volume of *The Theory of Communicative Action* Habermas offers a most perspicacious view on the question of institutionally determined sense of culture.

In advanced western societies conflicts have developed in the last ten to twenty years that deviate in various respects from the social-welfare-state pattern of institutionalized conflict over distribution. They do not flare up in areas of material reproduction; they are not allayed by compensations that conform to the system. Rather, these new conflicts arise in the areas of cultural production, of social integration, and of socialization; they are carried out in subinstitutional, or at least extraparliamentary, forms of protest; and the deficits that underlie them reflect a reification of communicatively structured domains of action, which cannot be gotten at via the media of money and power. It is not primarily a question of compensations that the social-welfare state can provide, but of protecting and restoring endangered ways of life or of establishing reformed ways of life. In short, the new conflicts do not flare up around problems of distribution but around questions concerning *the grammar of forms of life*.[10]

Through Habermas, one may approach the second antinomy as being predicated on cultural plurality, difference, and questions concerning the grammar of forms of life. Within the broader discourse of regimes of rep-

Oladélé Ayiboyé Bamgboyé, *Homeward/Bound*, 1995. Installation at The Short Century: Independence and Liberation Movement in Africa, 1945–1994, Gropius Bau, Berlin, 2001. Photo by Werner Maschmann.

resentation, decolonization complicates the classical texts of international and global curatorial work, the art-historical work bound to the institutional domains of the museum and the academy, and the conception of the ideal public. Decolonization reorients and transforms the priority placed on the productive and representational values, as well as on the multifarious objects, texts, and images of Western artistic modernity. With decolonization, the emergence of postcolonial states, and the dispersion of many postcolonial subjects to far-flung places, a new figure of the modern subject in the global metropolitan circuit became much more visible and challenged, by his mere presence, such enlightenment concepts as liberté, egalité, and fraternité.

For the postcolonial state, the pressure to modernize and develop not only the superstructure of the state but also the substructure of culture became

Antonio Olé, *Township Wall*, 2001. Installation at The Short Century: Independence and Liberation Movement in Africa, 1945–1994, Gropius Bau, Berlin, 2001. Photo by Werner Maschmann.

the contemporary manual for exiting peripheralization. Modernity as such, and the desire to modernize—that is, to leave behind backwardness—became a tacit agreement to re-Westernize, to be reintegrated into a neocolonial scheme in the name of progress, institutional development, and access to technology. It is in light of these two movements—between modernity and modernization—that certain forms of mega-exhibitions and museums can be understood. The São Paulo Biennale, founded in 1952, certainly offers one key example, while the Havana Biennale offers a kind of counter-reformation logic to the mega-exhibition model. While São Paulo insistently looks toward the example of European modernism, Havana looks toward the revolutionary ideals of state Marxism to address the exclusion of the Third World. As such Havana Biennale was conceived as a critical third space amid the "prejudice" and "decadence" of Western neoliberalism and modernity.

Founded by a member of an immigrant Italian family and modeled after the Venice Biennale, the São Paulo Biennale was designed to mediate for a modernizing Brazil the idea of progress through the iconography and innovations of Western artistic avant-gardes, to bring to Brazil historical works of European art so as to demonstrate Brazil's cultural continuity and contiguity with European culture. This conceit of cultural continuity and contiguity is an interesting one insofar as the founder of the biennale wished to present Brazil in the company of advanced visual culture and therefore separate it from the other Latin American countries. The Havana Biennale, on the other hand, was founded in 1984, just six years before the collapse of the Soviet Union brought to an end Cuba's intricate economic, ideological, and political alliance with that other world superpower, and against the backdrop of large-scale emigrations by many Cubans impoverished by the American embargo. The Havana Biennale not only defined itself as an alternative to Western and American power but, more important, offered emotional identification with artists working throughout the so-called Third World. The Havana and São Paulo Biennales, in their stark contrast to each other, demonstrate that not all biennales follow the same model.

However, they offer one lesson in understanding the function of the mega-exhibitions and the museum complex: how such institutions operationalize the discourse of modernity and modernization in relation to use and exchange value, to cultural and political ideology. Even mega-exhibitions in the West are not excluded from instrumentalizing the discourses of modernity and modernization. Two recent examples offer a view into an intricate form of cultural micromanagement. The emergence of global culture as supra-state policy in peripheral European locations is powerfully illustrated by the formation of Manifesta and the idea of "European cultural capital" wherein cities bid, as in the Olympic games, to host the avatars of advanced artistic and curatorial initiatives. The clear impetus for many large-scale international exhibitions as such is not necessarily to bring a more complex understanding of artistic movements to local publics through the symbolic use and exchange of forms and ideas of international, advanced art, but to propagate a certain will to globality. By so doing, such exhibitions seek to embed the peripheral spaces of cultural production and institutional articulation in the trajectory of international artistic discourse. Modernity and modernization mean, then, not only to develop greater proximity to the institutional patronage of the international artistic sphere but also to acquire and master the language of this international sphere, harvest its surplus resources, and ultimately to position and promote the periphery as a genuine destination of artistic modernity. I shall not speak here of some of the links to economics, tourism, regional revitalization, and nationalism, as it is self-evident that they all figure as part of the complex mechanisms at play in the formation of large international exhibitions or the building of new museums.

ENACTING THE DIASPORIC PUBLIC SPHERE:

MOBILITY, MEDIATION, AND PROXIMITY TO THE WEST

Even if the desire for modernity and modernization propel some of the institutions of international contemporary art, it would be misleading to think of them, especially those that exist outside the context of the large industrial centers of the West, as merely mimicries and pale imitations of something authentic, as constituted within the West. The very notion of proximity to the West as a strategy enunciated within the dialectical framework of global relations of power inherent in the development of the discourse of artistic modernity is a double-edged sword. Such a sword cuts a swath between the revolutionary and emancipatory portents of postcolonial critique of master narratives and the nationalist rhetoric of tradition and authenticity. But the periphery does not simplistically absorb and internalize what it does not need. Nor does it vitiate its own critical power by becoming subservient to the rules of the center. In the wake of the globalization of culture and art, the postcolonial response has produced a new kind of space, a discourse of open contestations which does not spring merely from resistance, but rather is built on an ethics of dissent. Therefore, in its discursive proximity to Western modes of thought, postcolonial theory transforms this dissent into an enabling agent of historical transformation and thus is able to expose some of the Western epistemological limits and contradictions.

In *Modernity at Large: Cultural Dimensions of Globalization* Arjun Appadurai puts more elegantly the issue of what I have called open contestations, when he describes the circuitous map of global cultural networks in the twin instances of mass mobility and mass mediation as paradigms of globality and locality.

Georges Adéagbo, *African Socialism*, 2001. Installation at The Short Century: Independence and Liberation Movement in Africa, 1945–1994, Gropius Bau, Berlin, 2001. Photo by Werner Maschmann.

As with mediation, so with motion. The story of mass migrations (voluntary and forced) is hardly a new feature of human history. But when it is juxtaposed with the rapid flow of mass-mediated images, scripts, and sensations, we have a new order of instability in the production of modern subjectivities. As Turkish guest workers in Germany watch Turkish films in their German flats, as Koreans in Philadelphia watch the 1988 Olympics in Seoul through satellite feeds from Korea, and as Pakistani cab drivers in Chicago listen to cassettes of sermons recorded in mosques in Pakistan or Iran, we see moving images meet deterritorialized viewers. These create diasporic public spheres, phenomena that confound theories that depend on the continued salience of the nation-state as the key arbiter of important social changes. . . . In this sense, both persons and images often meet unpredictably, outside the certainties of home and the cordon sanitaire of local and national media effects. This mobile and unforesee-able relationship between mass mediated events and migratory audiences defines the core of the link between globalization and the modern.[11]

What exactly does Appadurai mean, then, when he writes about diasporic public spheres? Who and what is the public that he refers to? Does not the very concept of diaspora as a historical condition through which global cultural processes are mediated present another antinomy in the dialectic between the tribal and modern, particularly in circumstances where diasporic cultures indigenize themselves on the soil of other entrenched values? I return now to the Brooklyn barbershop scene, but look at it from the purview of its pro-liferation, not on the occasion of the journey out into slavery and indenture, but on the basis of its inscription into and passage through the global scene of cultural translation. Today, the Brooklyn barbershop represents the site of another diasporic public sphere, a new transnational locality embedded in the networks of knowledge, labor (intellectual and manual), trade, tour-ism, immigration, technology, finance. Writ large, the diasporic public sphere articulates the distinctive travelogue of twentieth-century modernity while writing new concepts of translocalization and transnationalization of cul-ture within twenty-first-century globalizing processes. The diasporic public sphere offers the clearest example of what Néstor García Canclini in his book *Hybrid Cultures* calls strategies for entering and leaving modernity.[12] This to and fro movement predisposes Michel de Certeau's "everyday user" toward the instrumentalization of his or her own agency.

The diasporic delineates late modernity's transnational, transcultural, postcolonial, and global attitudes toward such concepts as identity, culture, nationality, and citizenship. It postulates an open-ended relationship with a variety of institutional productions and private experiences, between pro-fessional and personal identity models. The diasporic, through its twists and turns, from indeterminacy and contingency to indigineity, reveals, in a para-doxical sense, both the limits of identity discourse and the fate of all kinds of *Leitkultur* in the wake of the mass mobility not only of people traveling beyond home, nation, race, ethnicity, and continent but also of all forms of migratory knowledge, cultural iconography, artistic objects, and contempo-rary subjectivities, as well as the networks of their distribution, mediation, and interpretation.[13]

The diasporic public sphere is deeply intertwined with the conditions of the global, even when it objectifies the ceaseless contradictions and antagonisms between the two, especially in the ways in which questions of centers and peripheries, the local and global, national and regional, enlightened and backward, mobility and stasis, citizen and subject, cosmopolitan and provincial sit within them. One visible space where one often encounters these contradictions and antagonisms is in the social, political, and cultural sphere of the global city. As it emerges from the spatial and temporal disorientation of the global city, the diasporic public sphere becomes the space where the problem of translation for culture arises. Avid for critical incarnation of new forms of experimental production, cultural translation in the global present confronts one with a way to begin again, where the past is neither a foreign country, nor simply the authentic name for origin. The recent phenomenon of biennales in the periphery, then, should not be bemoaned as a ready-made example of biennale syndrome. Instead, one must see in the biennale phenomenon the possibility of a paradigm shift in which spectators are able to encounter many experimental cultures without wholly possessing them.

SPECTACLE, SPECTATORSHIP, AND MEGA-EXHIBITIONS

But what of the critique that biennales and other large-scale exhibitions foster an environment of speculative artistic enterprise that indulges in spectacle, and in so doing undercut the critical autonomy of artistic practices, subjecting them to the forces of the market, ideology, and media? I will address this critique through the idea of what I call "strategic globality" and through the idea of spectatorship, basing my argument on a partial reading of Guy Debord's *Society of Spectacle*; on Michel de Certeau's idea of the everyday user not as a passive consumer and receiver of culture, but as an active participant and agent whose critical engagement with culture makes the complexity of its meaning more focused; and on Pierre Bourdieu, who in *The Field of Cultural Production* imagines the field of culture as a habitus where position-takings among users and producers create a strong dialectical framework through which culture makes its institutional, ideological, conceptual, and other practices visible. Starting from these assumptions, I will address the question of multiculturalism as one moment in which the contradictory aspirations of users, agents, producers, institutions, and communities converge.

Installation view at "The Short Century: Independence and Liberation Movement in Africa, 1945–1994," Gropius Bau, Berlin, 2001. Photo by Werner Maschmann.

But, first, what about the question of art exhibitions as spectacle? It has been argued that the chief value of all institutional forms of mega-exhibitions (biennales, triennales, Documenta, cultural capitals, festivals of culture, blockbuster exhibitions of modern and classical European art, ethnographic exhibitions, World's Fairs, etc.) is grounded in the domain of spectacle and the spectacularization of art and culture through the process of diffusion and reproduction of excess.[14] While a certain case can be made for this view, such exhibitions address themselves not to the ideal viewer whose senses have already been co-opted and homogenized into the institutional logic of display and transformation, but to a general viewer who represents an unknown demographic in the fragmented network of global cultural exchange. This general spectator is lined up in the field of spectatorship which articulates itself, not inside Debord's critique of spectacle qua the delirium of capitalist excess, but as a new instance of spectatorial experience through diffusion and differentiation.

Thus, the general field of spectatorship as an active field of everyday users, agents, producers, and position-takings, in the context of recent postcolonial, post-imperial discourse inserts a new spectator whose gaze upon the mottled screen of modernity is counterhegemonic and not simply an instance of countercultural positioning. Postcolonial subjective claims (multicultural-ism, liberation theology, resistance art, feminist and queer theory, questions of third cinema, anti-apartheid, environmental and ecological movements, rights of indigenous peoples, minority demands, etc.) deviate from the hege-monic concept of spectatorial totality and render it fragmentary, because experiences of looking do not always apprehend the same meaning from what is being looked at or the same meaning from the effects of an image. For example, in the United States, the readings of the videotape of police offi-cers beating Rodney King and of the media depictions of the O. J. Simpson murder trial were different for African Americans than they were for white Americans. This divergence is based not on whether the depictions were fac-tual or not, but on a subtle set of codes embedded in the representations of race and African American masculinity. The question of the spectacle is never universal, but mediated, as Debord showed, by extraspectatorial issues. This brings up all sorts of counterhegemonic conceptions of looking and of how ideas of art and culture may be rearticulated and reimagined in the wake of the globalization.

Though there have been many celebrations of the death of multicultural-ism in the service of a higher, more exemplary Leitkultur, one must continue to remind oneself that the multicultural paradigm created a space of open deliberations around what James Clifford has noted as the "radically asym-metrical relations of power" which were the rule in most institutional prac-tices.[15] And despite some of the shortcomings of multicultural discourse, its ethical project of citizenship, recognition of difference, tolerance, and respect for other cultures and forms of living remains today quite salient. No more so than in the post-9/11 return to the asymmetrical clash-of-civilizations dis-course. Multiculturalism at its best is inclusive and makes clear the complex cultural and social maps of all globalizing societies. It unbinds the discourse of art and culture from the false natal bonds of ethnocentrism while showing powerfully and critically that relations of exchange between cultures are also necessarily adumbrated by strong relations of power. And it was in the realm of power that multicultural discourse showed that, when placed at the service of nationalistic identification, power could easily turn into tools of exclusion and marginalization.

As one rethinks the values of the emergent forms of spectatorship that offer new critical insight into the historical condition of globalization, one could invoke, through the political critique of imperialism by Michael Hardt and Antonio Negri in their book *Empire*, what a new horizon of spectatorship might mean for non-nationalist art and culture. In *Empire* Hardt and Negri claim that former domains of relations of social production have become untied from the nation-state apparatus and its imperial program. And with this unbundling, a new type of sovereignty, which they name "empire," has emerged. It is a movement that mobilizes the force of critical counterhegemonic movements whose sovereignty supercedes the nation-state's imperial claims to such things as territorial autonomy, self-determination, a view of economic totality, and the ability to regulate economic and cultural life. Empire has no boundaries, no limits, they claim. It encompasses what they call a spatial totality, which means that it is everywhere.

If, as their stellar work argues, "the sovereignty of the nation-state was the cornerstone of the imperialisms of European powers constructed throughout the modern era," how can one today situate the mega-exhibition format that still functions under the imprimatur of the nation-state's hegemonic view of culture?[16] While there can be no singular answer to this question, one can, *pace* Hardt and Negri, begin such a discussion by insisting that mega-exhibitions have adopted the idea of the global from the perspective of the imperial and colonial mode of differentiation and homogenization, absorption and diffusion. They have not been attentive enough to that differentiated position of general spectatorship that announced simultaneously the twilight of the nation-state and the dawn of empire. In light of this, Debord's notion of the "society of spectacle" was only partially attentive to the new sovereign power that was to come in the wake of "Empire." In Debord's scheme such a sovereign power was flattened out by the spectacle-producing effects of capitalism. Everything, all social life, was, from his perspective, caught in the optical haze of mediation, perpetually ringed by the fearful machines of media absorption. The logic of the spectacle was, on the one hand, a colonial one, as Debord rightfully showed; on the other hand, his reading of the symptomatic logic of imperial discourse did not completely displace its effect as spectacle. The society of spectacle was one concerned chiefly with the negative dialectic wherein the relations of production, circulation, dissemination, reception, and acculturation proper to the European domain of culture found their expression. Debord's notion of spectacle did not, however, probe deeply into the discrepant categories of spectacle whose energies and modes of articulating their strategic globality within domains of cosmopolitan networks and relations of social production are strictly anti-imperialist and counter-hegemonic. Such strategies of globality introduce to contemporary artistic and cultural circuits new relations of spectatorship whose program of social differentiation, political expression, and cultural specificity reworks the notion of spectacle and constructs it as the site of new relations of power and cultural translation. It is here that certain mega-exhibitions function in the sense of Mikhail Bakhtin's notion of the carnivalesque. The gap between the spectacle and the carnivalesque is the space where certain exhibition practices, as resistance models against deep depersonalization and acculturation of global capitalism, recapture a new logic for the dissemination and reception of contemporary visual culture today.

POSTSCRIPT: PAN-AFRICANISM OR INTERNATIONALISM

The phenomenon of mega-exhibitions, considered from the purview of their strategies across the globe, reveals the telling coherence of their discourse in the formation of local, national, and international cultural self-understandings within the globalist articulation of modernity. Mega-exhibitions are neither arbitrary nor processes of cheap mimesis of dominant modes of cultural and artistic commodification and homogenization. A number of historical and ideological impulses have spurred the development of the globalist enterprises of biennales and mega-exhibitions. But it would be equally presumptuous to think that the coherence of the discourse of biennales, as many erroneously believe, aims for the same results.

The history of large-scale exhibitions in Africa is relatively recent; much of it can be dated no earlier than the 1950s. In the last half-century a number of cities in Africa—from Bamako to Dakar, Cairo to Alexandria, Cape Town to

Johannesburg, Libreville to Abidjan, Ouagadougou to Grahamstown—are or have been hosts to different forms of biennales or art festivals. The Alexandria Biennale was first formed in the late 1950s, in the exuberant atmosphere of Gamal Abdel Nasser's revolution and Arab nationalism.

Among all the festivals of art in Africa, perhaps none rivals the Pan-Africanist First Negro Festival of Art and Culture, organized in 1966 in Dakar, Senegal, under the state patronage of Leopold Sedar Senghor, the first president of Senegal and the main ideologue and philosopher of Négritude. The 1966 festival was imagined by Senghor as a space and moment where cultural expressions and artistic achievements of the black world (African and diasporic) could be showcased for a broad international public. Moreover, the festival was designed to commemorate the utopian ideals of the post-independence period and the role of culture in the development of postcolonial African identity. But Senghor also was thinking about continuity and envisioned that in subsequent years (every three years or so) a different African country would host such a festival. In 1969 Algiers, Algeria, played host to the second version, which it called the Festival of Pan-African Culture, a subtle move from racial toward political formation. In 1977 Lagos, Nigeria, hosted the Festival of African Cultures (FESTAC), again with a subtle accent on politics and culture. FESTAC was the third, largest, and most extravagant of these festivals (and also its last).

If the political optimism of Nasser's Pan-Arab nationalism and the Pan-Africanism of post-independence Africa evokes a sense of the untethering of a bound-up sense of nationalist cultural vigor, the lugubrious shadows of apartheid were darkening the sun of cultural openness in South Africa. Given international opprobrium toward South Africa, whatever passed for advanced culture was either a clandestine affair, or otherwise state sanctioned. The political circumstances of post-independence and post-apartheid cultural formations gave distinctive but divergent shades to the ideological conceptions of both the Johannesburg Biennale in 1995 and Dak'Art in 1989. For Dakar, the Pan-Africanist ethos of the 1960s, whether still useful today or not, provided a ground through which the exhibition defined its global stance toward contemporary art. Moreover, throughout the years of Senghor's presidency, culture had a decidedly ideological role in fostering the notion of a cohesive Senegalese identity within the international context. And, in a crucial way, culture came also to define the Dak'Art Biennale as foremost a Pan-African affair that focused on the work of artists in Africa (though the biennale has increasingly opened up and become more international in terms of participating artists) in the way that the Asia-Pacific Triennale in Brisbane, Australia, provided a forum for a Pan-Pacific and Asian alliance.

Though short-lived, the Johannesburg Biennale was from the outset intent on defining its critical role in South Africa along the lines of international-ism. The reasons for this direction are obvious enough given the protracted cultural boycott, which not only isolated South African artists from the larger international world (1968 was the last year South Africa had an official repre-sentation at the Venice Biennale) but also forced the emigration of many im-portant artists. The biennale not only celebrated the end of apartheid but also registered the return of South African artists back into the international fold. Christopher Till, the director of culture for the Johannesburg Metropolitan Council, who spearheaded the founding of the biennale, makes this clear in the opening lines of his statement in the catalog of the first biennale: "South Africa's challenge to emerge from its recent history, heal its wounds and play a role in the affairs of the world is one which is being taken up in all aspects of human endeavour. The visual arts is no exception and Africus: Johannes-burg Biennale is the vehicle through which a start has been made to begin a process of reconstruction and development through artistic interchange and exploration."[17]

I suspect that all other biennales, museums, or festivals imagined and pursued their mission with the same idealistic belief in the communicative and discursive importance of contemporary art to prise open new spaces of possibility both for artists and for the public who come as witnesses to the transfiguration of art through mechanisms of political, cultural, economic, and ideological management. Despite this, the convergence of the local and the global now seems only part of the well-turned phrase of an advertis-ing campaign, given that the motivations of the mega-exhibitions once for-mulated have become more ambiguous. Today Dak'Art is globalizing, mov-ing inexorably beyond the hoary framework of Pan-Africanism toward an even more hoary idea of globalism, while the Johannesburg Biennale, which sought to combine a bit of Africana with internationalism, is now a relic of its own global ambitions.

NOTES

This essay was first published as *Großausstellungen und die Antinomien einer transnationalen globalen Form*, in the series Berliner Thyssen-Vorlesung zur Ikonologie der Gegenwart, no. 1, ed. Gottfried Boehm and Horst Bredekamp (Munich: William Fink Verlag, 2002). The version published here is slightly revised and extended. My thanks to Horst Bredekamp, Gottfried Boehm, Sarat Maharaj, and Andreas Huyssen.

1. For a more theoretically inflected discussion on the concept of the culture industry, see Adorno 1991, 98–106; see also Horkheimer and Adorno 2002, the great study of mass culture in which the idea of the culture industry was first introduced. Here I use the term *culture industry* to denote the mass phenomenon that seems currently to be overtaking museological presentation of art in the form of traveling-exhibition blockbusters of culture, exhibitions which can have both a legitimate mass appeal and a specialized appeal to connoisseurs and scholars. The increase in museum attendance across all categories of museological practice seems to bear this out. In the wake of the institutional success of art as part of the industry of mass culture and media is the rise of curatorial programs in universities and specialized art academies. Of note is the almost two decades of expansion that has led to the proliferation of international and local biennales as models of the commodity culture of global capitalism and its great appeal to the diffusion of artistic practice, with little heuristic function and content, but as pure visuality in relation to mass culture.

2. Surely, Antonio Negri and Michael Hardt (2004) have come to represent the fashionable theorists of this conjunction.

3. I wish to distinguish between the kind of resistance to globalization which is in relation to its current form, whereby the highly technological economies dictate the terms of global trade through forums they control, such as the International Monetary Fund, World Bank, World Trade Organization, and so on, while developing economies wield little policy leverage in determining the course of their economies. It is to be noted that much of the developing economies' resistance to globalization is not anti-market in character, but opposed to policies whereby supranational global institutions impose stringent structural-adjustment programs through such devices as Bretton Woods institutions.

4. de Certeau 1984.

5. Anderson 1991.

6. Castells 1996, 3.

7. Hall 2001b, 21.

8. Bourdieu 1993, 30; emphasis in original.

9. For a particularly insightful book on the subject of the Wunderkammer and spectacle, see Bredekamp 1995.

10. Habermas 1984, 192

11. Appadurai 1996, 4. Appadurai's deployment of migratory audiences through the figure of the mobile spectator whose encounter with the objective world is mediated

through forums of global technologies makes the same observation in relation to subjectivity and modernity as Manuel Castells. Within conventional narratives of globalization Castells locates "a fundamental split between abstract, universal instrumentalism, and historically rooted, particularistic identities" (1996, 3). From such a split, the coordinates of identity and subjectivity become enmeshed in the polarities between mobility and mediation, a position Castells sees as "a bipolar opposition between the Net and the Self" (1996, 3).

12. García Canclini 1995.

13. *Leitkultur* refers to a recent controversy in Germany, wherein a German parliamentarian advocated that for immigrants to become full citizens and therefore to assimilate and integrate themselves into the German cultural context, they should adopt German culture as the lead culture. In a manner of speaking, this means that whatever cultural context any immigrant may have originated from, and which thus represents a value that structures the deepest commitment of that immigrant's identity, should be suppressed or made secondary and subjugated within the proliferate presence of a German Leitkultur.

14. This kind of critique has been gleefully taken up in the United States based on what the *New Yorker* art critic Peter Schjeldahl calls "festivalism." I find nothing either intellectually useful or historically correct in his analysis.

15. Clifford 1997, 192, quoting from Pratt 1992, 7.

16. Hardt and Negri 2000, xii.

17. Till 1995, 7.

ASIA

Gyan Prakash
....

MUMBAI

THE MODERN CITY IN RUINS

On 26 July 2005 the rain gods attacked Mumbai with relentless intensity. Nearly thirty inches of monsoon rain lashed the city within a twenty-four-hour period. Water flooded many neighborhoods and clogged the city's drains, roadways, and suburban rail network. Transportation came to a standstill, flights were canceled, the stock exchange closed, schools and colleges shut down, and people waded or swam to safety.

The flood evoked a primeval image. The idea of a city under water is the stuff of myths. It was nature biting back, punishing humans, its fury leveling their prized creation—the city. Just a few months earlier, the business and political elites had been retailing dreams of turning Mumbai into a world-class city, of transforming it into another Shanghai. But those dreams literally went down the clogged drains. People recalled the experience with a shudder. Monsoon waterlogging was commonplace, but this was a frighteningly different sight—this was the city itself sinking, inch by inch. It produced a sense of being choked and trapped. Many described having walked for hours through water, negotiating past floating garbage, debris, and animal carcasses to reach their homes, only to find them inaccessible or inundated. Others recounted having been marooned in office buildings, frantically calling their relatives to reassure them and to inquire about their well-being. Phones went dead and the mobile networks were jammed. Stalled traffic, marooned buildings and neighborhoods, stranded families, and a powerless administration conjured up a frightening image of chaos and dysfunction. Mumbai appeared imperiled. It was an urban dystopia—not a dream city, but a nightmare.

Undoubtedly, the beating the city had taken brought on this mood of despair. But this dark sentiment also tapped into an existing discourse that portrayed the great city in ruins. Consider, for example, Rohinton Mistry's novel *Family Matters*. Set in contemporary Mumbai, it uses the story of an aging man in the city as an allegory for urban decline. Mr. Kapur, a businessman with a somewhat naïve and elitist belief in the city's cosmopolitan history, despairs that the angry tides of ethnic particularism have battered the legendary open shores of the Island City. Bombay has officially become Mumbai, the change having been effected in 1996 to assert a majoritarian Maharashtrian claim over a multiethnic city of immigrants, and Mr. Kapur is filled with sadness. "Nothing is left now except to talk of graves, of worms and epitaphs," he says bleakly to his employee. "Let us sit upon these chairs and tell sad stories of the death of cities," he continues, offering a melancholy invitation to mourn the demise of his beloved city. The ruins of old Bombay remind him that it was once a shining city on the sea, "a tropical Camelot, a golden place where races and religions lived in peace and amity."[1]

To the elites, the city appears under siege, imperiled by spatial mutations and occupation by the uncivil masses, a wasteland of broken modernist dreams. Bombay is now "Slumbay," say the elites. Beatriz Sarlo identifies similar perspectives in certain literary representations of Buenos Aires in the 1990s, wherein "slumification" produces images of the multitude spreading from the periphery to the interior of the city. The city, overtaken by migrants from the interior and other parts of Latin America, is emptied of its elite and appears to return to nature. The "ruins of buildings turn into demolition sites, the demolition sites into wasteland, the wasteland into countryside."[2] The elites can no longer recognize Buenos Aires, for it no longer conforms to the contours of the imagined city of the past.

The city is dead. Urban theorists claim that the city no longer exists as a distinct, bounded entity. Urban sprawl and globalization have turned cities into

City on the Sea
then: Marine Drive
in the late 1940s to
early 1950s. Photo
courtesy of Sharada
Dwivedi and Rahul
Mehrotra.

City on the Sea now: Marine Drive in the 1990s. Photo courtesy of Sharada Dwivedi and
Rahul Mehrotra.

barely legible nodes in vast urbanized systems of communication, in transnational flows of people, commodities, images, and ideas, in finance, labor, factories, and warehouses. As the divide between the city and the countryside is perforated beyond recognition, the urban form is visible everywhere. The world is now comprised of megacities with ever-extending reach and rapidly diminishing inner unity. As globalization produces different kinds of legal regimes and citizens, new hierarchies of cities and urban dwellers, it poses a new set of questions for citizenship, identity, and politics.[3] Contemporary urbanization and its global processes and representations have destroyed the idea of the city as an organism. Increasingly obsolete is the idea of the bounded city defined by an internally coherent civic life, organized as a public space inhabited by rational citizens, and structured by clear relationships to the region, nation, and the wider world. The nonlegal basis of urban existence and politics in the slums and squatter settlements of the global South mocks the classic notion of the city as the space of civil society and political discourse.[4]

I was to hear and read this description applied to Mumbai. Conversations with the city's residents, newspaper and magazine commentaries, and literary and academic writings portrayed the great city in ruins. Where once textile mills and docks had hummed to the industrial rhythm, there was now the cacophony of the postindustrial megalopolis. Bombay was no more, killed not by decay and stagnation but by choking urbanization. In place of the clearly defined city of mills, dockworkers, employees, and trade unions, there was now the socially amorphous world of the megacity, strung out tight between its rich and poor ends. Civic services were bursting at the seams under the pressure exerted by explosive and unplanned growth. Nativist passions, communal riots, the nexus between corrupt politicians and greedy businessmen had destroyed civic consciousness and wrecked the city as a coherent and cosmopolitan space.

Most of all, there was the ominous shadow cast by the Shiv Sena. Established in 1966, the Sena described itself as a "nonpolitical" organization formed to advocate the interests of the city's Maharashtrian population. Led by a fiery leader, Bal Thackeray, the Sena initially cut its teeth on violent anticommunist and anti-immigrant politics. Deindustrialization and the closure of the textile mills in the 1980s contributed to its campaign to destroy the modernist political and social fabric of the industrial city. Deploying a toxic brew of nativist and anti-Muslim rhetoric, Thackeray mobilized the discontent and resentment among the youth bred by urban crisis to fashion a masculinist and fascistic politics.[5] In the last few years, the Sena's fortunes have dwindled as internal squabbles have hobbled the party. Yet it has managed to insinuate majoritarianism in the city's political and cultural landscape. When the damage it has inflicted on the city's secular fabric is viewed together with the urban transformations associated with deindustrialization and the neoliberal economy advanced by globalization, the sense of doom gathers force. Like many other Third World megacities, Mumbai appears as a runaway metropolis, racing toward dysfunction and disaster. From this point of view, the flood—the human bodies, animal carcasses, and garbage floating in the water—appears merely to have exposed the malaise set deep in the city's body.

Etched in this portrait of death and ruin are the outlines of a remembered city. Its shape peers through the images of the damaged built environment, eroded institutions, and ethnic eruptions on the city's cosmopolitan skin. What was the Bombay that Mumbai had destroyed? If acts of mourning unsettle the present by dredging up traces of the past in contemporary Mumbai, then what was the city now cast aside as history? To understand the present imaginary it is necessary to discover the shape of the *imaginaire* it now remembers as its past.

COLONIAL GENEALOGY

The discourses of Bombay's demise locate the remembered city in the ruins of structures and institutions that crystallized under colonialism. So, a good place to start is the formation of the island city *as* modern society during British rule. The industrial-urban world of Bombay began to take a definable shape during the second half of the nineteenth century with the growth of manufacturing, transportation, and communications. Steamships, the opening of the Suez Canal, railroads, docks, and cotton mills turned what had been a colonial port built on trade into a throbbing commercial and industrial city. By the early decades of the twentieth century, Bombay's eastern shore had become a grid of wet and dry docks, open wharves, warehouses, railway yards, trading establishments, shipping agencies, and posh offices belonging both to public institutions and to private companies. Powering this transformation in the city's morphology was its rising consequence as a port: by 1920–21, 41 percent of British India's imports and 38 percent of its exports passed through Bombay.[6]

Maritime trade was not the only engine of expansion, however, and Bombay was not a typical colonial port city. Overseas trade fostered Bombay's early growth and played a pivotal role in its subsequent development, but the city was neither a mere hub in the network of European trade, nor principally an agent of colonial influence and control. Indeed, unlike in other colonial cities such as Madras and Calcutta, Indian merchants and bankers were vital to Bombay's economic life. The most advanced capitalist center in colonial territory was also the most "Indian" of its cities. Bombay flourished by drawing on social and economic resources in the hinterland.[7] Gujarat, a vibrant center of mercantile capital well before the start of colonial rule, naturally played a key role. Its merchants and bankers, faced with the growing European domination of the Indian Ocean trade, seized on opportunities in the opium and cotton trade. Jains, Parsis, Khojas, Memons, and Bohras, among others, flocked to Bombay. They made immense fortunes in opium and cotton exports and shipping, but soon faced the formidable reach and power of the British agency houses. Fluctuations in trade added to their difficulties. Once again, Indian capital sought alternative opportunities. This is how Bombay's merchants turned to cotton mills.

Taking advantage of the growing supply of raw cotton transported by railroads from the Deccan, Indian merchants began setting up mills. The first mill was founded in 1858, and by 1875 twenty-eight mills employed over 13,000 workers. Two decades later, there were seventy mills, employing nearly 76,000 wokers, and by 1925 the number of mills had risen to eighty-two, with 148,000 workers.[8] Built on shaky foundations, however, the industry depended on the supply of cheap labor. Thousands of migrants flocked to the city. As mills produced legendary industrialists—the Parsi entrepreneurs Byramjee Jejeebhoy and Cursetji Cama, the Bhatia magnate Varjivandas, and the Baghdadi Jew David Sassoon—they also drew a growing number of the rural poor from the immediate hinterland and beyond. By 1921 the city's population was nearly 1.2 million, 84 percent of whom had been born outside the city.[9] The mills, located in central Bombay, employed only 16 percent of the population, but their share of industrial employment as a whole was

30 percent.[10] Many other workers were employed as general laborers and as tradesmen such as petty grocers, peddlers, hawkers, tailors, cobblers, barbers, and domestic servants.

Drawing on imperial connections, but built with indigenous entrepreneurial initiative and labor, Bombay emerged, by the early twentieth century, as a bustling commercial and industrial city of migrants. Leading up to this was the filling of breaches, construction of bunds and roadways, and the theft of lands from the sea (called reclamation), which joined seven islets into a single island city by the middle of the nineteenth century. The commercial boom of the 1860s unleashed ambitious building projects. The ramparts of the old fortified town were torn down in 1862, signifying that the city had outgrown its origin as a colonial garrison. The next few decades witnessed the construction of a succession of Gothic buildings on the esplanade, fronted by the Oval Maidan (a wide expanse of green that stretched beyond the fort walls) and facing the western shore. Other reclamation projects got underway, adding 20 percent to the island's size in the arc from Colaba to Malabar Hill.[11] The establishment of the Bombay City Improvement Trust in 1898 signaled a determination to impart a planned urban form to Bombay. The trust undertook a number of projects. Founded in the wake of the devastating plague of 1896–97, its gave immediate, if short-lived, attention to providing sanitary housing conditions for the poor. More substantially, it built and widened roadways, thus improving the east-west and north-south flow of traffic. The trust also developed and reclaimed lands, including 90,000 square yards on the western foreshore of Colaba, on which the spacious and elegant Edwardian bungalows of Cuffe Parade, completed in 1905, expressed the trust's vision of urban design. European observers and residents extolled Bombay as a city of palaces and parks, of elegant bungalows and broad avenues, a cosmopolitan hub of many tongues, races, ethnicities, and religions. G. W. Stevens wrote in 1899 that as one drives through the city, "all India is unfolded in one panorama." Bombay was a "proud and comely city," and "the Briton [felt] himself a greater man for his first sight of Bombay."[12]

Following Max Weber, it has become customary to view modern life as disenchanted, as freed of gods and myth, but what was colonial Bombay if not the space of new gods and new myths? The enchantment of the city was in its very material form; its physical, political, and social geography formed the "natural" landscape for a new mythic world. The spatial order laid out by

Edwardian bungalows on Cuffe Parade in the early 1900s. Photo courtesy of Sharada Dwivedi and Rahul Mehrotra.

the British imagined the city according to the ideals of European civilization and civic consciousness. Bombay's residents were expected to function under the authority of the colonial administration; earn their livelihood in docks, cotton mills, trade, and assorted capitalist institutions; settle their disputes in British courts; study in Western-style schools and colleges; receive treatment in Western medical establishments, travel on the new roadways and railways; write letters delivered by the postal system; walk along arcaded walkways; shop in modern stores; play cricket on the maidans; and value the public space of fountains and squares marked by the statues of imperial figures. There was never any doubt that entry into this urban order was conditional on the acceptance of colonial authority, that alien power and culture underpinned the public space of avenues, parks, educational institutions, and learned societies. There was also little likelihood that the poor could live the ideal of colonial urbanism, but then this ideal was staged as the pedagogic model that the natives were expected to learn from and emulate.

COLONIAL URBANISM

The indigenous elites were quick to learn from the colonial model, none more rapidly and completely than the Parsis. The Parsis developed a close relationship to the British as early as the seventeenth century when they began acting as the company's brokers and employees. As they accumulated wealth as shipbuilders, brokers, merchants, bankers, and mill owners, the Parsis also became the most Anglicized community in India, even as they zealously maintained their religion and identity. Their homes were furnished in European style, they dressed in English clothes, their education was Western, and cricket, golf, tennis, and bridge became their pastimes. Identifying with the British, the Parsis also bought into the colonial urban ideal. They contributed handsomely to various charities and donated funds for several public institutions. The evidence of their philanthropic investment in the city is visible all over Bombay today; several neighborhoods, squares, statues, and public buildings are named after the nineteenth-century Parsi families, as are, for example, the JJ School of Art, Jeejeebhoy Hospital, and Jehangir Art Gallery. Equally prominent in contributing to this imaginary was the Baghdadi Jewish family of David Sassoon. Embracing the idea of the city as a society founded in bourgeois relations, the Sassoon family founded public institutions, such as the David Sassoon Public Library and the Sassoon Mechanics Institute, designed to train the city's residents to be productive and enlightened subjects.

A text that captures the social imaginary projected by the colonial spatial order is Sir Dinshaw Wacha's *Shells from the Sands of Bombay*, which contains his recollections of the city between 1860 and 1875, as well as a survey of Bombay's history.[13] Scholars have mined his book for information on Bombay's history, but it also merits reading as a text of urban discourse. Wacha, born in 1844 and educated at Elphinstone College, lived through the period of Bombay's expansion and building boom. He worked as an accountant in the mills and became one of the most prominent Parsi politicians and writers of his time. Having grown up in Bombay, he wrote about it as a native. He evoked the remembered past and chronicled the changes that he witnessed. The urban form that the British and Indian elites had assembled left a deep impression on him, and he therefore described in great detail and with obvious affection the founding of the mint, post office, police, civil and criminal courts, railways, telegraph, mills, trading houses, chamber of commerce, and Western educational institutions.

Referring to the introduction of railways and telegraph — "two marvels of applied science discovered by the occidental mind and implanted on the Oriental soil"—he wrote, "Let the reader stretch his imagination and ruminate on the condition of semi-darkness which was prevalent in all India."[14] He described the development of the postal system as a "glorious evolution" and noted the introduction of undreamt of facilities: money orders, post savings bank, postal insurance, and the postcard. "And yet one's appetite grows on what it feeds. Here we are in the year of grace 1920, clamouring for a bi-weekly mail and still further improvements and facilities" (560–61). The construction of wet docks and the pioneering role played by the Sassoons in building the Sassoon Docks merited fulsome praise.[15] Efforts to provide water and build an adequate drainage and sewage system, on the other hand, did not pass his standards. He wondered why a breakdown of even a few hours created acute water scarcity for the poor in spite of the vast increase in piped water supplied by the Vehar Lake and Tansa reservoir. Open sewers and drains received severe censure.[16] His tone changed as he described Crawford Market, a central shopping complex "as [it was]known in the more civilized and progressive cities of the West" (331). As one reads his breathless praise and stern criticism, it becomes clear that the urban form forged by colonial modernization was firmly lodged in his consciousness. He mourned the passage of coconut groves and gardens caused by industrial sprawl, but the landscape shaped by capitalism and colonialism appeared natural to him. Not surprisingly, then, he took great satisfaction in his community's participation in the development of the network of institutions that made up colonial Bombay, proudly recording the commercial and civic accomplishments of the leading Parsi personalities and families.

The imprint of the colonial urban form on Wacha's text is evident, but he was no mere chronicler of Britain's work in India. He wrote as an urbanite, deeply conscious of his city as a distinct form of social existence. Watching Bombay change before his eyes convinced him that it was no longer just a colonial outpost but also a dynamic city that had assumed a life of its own. Though developed and shaped by alien rule, it had vitality and an identity derived from commerce. It was an upstart city, a parvenu, whose buildings lacked the stately dignity that only the possession of a deep past could provide.[17] Bombay was defined by its newness. Even the Gothic revival buildings had not succeeded in dressing it with grandeur and grace; no "Wren or Gilbert Scott" had designed them, nor was there a "single edifice which could rejoice the heart of a Ruskin or Ferguson" (315–16). So strongly rooted was the city in the worship of commerce that its temples and mosques inspired neither reverence nor awe, neither a sense of beauty nor joy.[18] What is important here is not the truth of Wacha's architectural judgments, but his strong consciousness of Bombay's ordinariness. Over several centuries of its history, the island, in his estimation, had not evolved into something grand or monumental. Subjected to the flux of change, and made over by the mundane forces of commerce and industry, Bombay's identity resided in its commonplaceness.

Matching his suggestions of ordinariness were sketches of everyday bourgeois life. One such sketch concerned "air eating" by the Parsis on the Maidan.[19] Here, groups of young and old, "but almost all of the sterner sex," could be seen sitting on China mats in circles. In the middle a large lantern or an oil lamp would shed its white-brown light on the "air-eating" group. The men on mats played cards or chess and engaged in the "*goube-mouche* of the day, replete with town gossip and light criticism on men and things happening during the day" (85). Another group could be seen listening with keen curiosity and bated breath to the thrilling legends of ancient Persian heroes read by a Parsi priest or layperson well versed in Gujarati and Persian. While adults amused themselves in these activities, "boys and girls, in their silk frocks, and quaint caps of *kinkob* from Surat, or embroidered in Berlin wool, would carry on their gambols all innocent in their happiness" (86). Vendors, also Parsi, would move from group to group, selling sugarcane by "calling out 'Ganderi, goolab ganderi' ['Sugarcane, rosy sugarcane']" (87). The next morning, the sweeper could be seen sweeping away the chewed remains. Wacha remarked that sugarcane, not ice cream, was then the popular refreshment, though there were a few vendors who had learned the art of ice confectionary: "Morenas was a name to be conjured with for ice creams" (88). After this "delightful little digression" on ice creams, Wacha continues his account of daily life, noting the confectionery favored by the lower classes and describing the brisk trade in toys. Apparently, English mechanical toys were in great demand. "A little doll, dressed up, smitting 'mamma' would fetch five rupees!" (92).

One should not think of Wacha's remembrance of the evenings on the maidan and the brisk trade in English toys as a compendium of meaningless facts. The quotidian, Henri Lefebvre writes, is where people are born, live, and die. "They live well or ill; but they live in everyday life."[20] The routines and objects of daily life are forms in which society is produced and reproduced. Wacha registers the existence of the city as society at the level of the everyday, its reality identifiable but also fleeting in daily recurrences. Thus, he registers how the division of social life between work and leisure is spatially reproduced in the "air eating" on the maidan. His descriptions of daily commerce on the maidan and on the streets—the sale of toys, confectionery, grocery, jewelry, etc.—produce a social map of the city in the daily exchange and consumption of commodities. He portrays the everyday space of work, pleasure, and consumption as the "natural" landscape of the city.

Wacha was no flâneur; he did not occupy an ambivalent position in relation to the modern city he observed, nor did he loiter and intentionally lose himself in the city's daily rhythms in order to offer critical commentaries with poetic sensibilities. Yet his writing is interesting because it reveals the power of the colonial urban imaginary. Wacha was completely at home in the bourgeois landscape of Bombay, immersed in the mythic world of the colonial city. The routines and objects of everyday life held him under their magical spell. Wacha's writing is animated by a strong conviction about Bombay's existence as a city, as a dynamic and cosmopolitan society that had grown beyond its colonial origins. His attention to the quotidian expresses his belief that the city existed in its daily routines, that it had a rhythm, a life of its own.

This was a powerful social imaginary. The city projected by and lived in the spatial order assembled by the British captivated not only Europeans and the Parsis but also Marathi writers. As early as 1863, one such writer noted with wonder the number of languages spoken and the range of communities that lived in the city. "Just the Marathi language comes in thirty or forty dialects," he observed with awe, estimating that there were about a hundred and fifty varieties of Hindus. "Then there are other communities—Parsis, Muslims, Jews, Arabs, . . . etc. In addition, the English, Portuguese, French, Dutch, Turks, Germans, Armenians, Chinese and such other hat-wearers are visible in all directions."[21] Hari Narayan Apte's 1889 novel *Pan Lakshyat Kon Gheto!* described a woman's expression of awe and wonder at the scale and style of buildings, the mills, "the chimneys touching the sky," and the sheer size of the city: "I had imagined Bombay only as a city far greater than Poona. . . . But the reality was incredible. What carriages! What tramways! O no! All was quite unimaginable."[22]

DIVIDED MODERNITY

The experience of the unimaginable, however, did not diminish the reality of colonial and European domination before Indian eyes.[23] Spatial divisions and order encoded racial dominance. While the nucleus of the European population lived in the south, Indians were clustered north of the old fortified town, with the east-west line of Churchgate Street demarcating the boundary between the natives and the foreigners. This basic division persisted even after the fort walls came down in 1862. Over time, however, class came to mute racial divisions as wealthy Indian merchants and industrialists built houses in European areas. Broad avenues and spacious houses set in gardens characterized the European areas where elite Indians also built grand bungalows. No European lived in the native quarters, which were crowded, mixed-use neighborhoods where merchants both lived and worked. Remarking on the dramatic change in the landscape as one crossed over from the British to Indian areas, Stevens wrote that it was as if a magician had suddenly turned his ring. The old was new, the plain was colored, and the East had swallowed up the West. "Cross one street and you are suddenly plunged in the native town. In your nostrils is the smell of the East. . . . The decoration henceforth is its people. The windows are frames for women, the streets become wedges of men."[24] If Stevens had traveled further north, to the mill district, the Briton may have had to reconsider his pride in the comely city. There, a smell of something altogether more unpleasant than the exotic East would have filled his nostrils, and he would have seen a landscape not conjured up by a magician, but visited by the Grim Reaper. Dark, ill-ventilated, tenements packed with impoverished workers, and cesspools of filth and disease made up the landscape of the mill wards. Land was abundant, but neither the capitalists nor colonial authorities were willing to sink enough money to build even an inexpensive and merely adequate transportation infrastructure. This forced workers to live close to mills and factories, where land was at a premium. Seeing opportunities for profits with little investment, landlords recklessly erected slums and tenements. Thus, dense clusters of overcrowded *chawls*, as

Workers' tenements (*chawls*). Photo courtesy of Sharada Dwivedi and Rahul Mehrotra.

well as stables and warehouses, set between narrow lanes and open drains, came to define the central and northern districts of the island.

This was the other city; it represented a different experience of modernity. In developing as a colonial outpost and as a hub in the colonial exploitation of Indian resources, Bombay had acquired the façade of a European city. But outside the elite precincts, the island had developed different urban forms. Gillian Tindall, in her evocative biography of colonial Bombay, calls these forms "non-European." She writes that "every mill that has been built has created mud-shanties somewhere near to hand; every block of flats that has been built, from the ponderous 'Hindustan Chambers' or 'Dharbanga Mansions' of the high Edwardian era to the glass towers of the present, has attracted into the city yet more up-country people with country standards and country ways."[25] This is true, but classifying these urban forms as "non-European" conceals their life as the other side of the modernity that she implicitly identifies in the twin birth of mills and mud-shanties. Slums and tenements were not alien to modern Bombay, but its intimate other; they held a mirror to elite spaces, reflecting the grotesque other side of colonial and capitalist spatial-ization.

Contemporary reports and modern scholars have described in detail the congested and miserable slums and chawls in which workers lived.[26] In addi-tion, the experience of periodic unemployment and chronic underemploy-ment was common; even in the mills, as much as 28 percent of the workforce was employed on a daily basis.[27] The combination of undercapitalization, the high cost of imported machinery, competition from foreign manufacturers, and the limited purchasing power of the domestic consumers caused sharp fluctuations in the fortunes of cotton mills, which affected the stability of employment. Moreover, a large percentage of the working population was employed as casual laborers and domestic servants, whose conditions of employment were even more unsteady. Workers coped with these uncertain conditions of urban life by maintaining their rural links. Many returned an-nually to their villages to help with harvesting. Connections based on the village, caste, and kin were also crucial in finding one's feet in the city. Male workers from the same village rented rooms together. Caste and kin members could be persuaded to make a few feet of space available in their crowded, one-room tenements. The social patterns of the working-class neighborhood imparted the appearance of a village. Not surprisingly, the mill district be-came known as "Girangaon," the village of the mills.

These facts of worker life have been taken to suggest that the migrants re-mained determinedly rural in their hearts, that their dream was to return one day permanently to the village.[28] There is something to the interpretation that the countryside carved out a powerful place right in the heart of the city. But the social and cultural resonance of the rural forms in the urban setting did not signify the persistence of tradition in the face of modernity.[29] Workers summoned "traditions" to manage the conditions of urban modernity; they erected village-like structures in response to housing and labor conditions in the modern city. If mud-shanties were born as the mill's inseparable twin, then the village also emerged as an aspect of the city's formation. Instead of following the ordered sequence of tradition and modernity, Bombay de-veloped by intertwining and interweaving different histories. Strategies of survival fashioned it into a place of porosity and hybridity, a swirl of intensi-ties and movements that brought different forces and agents into relationships and shaped the city as a social space. Migrants from near and afar traversed and marked the urban landscape with the footprints of the village, language, ethnicity, region, and religion. They used the imagined warmth and community of the countryside to represent the city as cold and alien. Yet few migrants returned to their village or region permanently; rather, they used the idea of a community based on village, language, ethnicity, and region to negotiate the city on their own terms.

This city of mills and the Indian neighborhoods were worlds apart from the European enclaves of the city; the bourgeois world sketched by Wacha was far removed from the village of the mills. In light of these sharp divisions, the idea of the cosmopolitan city, the "shining city on the sea," appears as a myth. Yet, as Wacha's text shows, this mythic world was real to the bourgeois city dwellers, just as real as the modern lives lived by poor migrants in tenements. These sharply distinct and segregated realities were drawn together in the city's public spaces, where communities and classes interacted in everyday life. Marketplaces, bazaars, civic and judicial institutions, commercial establishments, public open spaces, streets, tramways, and seashores were places of transactions across divides. Bombay's cosmopolitanism is usually identified and proudly recalled in such public spaces. People from the rest of India and beyond who washed up on the shores of the Island City to earn livelihoods, transact business, and seek adventures rendered its public life a mélange of languages, cultures, and experiences. Not only did mills, docks, and commerce bring migrants of diverse backgrounds in contact with each other, but even prostitution drew poor women, pimps, and hustlers from throughout India and Europe to Bombay. Lewis Mumford spoke of the city as a place for conversation; Bombay actually fashioned a mongrel street language—Bambaiya—for everyday conversation and exchanges.

Cities may be where strangers live together, but they are also spaces of collision and confrontation. This was eminently so in Bombay, where public space threw together groups with sharply divergent and contradictory experiences of modernity. The British sought to secure this public space of indeterminacy and confrontation with a spatial design and order intended to reproduce social and racial hierarchies. Thus, when Stevens felt pride as a Briton in Bombay, it was no doubt due to the staging of the city as imperial spectacle. Enacted along a north-south ceremonial route, this spectacle was

The Gothic parade and the Oval Maidan. Photo courtesy of Sharada Dwivedi and Rahul Mehrotra.

cast in the Gothic architecture of the High Victorian style. Although much has changed in and around the southern core of the city, Gothic buildings from the late nineteenth and early twentieth centuries still stand at attention as one walks up the old esplanade. The Gothic parade begins right after the College of Science, built in Renaissance style, and the Romanesque Elphinstone College with its arcaded walkways. Walking northward from their invocation of the secular rationalism of antiquity, one is confronted with a string of buildings that project the sculpture of imperial dominance: the elephantine secretariat, in Venetian Gothic style, expressing the remoteness of colonial power; the Oxbridge pretensions of the Bombay University buildings, set in neatly manicured lawns and including the university library in yellow sandstone topped by the soaring Rajabhai clock tower; the high court, its weighty authority cast in a fortress-like structure (though, curiously, a one-eyed monkey holding the scales of justice stands on one of the pillars); and finally, the public-works office and the Bombay, Baroda, and Central Indian Railway headquarters, designed in what is called Oriental Gothic. The desire to clothe the industry-driven growth of Bombay in Gothic garb is evident elsewhere, too—in the Gothic towers and onion domes of the Bombay Municipal Corporation Building, as well as in the arcaded walkways on Hornby Road (now Dadabai Naoroji Road), which leads up to Victoria Terminus, a lavish riot of towers, domes, spires, cornices, and gargoyles that graces the spot where dhobis once walloped the city's clothes on the washermen's stone. The construction program was immense, and it created a new spatial complex of imperial spectacle whose assertion of colonial power over public space was underscored by British street names and by intersections bedecked with statues and fountains that commemorated colonial figures and European cultural symbols.

The instantiation of colonial dominance in the imperial spectacle rendered and recognized the public spaces of the city as sites of power. But streets, bazaars, and public institutions were also spaces where Bombay's modern divides, secured in the private sphere through residential segregation, were crossed. As places where interactions took place across inequality and difference, the city's public spaces reproduced the social and political hierarchy — which meant that they *also* bred resistance and confrontation. The other city of modernity frequently spilled onto the streets and sought to reclaim and reinscribe them, which sparked clashes with the dominant order. Thus, when the annual Mohurrum processions by shia Muslims to commemorate Hussain's martyrdom at Kerbala provoked clashes among Muslims in the early twentieth century, the colonial authorities swung into action. S. M. Edwardes, Bombay's police commissioner, believed that the "orgiastic method of celebrating the festival was an anachronism, not countenanced by Islamic teaching and gravely injurious to the City."[30] He prohibited the processions from playing music while passing Bohra streets, and later effectively banned them from taking out *tabuts* altogether.[31] Something similar occurred with the Ganapati festival.

Until 1895, Ganapati worship was largely a domestic ceremony, though the immersion of the clay image in the sea did involve street processions, which provoked clashes. When Bal Gangadhar Tilak, the militant nationalist leader, instituted the public worship of Ganapati as a patriotic celebration in 1895, its claim on public spaces became both more assertive and more systematically regulated. Nationalism made confrontations over public spaces more general as open public spaces like Chowpatty Beach, parks, and the courtyards of chawls and *baghs* became venues for political mobilization.[32] Similarly, the communist-led trade unions, drawing on social patterns in the mill neighborhoods, brought conflicts in the workplace into the public spaces of the city and made working-class strikes and other actions part of Bombay's ex-

Ganapati festival now. Photo courtesy of Sharada Dwivedi and Rahul Mehrotra.

perience.[33] This was particularly the case in the 1950s, when, following Indian independence in 1947, radical activists and intellectuals represented the city as the space to realize the ideals of postcolonial citizenship and social justice. Hindi cinema of this period, for example, projected the street as the space where both the promises and failures of postcolonial urban citizenship were played out.[34]

The emergence of the Shiv Sena in 1966 opened a new chapter in the history of Bombay's public spaces as sites of confrontation. As Thomas Hansen shows, the Sena's political rhetoric and methods generalized social conflicts between dominant and popular classes as a confrontation between the natives and outsiders—immigrants, communists, and Muslims—at the level of the city.[35] The Sena has sought to appropriate the city's public spaces through day-to-day mobilization, by renaming streets, public institutions, and Bombay itself, and through religious and political processions and celebrations. While these actions seek to appropriate the city ritually and symbolically, the Sena's use of violence in daily political activity and in bloody spurts of communal pogroms against the Muslims, as in 1992–93, asserts control as revenge, as an act of cleansing the native soil of the "alien." Tempting as it is to see the Sena's rise as an irruption of archaic and atavistic energies, in fact its origins lie in Bombay's divided history of modernity. It was precisely in the public space of the city that the Sena reconfigured interactions across social divides into confrontations between the Marathi *manus* (man) and the "outsider."

THE LAYERED CITY

Clearly, the Shiv Sena's nativist rhetoric and its orchestration of anti-Muslim violence have changed the city decisively. Described as "de-cosmopolitization" and "provincialization," the Sena's attempt to replace universal citizenship with exclusivist regional and communal conditions for rights to the city is ironically related to globalization's growing presence in Bombay.[36] Both have arisen on the ruins of the modernist projects. The destruction of the industrial city and radical working-class politics, the dismantling of the postcolonial developmentalist state and the shattering of the dreams of universal citizenship and social equality have set the context for the rise of both the ethnic particularism of the Shiv Sena and the globalization of capital. In place of the cosmopolitan and secular-nationalist modern city, Bombay's residents are now asked to embrace the exclusivist ideology of regionalism and Hindu chauvinism. Globalization has also added new urban forms and practices: shopping malls and multiplex cinemas; the growing circulation of global media and images; the functioning of media, advertising, and commodity-exchange as a nexus; the increasing importance of entertainment and consumption; and the expansion of call centers, outsourcing, and the informalization of labor. These developments project the neoliberal fantasy that economic modernization and consumption will "free" Bombay from the shackles of the nation-state's developmentalism and turn it into a "world-class" city.[37] The fact that critiques of this vision have not consolidated into a radical oppositional movement or social bloc seems to affirm the portrait of Bombay's demise as a modern city.

However, there is something deeply problematic in this rise-and-fall story. Foucault wrote, "The great obsession of the nineteenth century was, as we know, history: with its themes of development and suspension, of crisis and cycle, themes of ever accumulating past."[38] Speaking this language of development, the discourse of the death of the city suppresses history's spatiality, its internal differentiations and asymmetries in favor of a narrative of evolution, progression, crisis, and death. The history of the modern city as a space of porosity, multiplicity, difference, division, and disruption is concealed when urban change is represented as the unfolding of one historical stage to another, from the bounded unity and identity of the city of industrial capitalism to the "placeless" and "generic" city of globalization, from modernity to postmodernity. The mourning for the remembered city fails to identify the layers of contradictory and conflicting practices and desires in the ruins of Bombay's urban modernity.

Henri Lefebvre writes that urban space has a structure more like that of flaky pastry than the homogenous and isotropic space of classical mathematics.[39] Bombay's history as a space contains several patterns and layers in its flaky structure. It developed as a city of colonial and capitalist domination that attracted millions, a city where communities and classes interacted in public spaces while living separately in enclaves. It grew into a big city, but with village-like neighborhoods and identities. Its public spaces have been sites of ritual and political confrontations, of aspirations of democratic and nationalist citizenship, and of the politics of nativist and communal revenge. The city, its forms and order, must be understood as the spatial expression as well as the enabling condition of these changing and interrelated layers of modern practices and imaginations. The discourse that grieves Bombay's death overlooks the internal relationship between these layers. Besides misreading as evidence of decline the problems produced by Bombay's dynamic though haphazard growth, this discourse also fails to recognize the relationship between the modern city and its others, between Dinshaw Wacha's mythic city of daily life on the promenade and the everyday tactics of urban habitation by rural migrants in Girangaon. Urban modernity in Bombay developed by living a double life; the cosmopolitan city was also experienced as an alien city. It was neither only one nor only the other, but both, and held together by lines of power.

Mr. Kapur in Mistry's *Family Matters* has no experience or memory of modernity's doubleness and believes that his beloved city's era of brilliant and Olympian cosmopolitanism has been succeeded by the dark phase of ethnic intolerance and violence. But Bombay's history as a structure of layered spaces and experiences resists this evolutionary representation; it suggests that what one is witnessing today is not the death of the city, but the demise of the idea of the city as an organism, of modernity as a singular project. Bombay has experienced far-reaching transformations, an important aspect of which has been the erosion of the ideal of the modern city as a unity—a unity that was secured through elite domination and was met with confrontation and resistance. The ruins of the elite imaginary bring Bombay face to face with its divided history of urban modernity. They also pose a challenge to reimagine urban life, to think afresh about how the layered, divided, and porous spaces of the modern city, now worked over by globalized capitalism, can constitute a place for strangers to live together. This is the ethical responsibility presented by the ruins of the modern city.

NOTES

1. Mistry 2002, 263–64. See also Salman Rushdie's bleak portrayal of Bombay in *The Moor's Last Sigh* (1995).
2. Sarlo 2000, 119.
3. Appadurai and Holston 1999b, 1–20.
4. Chatterjee 2004.
5. See Hansen 2001.
6. Kosambi 1986, 50.
7. Chandavarkar 1994, 29, 55.
8. Ibid., 250.
9. Ibid., 125.
10. Kosambi 1986, 56.
11. Edwardes 1909, 2:170.
12. Stevens 1915, 82.
13. Wacha 1920.
14. Ibid., 558. Page numbers from Wacha's *Shells from the Sands of Bombay* cited parenthetically.
15. Ibid., 566–67.
16. Ibid., 461–84.
17. Ibid., 318.
18. Ibid., 319.
19. The following description is derived from ibid., 82–93.
20. Lefebvre 1971, 21.
21. Madgavkar 1961 [1863], 1–2. Cited in Kosambi 1995, 17–18.
22. Cited in Kosambi 1995, 18.
23. Kosambi 1995, 18–19.
24. Stevens 1915, 82–83.
25. Tindall 1992, 204.

26. Burnett-Hurst 1925.

27. Chandavarkar 1998, 105.

28. See, for example, Tindall 1992, 252–53.

29. Chandavarkar 1998, 107.

30. Edwardes 1923, 186.

31. Masselos 1982, 59. *Tabuts* were wooden structures covered with silver and colorful papers and tinsel, representing Hussain's mausoleum in Kerbala.

32. Dwivedi and Mehrotra 1995, 211.

33. Chandavarkar 1998, 126–27.

34. Raj Kapoor's *Shree 420* (1955) is frequently cited as the paradigmatic cinematic imagination of the hopes and disappointments of postcolonial citizenship in Bombay (see, for example, Varma 2004, 65–89). But this was only one among many films made in the 1950s—among them the film noir projects starring Dev Anand—that explored the conditions of urban life in Bombay. Significantly, not all of them worked with the frame of the nation in representing different spaces of the city.

35. Hansen 2001.

36. The term *de-cosmopolitization* comes from Appadurai 2000, 627–51; *provincialization* is used by Varma 2004.

37. In 2003 a plan for making Mumbai into a "world-class" city by 2013 was prepared by McKinsey and Company for a pro-business civic organization, Bombay First, and received the cooperation of the municipal and state governments. Its chief recommendations were to boost economic growth, improve infrastructure, and provide affordable housing. See Bombay First–McKinsey Report 2003.

38. Foucault 1986, 22.

39. Lefebvre 1991b, 86.

Rahul Mehrotra

NEGOTIATING THE STATIC AND KINETIC CITIES

THE EMERGENT URBANISM OF MUMBAI

Cities in India, characterized by physical and visual contradictions that coalesce in a landscape of incredible plural-
ism, are anticipated to be the largest urban conglomerates of the
twenty-first century. Historically, particularly during the period
of British colonization, the different worlds—whether economic,
social, or cultural—that were contained within these cities occupied different spaces and operated under different rules, the aim
being to maximize control and minimize conflict between opposing worlds.[1] Today, although these worlds have come to share
the same space, they understand and use it differently.[2] Massive
waves of distressed rural migration during the latter half of the
1900s triggered the convergence of these worlds into a singular
but multifaceted entity. This, coupled with an inadequate supply
of urban land and a failure to create new urban centers, resulted in
extremely high population densities. Furthermore, in the 1990s,
with the emergence of a postindustrial, service-based economy,
the intertwining of these worlds within the same space became
even more intense.[3]

In this postindustrial scenario, cities in India have become critical sites for negotiation between elite and subaltern cultures. The

new relationships between social classes in a postindustrial economy are quite different from those that existed in state-controlled economies and the welfare state.[4] The fragmentation of service and production locations has resulted in a new, bazaar-like urbanism, which has woven its presence through the entire urban landscape.[5] It is an urbanism created by those outside the elite domains of the formal modernity of the state and is thus a "pirate" modernity that slips under the laws of the city simply to survive, without any conscious attempt at constructing a counterculture.[6] This contrasts with the many historic legacies of modernity in India where instruments such as the State Plan (referred to as the Development Plan), borrowed from Soviet socialist planning paradigms, controlled, determined, and orchestrated the built landscape. With the dramatic retreat of the state through the 1980s and 1990s, the space of the "everyday" has become the space where economic and cultural struggles are articulated. These common spaces have been largely excluded from the cultural discourses on globalization, which focus on elite domains of production and their spatial implications.[7]

Today, Indian cities comprise two components that occupy the same physical space. The first is the formal or Static City. Built of more permanent materials such as concrete, steel, and brick, it is comprehended as a two-dimensional entity on conventional city maps and is monumental in its presence. The second is the informal or Kinetic City. Incomprehensible as a two-dimensional entity, it is perceived as a city in motion—a three-dimensional construct of incremental development. The Kinetic City is temporary in nature and often built with recycled material: plastic sheets, scrap metal, canvas, and waste wood. It constantly modifies and reinvents itself. The Kinetic City is perceived not as architecture, but in terms of spaces which hold associative values and supportive lives. Patterns of occupation determine its form and perception. It is an indigenous urbanism that has its particular "local" logic. It is not necessarily the city of the poor, as most images might suggest; rather, it is a temporal articulation and occupation of space which not only creates a richer sensibility of spatial occupation but also suggests how spatial limits are expanded to include formally unimagined situations in dense urban conditions.[8]

The Kinetic City presents a compelling vision that potentially allows one to better understand the blurred lines of contemporary urbanism and the

Temporary construction for a festival. Photo by Rahul Mehrotra.

changing roles of people and spaces in urban society. The increasing concentrations of global flows have exacerbated the inequalities and spatial divisions of social classes. In this context, an architecture or urbanism of equality in an increasingly inequitable economic condition requires looking deeper to find a wide range of places in which to mark and commemorate the cultures of those excluded from the spaces of global flows. These don't necessarily lie in the formal production of architecture, but they often challenge it. Here, the idea of a city points to an elastic urban condition — not a grand vision, but a grand adjustment.

The Kinetic City, bazaar-like in form, can be seen as the symbolic image of the emerging urban Indian condition. The processions, weddings, festivals, hawkers, street vendors, and slum dwellers all create an ever-transforming streetscape — a city in constant motion, where the very physical fabric is characterized by the kinetic. The Static City, on the other hand, dependent on architecture for its representation, is no longer the single image by which the city is read. Thus, architecture is not the "spectacle" of the city, nor does it even comprise the single dominant image of the city. In contrast, festivals such as Diwali, Dussera, Navrathri, Muhharam, Durga Puja, Ganesh Chathurthi, and many more have emerged as the spectacles of the Kinetic City. Their presence on the everyday landscape pervades and dominates the popular visual culture of Indian cities. Festivals create a forum through which the fantasies of the subalterns are articulated and even organized into political action. In Mumbai, for example, the popularity and growth of the Ganesh festival has been phenomenal.[9] During the festival, which occurs in August or September, numerous neighborhoods transform themselves temporarily with lights and decoration. New public spaces are created to house the idols of Ganesh for ten days. During the festival period, family, neighborhood, and city events mark the celebrations. On the last day a large part of the city's population carries the idols in long processions to the sea, where they are ultimately to be immersed.

Each procession carries tableaux depicting images of both local and global concerns, with Lord Ganesh mediating the outcomes. These representations are not based on formal scriptures or predetermined rules; instead, human ingenuity breaches the boundaries between the local and the global, the historic and contemporary. The images convey the hybrid urgencies of metropolitan India.[10] The neighborhood processions weave through predetermined routes in the city, each vying with other neighborhood processions to showcase the intensity of their followers. Set against the backdrop of the Static City, the processions culminate with the immersion of the idols, which the followers bid farewell amid chants inviting Ganesh to resurrect his presence the following year.

Immersion becomes a metaphor for the spectacle of the city. As the clay idol dissolves in the water of the bay, the spectacle comes to a close. There are no static or permanent mechanisms to encode this spectacle. The memory of the city is in this instance an "enacted" process, a temporal moment, as opposed to a static or permanent entity in the form of buildings that contain the public memory.[11] The city and its architecture are not synonymous and cannot contain a single meaning. Within the Kinetic City, meanings are not stable; spaces get consumed, reinterpreted, and recycled. The Kinetic City recycles the Static City to create a new spectacle.

This transformative ability of the Kinetic City becomes even more vivid in the events that play out at Mumbai's town hall every year on 15 August, India's Independence Day. The Public Works Department (PWD) subverts the meaning and symbolism of the architecture of this classical building by reconfiguring it for an annual ceremony when the governor of the state addresses the

Immersion of the Ganesh idol. Photo by Rahul Mehrotra.

citizens. To ensure the ceremony is protected from the monsoon rains, the PWD builds a structure, a sort of large porch built overnight in bamboo and cloth, which attaches itself to the building. The decorative trim and other ornamental highlights graft on to this classical building a local and perhaps traditional sensibility that momentarily transforms the architecture. The conservationists in the city protest each year, decrying such construction as an abuse of the legislation that protects heritage buildings, but they ignore the fact that this is a reversible action, well within the bounds of even the holiest of preservationists' canons.[12] The intended image of this symbol of colonial power, a celebrated asset of the Static City, is subverted and recolonized by the Kinetic City. The PWD alters the significance of this building momentarily to expand the margins of the Kinetic City.

This notion of cultural preservation takes on a critical dimension when applied to the preservation of the built environment in these contexts. Debates about the conservation of the Static City have often revolved around the idea of "cultural significance," an all-encompassing concept that emerged clearly in the 1980s. To be more precise, it first emerged in what is referred to as the Burra Charter, one of the many resolutions made by the International Charter for the Conservation and Restoration of Monuments and Sites to define and guide conservation practice. Adopted in Burra, South Australia, in

Town hall of Mumbai, with its thirty-four steps. Photo by Rahul Mehrotra.

Town hall of Mumbai transformed on Independence Day. Photo by Rahul Mehrotra.

Victorian statues in the garden of the Bombay Zoo. Photo by Rahul Mehrotra.

1979, the Burra Charter defined cultural significance as the aesthetic, historic, scientific or social value for past, present, and future generations. Implicit in this definition is the belief that "significance" is static. It is a definition that is "object"-centric (devoid of life) with its roots in the debate propagated by the antiquarians of the Renaissance.[13] What is the validity of a notion where cultural memory is often an enacted process, as in the Kinetic City? Or where meanings are fluid like the Kinetic City itself and often complicated in postcolonial conditions by the fact that the creators and custodians of historic environments in the Static City are different cultures from those that created them?

What, then, might be one's cultural reading of the Kinetic City, which now forms a greater part of urban reality? In this dynamic context, if the production or preservation of architecture or urban form has to be informed by one's reading of cultural significance, it will necessarily have to include the notion of "constructing significance" in both architectural and conservation debates.[14] In fact, an understanding that cultural significance evolves will challenge as well as clarify the role of the architect as an advocate of change (versus a preservationist who opposes change)—one who can engage with both the Kinetic City and the Static City on equal terms. Under such conditions, a draining of the symbolic import of the architectural landscape leads to a deepening of ties between architecture and contemporary realities and experiences. This understanding allows architecture and urban typologies to be transformed through intervention and placed in the service of contemporary life, realities, and emerging aspirations. The Static City can thus embrace the Kinetic City and be informed and remade by its logic.

The phenomenon of bazaars in the Victorian arcades of the Fort Area, Mumbai's historic district, is emblematic of this potential negotiation between the Static City and the Kinetic City. The original use of the arcades was twofold: first, they provided spatial mediation between building and street; second, they were a perfect response to Bombay's climate, serving to protect pedestrians from both harsh sun and lashing rains. Today, with the informal bazaar occupying the arcades, the original intent of the area has been challenged. The emergent relationship between the arcade and the bazaar not only forces a confrontation of uses and interest groups but also demands new preservation approaches. For the average Mumbai resident, the hawker provides a wide range of goods at prices considerably lower than those found in local shops, and the bazaars that characterize the Fort Area arcades are therefore thriving. For the elite and for conservationists, the Victorian core represents the old city center, complete with monumental icons. In fact, as the city sprawls, dissipating the clarity of its form, these images, places, and icons acquire even greater meaning, for preservationists, as critical symbols of the city's historic image. Consequently, hawking is deemed illegal by city authorities that are constantly attempting to relocate the bazaars.

The challenge in Bombay is to cope with the city's transformation, not by inducing or polarizing its dualism, but by attempting to reconcile these opposite conditions as being simultaneously valid. The existence of two worlds in the same space implies that one must accommodate and overlap varying uses, perceptions, and physical forms. For example, the Fort Area arcades are a special urban component that inherently possesses a capacity for reinterpretation. As an architectural or urban-design solution, the arcades display incredible resilience; they can accommodate new uses while keeping the illusion of their architecture intact.

One design solution might be to readapt the functioning of the arcades,

restructuring them to allow for easy pedestrian movement and to accommodate hawkers at the same time. Restructured arcades, providing an illusion
of the disciplined Victorian arcade or the exterior façade, could contain the
amorphous bazaar within. With this sort of planning, components of the city
would have a greater ability to survive because they could be more adaptable
to changing economic and social conditions. There are no total solutions in
an urban landscape charged with the duality between permanence and rapid
transformation. At best, the city could constantly evolve and invent solutions
for the present through safeguarding the crucial components of historically
important "urban hardware." Could "Bazaars in Victorian Arcades" become
a symbol of an emergent reality of temporary adjustment?

Clearly the Static and Kinetic Cities go beyond their obvious differences to
establish a much richer relationship both spatially and metaphorically than
their physical manifestations would suggest. Here, affinity and rejection are
simultaneously played out, maintaining a state of equilibrium via a seemingly
irresolvable tension. The informal economy of the city vividly illustrates the
collapsed and intertwined existence of the Static and Kinetic Cities. *Dabbawalas* (literally, "tiffin men") exemplify the relationship between the formal
and informal, the static and kinetic. The tiffin-delivery service, which relies
on the train system for transportation, costs about 200 rupees (four dollars) per month, with an annual turnover that amounts to roughly 50 million
rupees (around a million dollars). Approximately 4,500 dabbawalas deliver
an estimated 200,000 lunchboxes every day. A dabbawala picks up a lunch
tiffin from a house anywhere in the city. He then, through a complex network,
helps deliver the tiffin by lunchtime and return it to the house later in the day.
The network involves the *dabba*, or tiffin, being exchanged up to four or five
times between pickup and return, with the average box traveling about thirty
kilometers each way. The efficiency of Mumbai's train system, the spine of the
linear city, enables this complex informal system to work. The dabbawalas
have thus innovatively set up a network that enables an informal system to
take advantage of a formal infrastructure.[15]

Entrepreneurship in the Kinetic City is an autonomous and oral process
that requires the ability to fold the formal and informal into a symbiotic relationship. The dabbawala service—like other informal services, which range
from banking to money transfers to couriers to electronic bazaars—lever-

ages community relationships and networks and deftly uses the Static City and its infrastructure beyond its intended margins. These networks create a synergy that depends on mutual integration without the obsession of formalized structures. The Kinetic City is where the intersection of need (often at the level of survival) and of the unexploited potentials of existing infrastructure engenders innovative services. The trains in Mumbai are emblematic of a kinetic space that supports and blurs the formal and the informal, slicing through these worlds while momentarily collapsing them into a singular entity. In this space the self-consciousness about modernity and the regulations imposed by the Static City are suspended and redundant. The Kinetic City carries local wisdom into the contemporary world without fear of the modern, while the Static City aspires to erase the local and recodify it in a written "macro-moral" order.[16] Inspired by modernist urban-design tenets, the Static City periodically remakes the Kinetic City in its own image.

The issue of housing most vividly demonstrates the process by which the Static City reorders and remakes the Kinetic City. In Mumbai, for example, approximately 60 percent of the city's population does not have access to formal housing. This population lives on approximately 10 percent of the city's land in settlements that are locally referred to as slums. It is estimated that about 70 percent of the city's population works in the informal sector. This number has risen with the new liberal economy, which curtails bargaining capacity by fragmenting labor. Despite its informal nature, the subaltern population's productivity allows Mumbai to be competitive on a global scale.[17] This population lives in the interstitial spaces of the cities—road edges, drainage channels (*nalla* spaces), edges of railway lines—and must engage in innovative means of negotiating everyday life. Dish antennas and a web of electrical wire and cables are juxtaposed with homes covered by plastic sheets or with walls made of empty drums—a kaleidoscope of the past, present, and future compressed into an organic fabric of alleys, dead ends, and a labyrinthine, mysterious streetscape that constantly modifies and reinvents itself. The Kinetic City, like a twitching organism, locates and relocates itself through perpetual motion. Flow, instability, and indeterminacy are basic to the Kinetic City. Regular demolitions exacerbate the tenuous occupation of land by the inhabitants of these settlements, inhibiting any investment the occupants might make in their physical living conditions.

Thus, the Kinetic City is fluid and dynamic, mobile and temporal (often as a strategy to defeat eviction), and leaves no ruins. It constantly recycles its resources, leveraging great effect and presence with very little means.

The expansion of the Kinetic City only heightens the growing contradictions evident in the islands of concentrated wealth that are increasingly manifest in gated communities throughout the city and the edge-city suburbs. The popular metaphorical reference to "making Bombay Shanghai" is emblematic of the one-dimensional imagination that planners and politicians bring to bear on decisions about the city's development.[18] An obvious extension of the Shanghai metaphor is the notion of remaking the city in a singular image and using architecture as the spectacle to represent a global aspiration. The radical transformation of the physical nature of the city is seen as the most immediate method to make the city viable for integration in a global network of cities and economies. New highways, flyovers, airports, corporate hotels, and convention centers (followed by the secondary development of museums, galleries, parks, and progressive urban regulations to demonstrate further compliance with international urban standards) are all critical elements for the Static City to achieve this perceived integration. Such global implications also raise political questions that challenge the democratic processes of city governance.

Ambiguity regarding the urban form of Mumbai and the dominant image of the city prompts the question "Whose city is it anyway?" This question goes beyond the politics of occupation and challenges the processes by which the city is made. The making of the city is perhaps most critical when negotiating between the Static and Kinetic Cities, for it is also an effective point of intervention. Through the city-making process, globalization and its particular transgressions in the urban landscape are realized, but that process is also how the Kinetic City can resist or participate in globalization as well as reconfigure itself socially, culturally, and spatially.

The growing movement of slum associations and networks in Mumbai is a potent illustration of effective intervention. These associations engage with the formal world of the Static City while mediating the contradictions inherent in issues of legality, informality, and the mobile and temporal strategies of the Kinetic City. One such successful movement is the alliance between the nongovernmental organization Society for the Promotion of Area Resources, the community-benefit organization National Slum Dwellers Federation, and the Mahila Milan, an organization of poor women. This alliance is essentially united around concerns for securing land and access to urban infrastructure. It has successfully negotiated between the formal and informal worlds in the city, as well as across national boundaries through a network of alliances working with slum dwellers around the world. Besides representing efforts to reconstitute citizenship in cities, these alliances form what Arjun Appadurai calls a "deep democracy," referring to "[a] model that produces poor communities able to engage in partnership with more powerful agencies—urban, regional, national and multilateral—that purport to be concerned with poverty and citizenship. . . . [V]ertical collaborations and partnerships with more powerful persons and organizations together form a mutually sustaining cycle of process. This is where depth and laterality become joint circuits along which pro-poor strategies can flow."[19] It is through this restructuring of the city-making process that the Kinetic and Static Cities can be intertwined beyond the physical and thus better engage the inhabitants of the city.

In such conditions, the urbanism of Mumbai represents a fascinating intersection where the Kinetic City—a landscape of dystopia, yet a symbol of optimism—challenges the Static City—encoded in architecture—to reposition and remake the city as a whole.[20] The Kinetic City forces the Static City to re-engage itself in present conditions by dissolving its utopian project to fabricate multiple dialogues with its context. Could this become the basis for a rational discussion about coexistence? Or is the emergent urbanism of Mumbai inherently paradoxical such that the coexistence of the Static and Kinetic Cities and their particular states of utopia and dystopia are inevitable? Can the spatial configuration for how this simultaneity occurs actually be formally imagined?

In spite of these many potential disjunctures, what this reading of the city does celebrate is the dynamic and pluralist processes that create the urban Indian landscape. Within this urbanism, the Static and Kinetic Cities necessarily coexist and blur into an integral entity, even if momentarily, to create the margins for adjustment that their simultaneous existences demand.

NOTES

1. King 1976.

2. This unprecedented demographic shift has not only transformed the social make-up of Indian cities but has perpetuated an incomprehensible landscape charged with intense dualities—which are cultural and social, as well as economic. This new demography comprises mainly rural migrants, who form the urban poor, bringing with them new skills, social values, and cultural attitudes that not only determine their ability to survive in an urban environment but are also, in the process, altering the very structure of the city. The different attitudes of rural migrants that influence the way the city is used and perceived are also emblematic of the more universal phenomenon of global flows that are transforming cities across the world and of local resistances which emerge in landscapes characterized by uneven development. Furthermore, the presence of the urban poor makes explicit another crucial divide—that between those who have access to the formal city and the infrastructure that goes with it, and those who do not have this access and therefore lack the basic amenities in the urban system.

3. Distinct manufacturing zones and segregations have now shifted spatially to services and manufacturing occurring in fragmented areas in the city, which are networked through the efficient transportation system the city offers. Similarly, the markets on which these economies are dependent have been fractured, giving rise to adjacencies of use and urban form previously not experienced in the city. See Shetty 2005.

4. Chatterjee 2003.

5. The fragmented nature of the new economy in Mumbai was well documented by Prasad Shetty (2005). One interesting observation had to do with the changing patterns of mobility in public transportation, particularly with regard to trains. While the city's population between 1991 and 2001 grew by 22.40 percent, train travel increased by 42.37 percent (from 4.95 million to 6.4 million passengers). This was largely due to significant changes in work and production patterns. Small-scale operations and individual agents now connect manufacturing nodes that are fragmented across landscape of the city.

6. Sundaram 2001.

7. Chatterjee 2003.

8. Weddings are an example of how the rich, too, are engaged in the making of the Kinetic City. The lack of formal spaces for weddings as the cultural outlet for ostentation has resulted in public open space being temporarily colonized for consumption by the rich as spaces for the spectacle of elaborate weddings. Complex wedding sets are often constructed and removed within twelve hours—a transitory spectacle set up by the rich in the public domain for private consumption. Again, the margin of the urban system is momentarily expanded.

9. In its present form the Ganeshotsava, as the festival is referred to locally, was re-

invented in the late nineteenth century, by Lokamanya Tilak, as a symbol of resistance to the British colonial regime. Tilak took a domestic and private idiom of worship and translated it into a collective and public rite of self-assertion.

10. Ranjit Hoskote, "Scenes from a Festival," *Hindu Folio*, 14 January 2001, 18–21.

11. Mehrotra 2002.

12. Conservation legislation was first introduced in Mumbai in 1995 and was the first of its kind in India. Over the last ten years of the legislation's existence, the debate about historic preservation — or conservation, as it is more commonly referred to in Mumbai — has become a well articulated one. A number of nongovernmental organizations are involved in activism and advocacy to lobby for the protection of the listed buildings. Unfortunately, most of these debates are biased toward British conservation practices because a large number of Indian architects trained in conservation were educated at universities in the U.K. and thus tend to bring a British-centric view to the protection of colonial buildings, a view that is largely out of sync with contemporary Indian urban realities. The benchmarks for these architects are British and European standards, which often steers conservation practice into the realm of the elite patrons (banks, government agencies, etc.), which is seen as an exclusionary activity.

13. These ideas were first presented at the "Cultural Significance: Construct or Criterion?" seminar held at the Center for Architecture and Middle Eastern Studies, University of Adelaide, in July 2000. I am grateful to Peter Scriver for his help in developing these ideas.

14. For examples of works or projects that have attempted to translate these ideas, see Mehrotra 2004.

15. Venkatraman and Mirti 2005.

16. Khosla 2002.

17. As organized manufacturing left the city of Mumbai, skilled laborers were left no choice but fend for themselves. Small manufacturing centers with agents working to network them have become the emergent paradigm. This system allows for an incredible web of distribution, with the slums serving as centers of production.

18. Before Shanghai — that is, until the late 1990s — Singapore was the metaphor for a successful city, as implicit in the question politicians asked: "Why can't Mumbai become like Singapore?" Singapore's levels of hygiene, cleanliness, efficient functioning, all set in a tropical landscape — Mumbai and its citizens could easily imagine these things for their city. Their imaginings were fueled by big businesses, as represented through organizations like Bombay First, to prepare the city to participate in the global economy.

19. Appadurai 2001, 42–43.

20. Charles Correa, the eminent Indian architect, has described Mumbai as "a Great City, Terrible Place." As I intend it, utopia is the cultural and economic landscape of the city, and dystopia the physical landscape.

Yingjin Zhang

REMAPPING BEIJING

POLYLOCALITY, GLOBALIZATION, CINEMA

Remapping has become a sheer necessity these days in any metropolitan Chinese city, not least because hasty, large-scale urban development since the early 1990s has demolished much of the old cityscape and replaced it with nondescript high-rises and commercial districts, thereby rendering printed maps inadequate or irrelevant in a matter of months. In this frenzied age of "globalization"—a magic word sanctioned by Chinese bureaucracy and mass media—Chinese cinema has participated in various projects of remapping the city, of producing urban imaginaries that articulate new urban visions, negotiate changing urban values, and critique problematic urban transformation. In this essay I investigate "cinematic remapping" as a particular mode of urban imaginary, a mode that combines motion, emotion, and commotion in an intensified, often visceral representation of temporality, spatiality, locality, equality, identity, and subjectivity. With an emphasis on *moving* images—images set in motion, marked by mobility, and charged with affect—of a local/global dynamic, my investigation differs from Fredric Jameson's remapping of Taipei in terms of postmodernity, Ackbar Abbas's remapping of pre-1997 Hong Kong in terms of a postculture of disappearance, and Dai Jinhua's remapping of Chinese cinema of the 1990s in terms of postcolonialism.[1] Rather than "cognitive mapping" conceived at a high level of abstraction, I am interested primarily in instances of cinematic remapping that favor street-level views over cartographic surveys, contingent experience over systematic knowledge, and bittersweet local *histoires* over grand-scale global history.

A LOCAL/GLOBAL DYNAMIC

Three theoretical issues related to the global, the national, and the local have informed my investigation of cinematic remapping in Chinese cinema of the twenty-first century. First, one should bear in mind questions Anthony King raised in 1989: "Does [globalization] imply cultural homogenization, cultural synchronization or cultural proliferation? What does it say about the *direction of cultural flows*? Is it the interaction of the local and the global, with the emphasis on the former, or vice versa?"[2] Even if one grants globalization the status of the dominant in contemporary China (as the Chinese State is now fundamentally complicit with transnational capitalism centered in the West), its homogenizing tendency does not always work wonders at the level of local culture. Indeed, as Stuart Hall writes of a global mass culture, "The homogenization is never absolutely complete, and it does not work for completeness."[3] Not surprisingly, urban imaginaries produced in contemporary Chinese cinema tend to *emphasize the local* in its interaction with the global, and they prefer cultural hybridization and "global mélange" more than cultural synchronization or homogenization.[4]

Second, as the foremost Chinese metropolises like Beijing and Shanghai aspire to the coveted status of the global city, the national continues to play a vital role in China's integration into a globalizing world. Saskia Sassen asks, "What happens to the relationship between state and city under conditions of a strong articulation between city and the world economy?"[5] It is known with certainty that the Chinese state has so far maintained its overriding power over the city, and the national is structured into China's program of globalization as Beijing prepares itself strategically for the 2008 Olympic Games and Shanghai for the 2010 World Exposition, both enterprises blessed with an influx of global capital. True, in the realms of economics, finance, technology, and the like, Beijing and Shanghai are increasingly connected in global and globalizing networks; however, instead of eclipsing the national, the city has remained indispensable, a site where the local enlists the national in negotiating with globalization while the national still counts on the local in exploiting cultural symbolism and popular memory.

Third, one must not forget that the local, despite its frequent idealization as the space of authenticity, appropriation, and resistance, is itself in many ways *translocal*. The notion of the translocal acknowledges the coexistence of different locals in the same urban area, albeit in different spaces and places; it also means that not all locals are equally indigenous to a locality, thereby leaving room for questions of migration and diaspora. In fact, a recurring motif in Chinese cinema of the new century is precisely the tension of the multiple translocal, or polylocality, in the city, a tension drastically complicated by the steady rural-to-urban migration on a national scale and by stringent demands of globalization on a transnational scale.[6] Given such tension-filled circumstances, urban imaginaries in Chinese cinema often foreground the glorious façade of globalization as a mere pretext to figure out a rapidly shifting urban landscape in which alien economic power—alien to China's socialist memory—reigns supreme and local individuals' experiences are repeatedly frustrated, fragmented, and fractured in seemingly insignificant details of everyday life. What is more, even the "everyday" can no longer function as a fixed local; rather, it constitutes what David Campbell calls "a transversal site of contestations"—contestations, that is, among the local (or translocal), the national, and the global.[7]

This essay focuses on Beijing precisely as such a salient polylocality in contestation. My bracketing of Shanghai in this study of cinematic remapping is in part to follow Joseph Esherick's call to redirect academic attention beyond Shanghai, Shanghai having dominated research agendas since the early 1990s, especially in modern history, but likewise in cinema and urban culture.[8] The concentration on Beijing is additionally motivated by my interest in the extent to which previously prevailing imaginaries of Beijing as a traditional walled city and a sacrosanct site of China's imperial power and socialist enterprises have been transmuted by the forces of globalization and transfigured into new imaginaries of Beijing as a global city wrought with ambivalences and contradictions. Before examining contemporary attempts at cinematic remapping, however, one should first look back at representative imaginaries of Beijing in film history.

When it comes to China, Western films typically project Orientalist and salvationist fantasies filtered through the imagination of bygone imperialist conquistadors and the vestiges of Cold War ideology. From D. W. Griffith's *Broken Blossoms* (1919), Frank Capra's *The Bitter Tea of General Yen* (1933), Mark Robson's *The Inn of the Sixth Happiness* (1958), and Robert Wise's *The Sand Pebbles* (1966), to David Cronenberg's *M. Butterfly* (1993) and Jon Avnet's *Red Corner* (1997), a tradition of cinematic Orientalism and salvationism is easily traced through American film history.[9] Three examples from this long history help probe the deep recess of widespread Western imaginaries of Beijing.

The first example comes from Joseph von Sternberg's *Shanghai Express* (1932), a film deliberately contrasting Western "civility" (honesty, etiquette, romance, as embodied by a British officer, Doctor Harvey) and Chinese "barbarism" (betrayal, torture, murder, as embodied by a Chinese warlord, Chang). In spite of its titular reference this star vehicle for Marlene Dietrich (as "Shanghai Lily," self-acknowledged as the notorious "white flower of China") shows no images of Shanghai's cityscape. Instead, it starts with the railroad journey from Beijing, which is projected as primitive, backward, and vulnerably locked inside its formidable, ancient city walls. As the screenplay describes it, "The Shanghai Express has drawn out of the station and is slowly puffing down the middle of a Chinese street decorated with banners and dragons. We have left modern China behind at the railroad station and are entering a China that is age-old. The street is teeming with ancient traffic.... Hucksters cry their wares."[10]

In this chaotic sequence the express train—the marvel of Western technology—crawls through an overcrowded neighborhood, incredulously led by fleeting pedestrians and a flock of chickens, and then temporarily blocked by a cow calmly nursing a calf right on the tracks. The train's sirens and bells have no impact on the stubborn animals, and it takes the brakeman a long time to clear the tracks for traffic. "You're in China now, sir," Chang tells Carmichael, a fellow traveler, "where time and life have no value." Among other things, *Shanghai Express* configures Beijing as a city paralyzed by agrarian lifestyles, abandoned by historical progress, and utterly indifferent to Western modernity.

The second example comes from the end of Nicholas Ray's *55 Days at Peking* (1963), where Empress Dowager Tzu-Hsi concedes that the dynasty is over after the foreign troops have stormed into Beijing and ended the fifty-five-day siege of the international legation during the 1900 Boxer Rebellion. As the eight powers gather their troops outside a Beijing gate tower in preparation for a victory parade, the American officer Major Matt Lewis (Charlton Heston) tells his British friend, Sir Arthur Robertson (David Niven), that he has yet to "make a home" for himself. He mounts his horse and looks at a silently admiring Chinese teenage girl, who beams into a radiant smile when she catches his attention. "Here, take my hand," Major Lewis says, reaching down to her, and cheerful nondiegetic music starts as the ecstatic girl climbs up and rides behind him. To the upbeat tune of "Yankee Doodle," the American troops march triumphantly through a decorative street arch. What is noteworthy here is not only the image of military conquest but also the sense of moral justification: the violence of a foreign invasion in an ancient empire is justified insofar as a token innocent Chinese girl is "rescued" from misery and "adopted" into the American way of life. Ultimately, *55 Days at Peking* imagines Beijing—a synecdoche of China—as an empire in ruins, a collapsed civilization desperately awaiting rescue or salvation from the West.

The extent to which Western filmmakers insisted on reliving the past glory of imperialist conquest at the heights of the Cold War was demonstrated in the production of *55 Days at Peking* in the early 1960s, which ran into financial difficulties from the start. In the name of cinematic realism, a full-scale sixty-acre replication of Beijing circa 1900 was built outside Madrid, and thousands of Chinese extras were hired from all over Spain and even from other parts of Western Europe. A number of costumes for the imperial Chinese court were believed to be authentic because they reportedly "were loaned by an illustrious Florentine family which wished to stay anonymous but was able to rescue them from the collapse of the dynasty right after the Boxer rebellion."[11] The usage of the word *rescue* in this trivia is particularly revealing, if not shocking, because what in the eyes of the Chinese was the Western conquistadors' barbaric looting of cultural treasures from Chinese imperial palaces in 1900 is unproblematically valorized as "rescue" or salvation in the Western imagination.

The third example comes from Bernardo Bertolucci's *The Last Emperor* (1987), an epic film shot on location in Beijing's Forbidden City and centered on the life of Pu Yi, China's last emperor, through a tumultuous century in modern Chinese history. In a scene echoing that in which Major Lewis offers his hand to a nameless Chinese girl, Reginald Johnston (Peter O'Toole) comes to the rescue when Pu Yi (Jone Lone), distressed by his birth mother's death, climbs up to the top of the palace wall and shouts, "I want to go out!" He slips and lies down on the edge of the wall while Johnston, aided by several eunuchs holding each other's hands and forming a human chain atop the wall, reaches out to Pu Yi: "Give me your hand, sir." The following scene shows Pu Yi having an eye examination by a Western optometrist, and his blurred vision is then corrected by superior Western technology. These two scenes complicate Bertolucci's professed intention of "seeing things through Chinese eyes" due to his conviction that "every time we [Westerners] try to read a Chinese event with our mental structure, we are wrong."[12] Abundant Orientalist displays notwithstanding, *The Last Emperor* features Johnston as a private English tutor who enlightens Pu Yi with Western knowledge and physically rescues him because he, Johnston, understands the double meaning of the gigantic walled city: protection (safety, security) and restriction (imprisonment, suffocation).

Sure enough, in Chinese cultural imagination of the early twentieth century, the ambivalence of the walled city of Beijing was widely recognized, and the "ancient capital" (*gudu*) loomed largely as a traditional city teeming with rural values, personal relationships, leisure, and an articulate disdain for Western values. In contrast, Shanghai was imagined as a metropolis dominated by money and exchange values, frantic activity, and the pursuit of pleasure, diversity, and Western lifestyles.[13] Because the Chinese film industry was concentrated in Shanghai before 1949, Chinese films of the time tended to privilege Shanghai over Beijing, and Beijing thus functioned as the other to cosmopolitan Shanghai. Instead of using rapid-fire montages of the cityscape as they did in films about Shanghai, Chinese filmmakers entertained a rather nostalgic vision of Beijing as a safeguarded hometown relatively intact from the onslaught of modernity.[14] Rather than the car or the tram that zigzags through Shanghai streets, the preferred images of Beijing included the teahouse, where the locals indulge in leisure talks, and the rickshaw, which brings residents through a maze of narrow back alleys (*hutong*). As late as the 1980s, and despite decades of socialist propaganda, Chinese filmmakers were still delighted at the sight of the teahouse, the rickshaw, the hutong, and the *siheyuan* (a traditional one-storey residential compound typically shared by several families), all of which tend to evoke nostalgia for the lost or disappearing hometown in the popular imagination.

In the era of globalization the hutong and the teahouse decorate an urban landscape of cultural disappearance in Beijing, and a new generation of Chinese filmmakers must negotiate between local, national, and global discourses and practices.[15] Understandably, not all imaginaries of old Beijing are obsolete, for new configurations are frequently developed in counterposition to the old. Cinematic remapping of Beijing thus acknowledges the older imaginaries of Beijing and at the same time endeavors to invent new ones. More than in "mapping"—an attempt to formulate a rigidly coordinated mental map of the cityscape—Chinese cinema of the new century seems to have discovered in *drifting* an aesthetically gratifying, cognitively challenging, and psychologically complicating mode of urban imagination. Drifting captures a raw documentary effect, projects fantastic kaleidoscopic images, and enables incessant psychological and emotional flows; in its conceptual indeterminacy and sensory immediacy, drifting facilitates boundary crossing (local/global), class commingling (rich/poor), and cultural mixing (Chinese/foreign), although it implies a disturbing deprivation of agency that engenders a crisis in subjectivity. Drifting thus carries with its images unresolved (or yet irresolvable) ambivalences and contradictions. As such, it has become a preferred mode of cinematic remapping, in the sense of both rewriting the previous maps and anticipating being rewritten shortly after—a self-reflexive mode of capturing a fast-changing cityscape in a globalizing world.

The conceptualization of drifting as a new mode of cinematic remapping can be substantiated by elaborating on the cultural significance of four means of transportation that appear in four recent Chinese films: the bicycle in Wang Xiaoshuai's *Beijing Bicycle* (2001), the motorcycle in Feng Xiaogang's *Big Shot's Funeral* (2001), the taxi in Ning Ying's *I Love Beijing* (2000), and the airplane in Jia Zhangke's *The World* (2005). With recourse to drifting via these four means of transportation, Chinese filmmakers interweave a variety of intriguing urban imaginaries in their continuous remapping of Beijing in a tension-filled local/global dynamic.

An interesting attempt at remapping Beijing takes place at the beginning of *Beijing Bicycle*. Against a giant Beijing map that covers an entire office wall, a group of freshly recruited migrant workers (*mingong*, i.e., those who have migrated from the rural area to work in the construction, manufacture, and service sectors in the city) line up and listen to their manager, who orders them to memorize the location of every residential hutong and every commercial street in Beijing. Equipped with new haircuts, new uniforms, and new mountain bikes, they are transformed from ragged outsiders (*waidiren*) into acceptable representatives of an express-delivery company. After reminding them to maintain the company's good image, the manager announces, "Starting today, you're the modern Rickshaw Boys."

The manager acts as if he were a commander dispatching his troops (migrant workers) to secure a territory (the market) so impeccably delineated on the Beijing map, but, significantly, his remapping takes a verbal detour through the reference to "Rickshaw Boy" (Xiangzi), a quintessential Beijing figure made memorable by Lao She's novel *Camel Xiangzi* (1936).[16] Like Xiangzi—an example of "homo economicus," who worked industriously, pulling a rented rickshaw along Beijing hutong in the early decades of the twentieth century, and who calculated his savings obsessively in the hope of buying a rickshaw of his own—Guei (Cui Lin), a migrant worker in *Beijing Bicycle*, keeps a record of his deliveries and anticipates the day he will earn enough money to own his mountain bike.[17] As Guei pedals through Beijing's infrastructure, monstrous high-rises and highway bridges tower behind or above him, visually rendering him a human relay in a series of drifting images of the alienating cityscape. Yet the bicycle proves to be an efficient means of transportation, allowing him to cut through congested traffic in Beijing and deliver business documents to office buildings and hotels furbished to the latest global standards of extravagance (e.g., revolving doors, marble floors, and a shiny ceiling that reflects Guei's dumbfounded image upside down).

In addition to featuring the bicycle as a daily necessity in Beijing (or, more generally, in China, which used to be called "a kingdom of bicycles") and conceptualizing the global business world as site of alienation (where a woman who receives Guei's delivery symbolically remains faceless), *Beijing*

Romance in *Beijing Bicycle*. Photo by Wang Xiaoshuai.

Bicycle introduces a more subtle level of remapping by juxtaposing the local and the translocal in Beijing and by differentiating the bicycle's associations with work and leisure. On the day Guei expects to own his mountain bike, it is stolen outside a public bathhouse, and Guei is fired for his negligence in delivery due to distress. By sheer coincidence, Guei discovers that the stolen bike has been purchased by Jian (Li Bin), a teenage vocational school student who lives in an old neighborhood. After much violence and negotiation in an empty floor of a high-rise under construction, Guei and Jian agree to settle the disputed ownership by sharing the bicycle on alternate days. Through this shared ownership, the bicycle functions as an intimate connection between two overlapping "ethnoscapes" — migrant workers from the countryside and local residents of Beijing, both living in an old neighborhood threatened with imminent demolition.[18]

The juxtaposition of Guei and Jian also foregrounds different associations with the bicycle in Beijing. For Guei, the bicycle is associated with work, and the mountain bike is crucial because of its efficiency (the lack of which is exemplified when Guei uses his friend's old bike and has to abandon it after it falls apart). For Jian, on the other hand, the bicycle is associated with

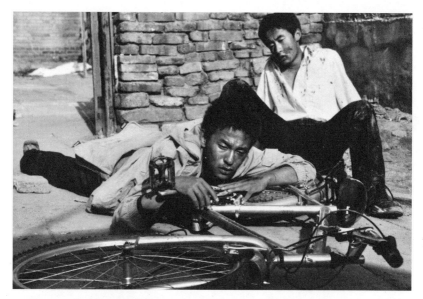

Bloody fight in *Beijing Bicycle*. Photo by Wang Xiaoshuai.

leisure, and the mountain bike is an expensive device (for he paid a hefty price of 500 yuan or US$60 for it) indispensable to his dating of schoolmate Xiao (Gao Yuanyuan). Parallel to Guei riding in hectic streets en route to delivery, Jian cycles cheerfully with Xiao along a lakeside covered with willow branches. After Xiao's compliment, "It's a nice bike," their romance is about to bloom, but Guei recognizes his secret mark on the bike and claims it as its original owner. The bicycle's intimate tie to eroticism works itself out as Xiao leaves the infuriated Jian for Da Huan (Li Shuang), a cool local youngster who handles his bike with acrobatic dexterity and who obviously treats it as a phallic symbol.[19] Given this symbolism, the bicycle may also function as what Slavoj Žižek elsewhere conceptualizes as "the link between the capitalist dynamics of surplus-value and the libidinal dynamics of surplus-enjoyment."[20]

Near the end of *Beijing Bicycle*, Jian seeks revenge by hitting Da Huan's head with a brick while the latter is riding with Xiao, and Da Huan's friends chase Jian and Guei through the labyrinthine hutong system, beat them up, and wreck the bike. The film ends as the battered Guei carries the ruined bike on his shoulder and walks (in slow motion) across a street intersection, where stopped traffic of cars and bicyclists witnesses his unfulfilled dream—like that of Rickshaw Boy decades before him and of millions of his contemporary migrant workers—of earning a decent living in the ruthless urban jungle.[21] Regardless of the bicycle's associations with work or leisure, the local or the translocal, Guei's and Jian's desires are frustrated, and their dreams crushed. In remapping Beijing via two parallel stories of drifting, *Beijing Bicycle* paints an alarmingly dystopian cityscape, where the glorious façade of globalization appears alien to the underprivileged local, the familiar hutong neighborhoods are threatened with demolition, and teenage romance is evoked with nostalgia as a lingering reminder of a past that is forever gone and a present bound to disappear soon.

THE TAXI: COMPROMISED AGENCY IN *I LOVE BEIJING*

I Love Beijing seems to start where *Beijing Bicycle* ends. A high-angle, extreme long shot presents a panoramic view of a Beijing intersection congested with multidirectional traffic flows of pedestrians, bicycles, cars, and buses. As a few jump-cuts get the viewer closer and closer to the congested intersection, patterns of slow traffic change, and at times, the flows appear to stop completely. Car radios announcing traffic and other news become audible intermittently, and after two minutes, the camera pulls back slightly to emphasize the grand scale and duration of Beijing's traffic nightmare. Right after the credit sequence comprising the traffic scene, the sense of stagnation is intensified by the divorce proceeding faced by Feng De (Lei Yu) and his wife. After his ex moves out, Dezi (as Feng De is nicknamed) is free to hit the streets in his taxi, and his adventures take the viewer in an aimless exploration of a changing Beijing.

Drifting characterizes Dezi's mode of existence: as a taxi driver, he travels around town, drifts in and out of strangers' lives, and connects public and private spaces. His own private affair, the divorce, is made a public spectacle when his mother slaps his ex as the latter is leaving with her lover, one of Dezi's fellow taxi drivers. Although otherwise considered a public space, his taxi is sometimes used to satisfy his customers' private sexual desires, as when he takes their instructions to circle around the Third Ring and ignore the shrill giggles from the unfolding backseat romance. Like Rickshaw Boy from old Beijing, Dezi is for hire from dawn to midnight: his service takes him any way his customers dictate, and his life therefore promises no preset direction and little individual agency.

In depictions of Dezi's many nocturnal adventures, drifting images of Beijing's cityscape and ethnoscape add to the feelings of alienation, frustration, and restlessness that permeate the entire film. Dimly lit Tiananmen Square is stripped of its daytime grandeur; eerie blue lights shine above dozens of high-rises under construction; seemingly nonstop, poorly marked road construction poses dangers to both drivers and pedestrians. One rainy night, Dezi brakes abruptly to a shrieking stop as a horde of exhausted migrant workers carry their baggage and walk across a dark street, disappearing out of view like ghosts. The next morning, when Dezi wakes up in his taxi, he is greeted by strange sounds, which he traces to a public park where seniors are exercising in a pine grove—one of few peaceful scenes in this film, each of which seems to catch Dezi utterly unprepared.

Such is the transformative power of globalization that traditional leisure life appears out of place to a local taxi driver. Constantly drifting into view are spectacles of high-rises (which recede fast behind the taxi and look distorted from the car windows) and nightclubs (which gather businesspeople, gangsters, party girls, and foreign expatriates). The taxi as a drifting vehicle that connects contrastive ethnoscapes in Beijing is best exemplified in three scenes. First, Dezi drives a group of gangsters, weapons in hand, to a suburban residential area to carry out their extortion or revenge plan; instead of being paid for a day of hard work, Dezi is beaten up outside a nightclub, where the gangsters celebrate their victory. Second, Dezi picks up two rural passengers, a father and his toddler, as he listens to the radio announcing the ranking of the richest men in the world (John Rockefeller and Bill Gates); when he learns that the father cannot pay, Dezi kicks them out, orders them to strip, and leaves them standing naked by the roadside. Third, after driving the host of a popular radio program on dating to an upscale Western-style nightclub, Dezi enters the club himself and is completely lost in a multinational crowd wherein English, French, Italian, and Chinese are exchanged at the same time. A former bartender, who once had been forced to drink bottle after bottle of beer until she threw up, tells Dezi that she is very happy now because she is married to an Italian. A half-drunk white woman pops her face to the camera and asks, in accented Mandarin, "Do you like me?" As this predominantly Euro-American crowd starts to dance, Dezi becomes intoxicated and is thrown out by the nightclub's uniformed Chinese staff.

These three scenes indicate that, just as the global itself is by no means homogeneous—the expatriates at the nightclub come from various nations (many of them probably descendents of bygone conquistadors)—so the local consists of people of different social, educational, and geographic backgrounds. Xiaoxue, Dezi's former girlfriend, had come from the now bankrupt industrial area in northeast China with the hope of securing a better future in Beijing (as symbolized by a decorated kite Dezi once flew with her in Tiananmen Square), but she, as a transient local working as a restaurant waitress, had been raped and eventually murdered, her dream devastated like that of Guei's in *Beijing Bicycle*. Zhao Yun (Tao Hong), on the other hand, is an educated local whose parents teach at a university and who seeks a one-night affair with Dezi, but she volunteers to introduce Guo Shun, a female migrant worker from Hunan province, to Dezi as his legitimate lover: in spite of his decent income, a taxi driver is still not allowed to marry into the educated circles.

What gradually emerges from the cinematic mapping in *I Love Beijing* is a cityscape plagued by class and gender tensions, besieged by disaffection, dislocation, and displacement. Almost all of its characters are out of place, including those expatriates who feel at home in an alien and alienating capital. The director's docudrama style heightens the sense of drifting, contingency, and irrationality in the globalizing city—a sense further substantiated in two depictions of "hysteria" that appear near the end of the film. In the first, an unknown party girl wearing a light-blue skirt, leather boots, and dark sunglasses hops on Dezi's taxi after exiting the nightclub, and when Dezi stops by a roadside, she starts dancing alone ecstatically before falling drunkenly to the ground. In the second, another unknown female passenger sings a melancholy song about the loss of love and asks Dezi, "Did you ever break up with a girlfriend?"

Because the film ends with Dezi's silent refusal to answer the question, the film's English title—*I Love Beijing*—becomes a statement of profound irony: to say the least, this sentiment is out of place, its enunciator unspecified, and its agency unrecognizable. By comparison, *Summer Heat*—the alternative English title that appears in the Chinese DVD version—better captures the feelings of frustration and restlessness that saturate the entire film. Furthermore, the Chinese title, *Xiari nuan yangyang*, is largely nondescript, referring to warm summer days when people feel comfortable, drowsy, and even apathetic. The Chinese title thus invites the viewer to hop on a hired taxi, disarm oneself temporarily, and let one's life drift along in a globalizing city.

THE MOTORCYCLE: PHANTASMAGORIC COMMERCIALISM
IN *BIG SHOT'S FUNERAL*

The pessimistic view of globalization that underlies *Beijing Bicycle* and *I Love Beijing* is given a hilarious twist in *Big Shot's Funeral*, where the local not only proves equal to the global but also outsmarts the latter on numerous occasions. Yoyo (Ge You), a freelance Beijing cinematographer recently laid off by a state-owned film studio, wears a black-leather jacket and rides his motorcycle to work for Don Tyler (Donald Sutherland), a world-famous Hollywood director who is shooting a remake of *The Last Emperor* in Beijing, but who has lost his interest in recycling hackneyed Orientalist motifs, such as gorgeous costumes, obedient servants, and spectacular palaces inside the Forbidden City. A street-smart local, Yoyo receives instructions from Tyler's Chinese-American personal assistant, Lucy (Rosamund Kwan): "You are just a pair of eyeballs . . . and the last thing we need is your creativity." The local, according to this division of labor, is restricted to providing a mechanical, documentary account of what global capital (in this case, Hollywood and its Japanese partners) plans to achieve in China. However, the ingenuity of the local proves so vibrant and uncontainable that Tyler entrusts Yoyo to conduct a comedy funeral for him, as Tyler will soon lapse into a coma. The remarkable means by which Yoyo raises advertising money to fund the funeral preparation prompt the recuperating Tyler to admire Yoyo's "boundless" imagination, to consider him a genius, an angel, a messenger from heaven who brings a perfect movie for him to make.

The motorcycle provides Yoyo with a means of transportation much more reliable than a bicycle: it is motorized, which translates into greater freedom and better efficiency, and its small size helps Yoyo navigate through Beijing's notorious traffic, so he can get where he wants to go. He turns his tri-wheel motorcycle around easily to park outside his hutong apartment near the Wangfujing Catholic Church; he murmurs "comedy funeral" while riding his motorcycle in a moment of enlightenment after accompanying Tyler and Lucy on a tour through a Buddhist temple; he even gives Lucy a ride through narrow access lanes inside the Forbidden City, where he later parks his motorcycle beside a BMW X5 and other crew vehicles. Situated at a midpoint between the bicycle and the car, the motorcycle grants Yoyo upward mobility in a globalizing world. Indeed, this upward mobility proves so spectacular that Yoyo is almost beside himself at a high-profile, press-covered auction he organizes where billboard advertisements are bid at prices as high as a million yuan apiece. With the newly acquired money and publicity, a motorcycle-riding local is gleefully drifting into the vortex of globalization.

Drifting implies a sense of abandonment, indulgence, and excess. Thanks to Yoyo's ingenuity, the comedy funeral triggers a fierce bidding war for product placements, with companies fighting over every inch of visible space on the funeral ground in front of the most sacred site of the Forbidden City, the Hall of Ancestry. While touring to inspect the work in progress, Lucy is bombarded with black-and-white balloons that are to be labeled with a Korean cosmetic product, two frontal billboards for Outback Steakhouse and Cozy Cola (in mimicry of Coca-Cola), and a giant plastic column for Bad News Beer. On the funeral platform, a mannequin of Tyler is covered by disparate products: a contact lens, a pair of sunglasses, a gold necklace, a tea bag, a shampoo bottle, a gold watch, a sports jacket, a leather shoe, and a sports shoe for each foot. The logic of global capitalism is stretched to the extreme in this carnivalesque celebration of all-penetrating advertisements, which saturates the field of vision with drifting images of product logos and replicas.

Through the tropes of indulgence and excess, *Big Shot's Funeral* maps Beijing as an ancient capital transmuted by phantasmagoric commercialism, as an emergent cosmopolitan city marked by global mélange (Chinese, English, Japanese), and as a frantic business world populated by foreign expatriates and local entrepreneurs dealing in profitable sectors like finance, real estate, and Internet technology (some of whom have gone crazy as in a psychiatric hospital scene). The film thus maps a different species of the local from that depicted in *Beijing Bicycle* and *I Love Beijing*: by bootstrapping himself, Yoyo has ascended into an elite club of Chinese transnational brokers, who work with their foreign partners in securing economic and cultural transactions that typically cross national and regional borders, and whose definition of success is proudly enunciated in the film by an insane real-estate mogul: "Buy the most expensive things, not the highest quality."

A parody of rampant commercialization not just in Beijing but also across

China, *Big Shot's Funeral* ultimately exposes its own metacinematic structure.[22] At the end of the psychiatric hospital scene, which seems to be just another scene from Yoyo's real life, Tyler suddenly shouts "cut." The scene is thus revealed to be, in fact, a filmed episode within a film—Tyler's latest project, which is about a Beijing drastically changed since Bertolucci's time there. This metacinema problematizes the agency of the Chinese local engaged in transnational cultural brokerage. After all, Tyler is reinstated as the authoritative behind-the-scenes director of this hilarious comedy funeral, and Yoyo is but a puppet-like actor who just happens to have helped broker lucrative transnational deals to secure funding for the extravagant comedy funeral show. Tyler's producer wants him to procure a "happy ending" for the film within the film, an ending where two lovers end up in bed, so Yoyo volunteers to conclude what has been his ingenious performance with an intimate scene with Lucy; although Yoyo clumsily moves around Lucy to find the best position during filming, the two eventually kiss off-screen—a romantic union between the local (Yoyo/Beijing) and the transnational (Lucy/Hong Kong), fantasized in such a clichéd way as to better serve the interest of the global (Tyler/Hollywood).[23]

THE AIRPLANE: IMAGINED FREEDOM IN *THE WORLD*

In an uncanny way, the motorcycle appears in Jia Zhangke's *Unknown Pleasure* (2002) as a vehicle that gets unemployed youngsters in China's hinterland practically nowhere. A sense of "trapped freedom" is metaphorically represented in a highway under construction, which ends abruptly, allowing no access to the promised freedom of globalization beyond a small town in the mountainous Shanxi province.[24] The bicycle is also used in *Unknown Pleasure* as a vehicle for articulating frustrated desires, as in a deserted bus station where Bin Bin refuses to kiss his college-bound girlfriend because he has recently been diagnosed as hepatitis-A positive and is afraid of transmitting the disease to her. This hidden disease has disqualified him from enlisting in the army and trapped him in a bankrupt industrial town with no prospects at all: his girlfriend rides the bicycle alone, circles around in the empty bus station, and eventually disappears from his vision.

Trapped freedom and frustrated desires are visualized with more existential angst in Jia's next feature, *The World*, which depicts migrant workers from

Distant view in *The World*. Photo by Jia Zhangke.

the Shanxi province who are employed by a Beijing theme park as helplessly incarcerated behind the phantasmagoric façade of globalization. The sprawling theme park boasts of over a hundred acres of land and 110 scaled-down replicas of world tourist attractions, such as the Tower Bridge in London, the Leaning Tower of Pisa in Italy, and the Taj Mahal in India. After an extended tracking shot of Tao (Zhao Tao) walking through the backstage rooms in search of a band-aid, a glimpse of the park's daily evening gala, and Tao's ride in a slick tour train over the park's greenery and a simulacrum of the Great Pyramid of Giza, the Chinese characters for the park's slogan appear—"Tour the entire world without ever leaving Beijing"—a slogan validated by the park's website address, www.worldpark.com.[25] An extreme long shot presents a panoramic view of the park from a distance, with the Eiffel Tower at the center and a few high-rises on the right. Suddenly, a garbage picker with a large hat and a heavy bag intrudes into the frame in the middle ground, then pauses near the center of the frame to face the viewer. After the credit "A film by Jia Zhangke" rolls, the garbage picker continues toward the right and walks outside the frame, and the film's title, *The World*, appears.

With this title sequence, Jia Zhangke executes his mapping of Beijing and globalization with intended irony and contradiction. While some critics may suspect his complicity in promoting the theme park (one of his sponsors), Jia nonetheless insists on introducing a disruptive moment in this apparently serene view of suburban Beijing. The garbage picker represents the unspeakable poverty and misery glossed over by the sheer spectacle of globalization:

on the one hand, he appears as a nameless eyesore to the glorious image of a globalizing city; on the other hand, both the actual world and its selective simulacra are simply too far away and too irrelevant to his concerns of daily subsistence.

Jia's mapping of Beijing in relation to the unevenly developed world continues when Tao receives an unexpected visit from a friend from Shanxi who has obtained a passport and is going to work in Ulan Bator, the capital of Mongolia. The era of globalization has seen massive migrations in multiple directions, in both transnational and intranational contexts. Anna, a Russian performer, joins the gala show in the theme park; after her passport is taken away by her sponsor, she is forced into prostitution and winds up working in a fancy karaoke parlor. More and more young people migrate from Shanxi to Beijing in search of a better life, which they don't always find; an unsophisticated young migrant worker, for example, dies in a construction accident, leaving behind a list of the meager amounts of money he owes to his equally low-income friends (due to the company's delayed wage payments). To the majority of migrant workers, the ersatz world of the theme park embodies a world of leisure and wealth beyond their imagination. "This is the United States, Manhattan," says Tao's boyfriend, Taisheng, who works as a security guard, proudly showing the attractions to his native Shanxi folks — proud because the replicas include miniatures of the twin towers that no longer exist in New York City. The newly arrived Shanxi folks, however, are more interested in the salaries of their friends (as low as 210 yuan or US$26 per month) than in the symbol of global capitalism.

As a recurring motif in *The World*, the airplane articulates migrant workers' frustrated desires and imagined freedom. Tao, dressed in a blue uniform, acts as a flight attendant in a grounded passenger airplane, which serves as a tourist attraction in the theme park. At one point, the camera pans through the empty plane and zooms in on Tao and Taisheng embracing each other on the pilot seat. Not much passion is demonstrated, however, as Tao is worried about tourists coming in. Neither of them has traveled on an airplane before, but a text message to Taisheng's cell phone triggers Tao's imagination. "I am bored to death here," so Tao pleads with Taisheng to take her out of the park. In one of several animated sequences following a cell-phone call or text message, Taisheng is depicted in the cockpit as the airplane flies away, passing

Animated flying in *The World*. Photo by Jia Zhangke.

Tao as she drifts in the air all by herself, still in the flight attendant's uniform, gliding over the cityscape of Beijing in a bird's eye view. Her flight in the sky, however thrilling, nevertheless serves as a chilling metaphor for the freedom denied to low-income migrant workers in Beijing.

The airplane appears in another scene, when Tao visits her Shanxi folks on the top floor of a high-rise under construction. Above a concrete jungle of unfinished pillars, an airplane quietly flies over at sunset. A medium shot of two workers admiring this beautiful scene becomes an emphatic comment on the gap between the rich and the poor in a globalizing world. Migrant construction workers risk their lives to build luxury apartments and offices to which they remain strangers (as in *Beijing Bicycle*), and the theme-park workers put up smiling faces and extravagant shows for tourists whom they never know. A group of actual flight attendants visits the park, and their giggling heightens the difference between the park as a leisure place for them and the park as a work place for underprivileged Shanxi migrants.

In a subtle, yet revealing way *The World* maps Beijing as a city of poly-locality, a city marked by translocal residents and their mobility, a city where the global (represented by miniature replicas) claims the attention of the local while the local dreams of traveling beyond the national borders. Such imagined freedom is typically set in motion by intermittent animated sequences, where a sense of drifting is magically conveyed through images of Tao flying over Beijing's skyline or passing over a street pedestrian bridge, of Taisheng riding a horse through a flurry of red rose petals, of a train speeding over the

Airplane flying over in *The World*. Photo by Jia Zhangke.

theme park, of a fish swimming freely in the water. The drifting metaphor returns in a pathetic fashion to conclude the film: the two lovers, having been exposed to a gas leak in a friend's apartment in suburban Beijing, drift out of coma after they are carried to the open air. "Are we dead?" Taisheng asks in a pitch-dark frame. "No," Tao answers, "this is just the beginning."

CONCLUSION: POLYLOCALITY IN A GLOBALIZING CITY

Although Jia Zhangke chooses not to identify what kind of beginning is in store for his beloved Shanxi characters, who are so helplessly trapped in a simulated world inside Beijing, it is evident that he intends *The World* to be a critique of globalization's negative impact on the local and the translocal. From the colorful, energetic beginning to the bleak, apocalyptic conclusion, *The World* shows globalization as an enticing façade, a Broadway-style gala, a series of physical and emotional dislocations that suggests that there is no bright future for the underprivileged. More than in *Beijing Bicycle* and *I Love Beijing*, the map of Beijing interwoven with the drifting mode of experience in *The World* appears not just fragmented, but virtually ruined. To a great extent, the characters in all these films seem to roam about Beijing on a *ruined map*, a map of physical and emotional ruins left behind by the globalizing forces. The ruined map thus necessitates renewed efforts to remap the "yitian yige shijie" (ever-changing world), as announced in one of the section titles in *The World*, with whatever means of transportation is available at any given time (bicycle, motorcycle, taxi, imaginary airplane). In addition, the ruined map serves a painful reminder that these characters' remapping efforts can only be provisional, fragmentary, and insignificant when perceived on the grand scale of the globalizing city.

The recurring pessimistic view of globalization in these four films brings one to Michael Smith's questions: Who has the power to make places of spaces? Who has the power of place making? Who produces or changes images of the place? Who consumes particular images and to what effects?[26] In most cases, the locals' power of claiming urban spaces as their own places has been radically eroded, and locals rarely care to consume the latest images of globalization that keep popping up on the new map of Beijing. What is worse, they either gradually become or remain out of place in the grandiose façade of globalization, as projected at the end of *Beijing Bicycle* and in the title sequence of *The World*.

The lingering pessimism in these Chinese films derives from a sense of powerlessness shared by the local vis-à-vis the national and the global, and this projection of power imbalance in turn motivates Chinese filmmakers to insist on experiencing the changing world from the perspective of the under-privileged local, thereby constructing a persistent mode of drifting in their cinematic remapping of the city. Instead of an intellectual who investigates the city as a modern-day flâneur and who enlightens the viewer with a cartographic survey or a panoramic view of Beijing, Chinese filmmakers prefer ordinary locals and translocals who are left behind by economic development and who must resort to makeshift tactics of drifting and surviving in the changing city. The filmmakers' insistence on the trope of drifting, therefore, can be regarded as a new kind of cinematic remapping that questions the validity of the dominant systems of thought and institutions of practices on the one hand and privileges ambivalence, contradiction, contingence, and improvisation on the other.

What emerges from the drifting cityscapes in contemporary Chinese cinema is a heightened sense of polylocality. Beijing no longer provides a set of fixed imaginaries of imperial or socialist grandeur, peaceful leisure life, and self-content residents; rather, it is a city caught in the whirlpool of globalization, a city crisscrossed by various spaces, temporalities, emotions, and ideologies, a city of ever-shifting landscapes, ethnoscapes, and mindscapes. This polylocality of Beijing is exemplified by the virtual-world tourist landmarks in *The World*, but it is more dramatically represented by the mobile localities embodied by millions of migrant workers and more subtly indicated by the fast disappearance of local landscapes and the increasing visibility of global symbols and transnational agents.

But there is another kind of polylocality: that of film production, distribution, and exhibition. Significantly, all four films analyzed herein involved transnational co-productions, and all were distributed abroad by overseas agencies, two of them by the heavyweight Sony Pictures.[27] The consideration of polylocality, therefore, should take into account the local/global dynamics of China, Taiwan, Hong Kong, Japan, France, and the United States. With the steady influx of global capital into Beijing and other places in China, the field of Chinese cinema has been reorganized, revamped, and strategically remapped in the twenty-first century. Ultimately, the project of remapping Beijing should move beyond the textual realm of urban imaginaries and extend critical attention to the circulation and reception of these imaginaries in polylocality. Here lies a new challenge to scholars of cinema studies as well as of urban studies.

NOTES

1. See Jameson 1994; Abbas 1997; Dai 2002, 49–70.
2. King 1997, 12, emphasis added.
3. Hall 2001a, 28.
4. On cultural hybridization or global mélange, see Pieterse 2004. On global mélange in Taiwan cinema, see Yingjin Zhang 2002, 299–305.
5. Sassen 1991, 14–15.
6. I would not go so far as to imagine the local as already "transnationalized," as Kwai-cheung Lo (2001) does for Hong Kong cinema. In mainland China the national—represented by the state and its programs of nationalism—systematically intervenes to preempt any large-scale convergence or coalition of the local and the transnational.
7. Quoted in Smith 2002, 125.
8. Esherick 2000, ix. For recent books on early Shanghai cinema, see Pang 2002, Yingjin Zhang 1999, and Zhen Zhang 2005; for Shanghai culture, see Lee 1999.
9. For Chinese images in American films, see Yingjin Zhang 2002, 240–44; Yingjin Zhang 2006, 66–78.
10. Furthman 1973, 67.
11. *Trivia for 55 Days at Peking* (1963), http://www.imdb.com/title/ (visited 2 January 2007).

12. Sklarew et al. 1998, 45, 50.

13. For an in-depth study of cultural differences between Beijing and Shanghai, see Yingjin Zhang 1996.

14. For instance, Yuan Muzhi re-edited a montage sequence of Shanghai scenes from *Cityscape* (1935) and included it as the initial credit sequence of *Street Angel* (1937).

15. The upscale teahouse now comes with chic interior design and furnishing, as in Zhang Yuan's *Green Tea* (2003). Images of hutong recur in many films by sixth-generation directors such as Wang Xiaoshuai and Zhang Yuan.

16. For an English translation of the novel, see Lao She 1979; for a film adaptation, see Ling Zifeng's *Camel Xiangzi* (1982).

17. The term comes from Liu 1995, 103–27.

18. On ethnoscapes and other kinds of "scapes," see Appadurai 1996.

19. Compare Bertolucci's perception in connection with *The Last Emperor*: "This bicycle is very . . . phallic, because it goes between the legs and it has two wheels" (see Sklarew et al. 1998, 39).

20. See Lin 2002, 268; the quotation is taken from Žižek 2000.

21. Jian Xu reads the film's ending as ambivalent: it could be either a celebration of "rural values endangered by urban expansion" or a criticism of "the mentality of the rural and the provincial for impeding the development of cosmopolitan China" (2005, 445). To me, the film endorses neither of these two binary readings, as the director's intention is not to formulate a fixed position, but to delineate a city of profound contradictions.

22. See Kong 2003.

23. Rosamund Kwan, who plays Lucy, is a famous actress in Hong Kong. The multinational cast in *Big Shot's Funeral* was clearly aimed at a maximum market appeal in various distribution territories. Not surprisingly, the film set a box-office record in China (see Wang 2003).

24. For more discussion of trapped freedom, see Lu 2006.

25. The official website address of the real-world theme park is www.beijingworldpark .cn. The theme park is located in Beijing's Fengtai District, off the southeast part of the Fourth Ring Road.

26. Smith 2002, 127.

27. *Beijing Bicycle* was co-produced by Arc Light Films (Taiwan), Pyramide Productions (France), and Beijing Film Studio (China). *I Love Beijing* was co-produced by Eurasia Communications (Italy-China) and Happy Village (China). *Big Shot's Funeral* was co-produced by Columbia Pictures (United States) and Huayi Brothers-Taihe (China). *The World* was co-produced by Office Kitano (Japan), Shanghai Film Corp (China), and Xinghui Productions (Hong Kong).

Ackbar Abbas

FAKING GLOBALIZATION

The Asian city (particularly the Chinese city), that city's relation to globalization, and the fake all have at least one characteristic in common: they are all hard to describe.

Transformed at unprecedented speed by new forms of capital, media, and information technology, the Asian city today (more so than other cities) threatens to outpace our understanding of it. It seems likely, though, that Asian cities are where the urban experiments of the twenty-first century will take place. They are the most "representative" urban forms because they are the most problematic. This does not imply that the Asian city is a homogeneous entity. Even if we restrict ourselves to studying the major Chinese cities (leaving aside the many "invisible cities" of the Chinese interior), it is clear that they are all unique: Beijing, the political and cultural city, is very different from Shanghai, at one time one of the most cosmopolitan cities in the world and today learning once again how to exploit its symbolic capital; and both are distinct from Shenzhen, the instant city, created as a Special Economic Zone to take advantage of its proximity to Hong Kong, a colonial/capitalist city like no other, once described picturesquely by Mao as "a pimple on the backside of China" and now returned to the mainland as a (cultured) pearl.

Nevertheless, what makes these cities comparable despite their enormous disparities is that we must come up with new terms and new frameworks if we are to describe them at all. They make it clear that the city exists not just as a physical, political, and economic entity that can be documented, but also as a cluster of images, a series of discourses, an experience of space and place, and a set of practices that need to be interpreted. Besides the physical city that we can observe and the cognitive city that we can map, there is something else that is simultaneously familiar and elusive, something that can be related at some level to what we might call the effect of the global, provided we bear in mind that the global always works in differentiated ways, even as it leaves its traces on everyday experience and urban forms.

Three concepts that in their interconnections might help open up the discourse on Asian cities, including their relation to globalism, are Gilles Deleuze's "any-space-whatever," which appears in his work on cinema; Mario Gandelsonas's "X-urbanism," which appears in his typology of the American city; and, as I extrapolate from Gandelsonas, "X-colonialism." These ideas can be related to that of the fake, which (if we are willing to suspend moral judgments for a while) can highlight in some unexpected ways many of the issues raised by the relation of Asian cities to the global system.

"ANY-SPACE-WHATEVER"

Deleuze's argument about "any-space-whatever" is not specifically about urban space or the Asian city; rather, it is part of a discussion about a class of cinematic images he calls the "movement image."[1] What the discussion shows, nevertheless, is not just how relevant but also how indispensable cinematic concepts are to an understanding of contemporary urban space. I have argued elsewhere that if the new Hong Kong cinema became so intriguing in the 1980s, it was because it had found the cinematic means to evoke a new cultural and political space where the paradigms of colonialism were overlaid by those of globalism in uncanny ways.[2] Such overlayings and, more important, our affective response to them provide a context for understanding what Deleuze calls any-space-whatever. Interestingly enough, his exposition of the concept occurs in the section on the affection image, which is one of three kinds of movement image, the other two being the perception image and the action image.

The concept helps not only to underline the important relation between

Pacific Place Shopping Centre, Hong Kong. Photo by David Clarke.

affectivity and space but also to differentiate between space and place, affectivity and emotion, along the following lines: as "space" refers us to places we do not yet understand, or no longer understand, so affect refers us to emotions we do not yet have, or no longer have a name for. In both cases, some kind of shift has occurred. As Deleuze explains it, any-space-whatever is the polar opposite of an actualized "state of things," which is always *framed* in terms of spatiotemporal-psychic coordinates that we tacitly understand.[3] By contrast, any-space-whatever involves a series of deframings. One of Deleuze's examples is the Gare de Lyon as shown in Robert Bresson's film *Pickpocket*, but an equally striking example is Hong Kong as portrayed in the opening sequence of Wong Kar Wai's *Chungking Express*: as a skyline of nondescript rooftops on nondescript residential buildings. Hong Kong as subject is not framed by an "establishment shot" with recognizable landmarks. What we see, as in *Pickpocket*, "are vast fragmented spaces, transformed through rhythmic continuity shots."[4] The "law of this space," Deleuze says, "is fragmentation."[5] It is "a matter of the undoing of space."[6] But it is through such an undoing that a precisely corresponding affect is caught. In the case of *Chungking Express*, it is the affect caught by the rhythmic alternation between frenetic speed and long moments of waiting and lethargy.

We can think about any-space-whatever as a particular and ordinary space, but one that has somehow lost its homogeneity and systems of interconnectedness. Such a formulation is remarkably generalizable, even to spaces outside the cinema. Deleuze himself speaks of the proliferation of any-space-whatever inside and outside cinema in a Europe during the aftermath of World War II, with cities demolished and reconstructed, and an abundance of waste grounds and shantytowns, unused or useless places, everywhere.[7] Chinese cities today are even more interesting along these lines, because what is spurring their urban reconstruction is not the aftermath of war, but rather the prospects of easy access to the global economy—the aftermath of peace. This is evident both in the Shanghai frenzy for building after Deng Xiaoping's southern tour in 1992, when he gave the unambiguous signal for transforming China into a "socialist market economy," and in the Beijing cityscape that is being transformed in anticipation of joining the World Trade Organization and hosting the 2008 Olympic Games. What is disorienting in these and other Asian cities is not so much the unfamiliarity of new places, but the way the coordinates of the old places seem to have shifted, the unfamiliarity not of the new, but of the old. Once again, the point can be made through cinema. For example, a futuristic film like *The Matrix*, in spite of all its sensational special effects, is in the end not disorienting at all, because the strange is presented as such: we expect and are expected to be surprised. By contrast, in a "retro" film like *In the Mood for Love*, set in 1960s Hong Kong, the past, like the affective mood of the main characters, is simultaneously familiar and hard to decipher. We move from a "period piece," placed in a specific era we thought we knew, to any-space-whatever, just as in Beijing and Shanghai many "traditional places" take on a quality of any-space-whatever.

X-URBANISM

To see the Chinese city deframed by any-space-whatever is to some extent to see it in terms of an avant-garde film. Let me now qualify this a little by turning to the idea of X-urbanism, introduced by Mario Gandelsonas, which has a darker, more noir quality to it.[8] Whereas Deleuze presents a typology of cinematic images, Gandelsonas presents a typology of urban forms. His book deals with the American city through drawings, but also through a text which gives us, in seven scenes, a history of urban mutations in America, each scene more traumatic than the one before. But what is the relevance of all this for Chinese cities? Picking up the argument from the middle, we can see how the city of skyscrapers engendered the suburban city, which in turn mutated into the X-urban city. The city of skyscrapers created a new urban structure made up of three concentric rings, with the core business district at the center, surrounded by a second ring of poor neighborhoods and factories, outside of which, in a third ring, lie the suburbs where the middle classes live. The suburbs' development into the suburban city is made possible by, among the other things, the motorcar and television; one extends the suburban house to the city, the other brings the city to the house. The urban scene is now doubled, consisting of the pairing of the urban and the suburban.

Of most concern is the final scene, what Gandelsonas calls Scene X: the mutation of the suburban city into the X-urban city. It comes about when the global finance and service industries begin to relocate their offices to the suburbs. This gives rise to the office campus and a blurring of the opposition between suburb and core city, home and workplace. In the office campus we find not only offices but also shopping malls, entertainment centers, and residential areas, that is, the kind of multi-use urbanism characteristic of X-urbia. Unlike the suburban city, X-urbia develops not in opposition to the center, but in contiguity and in tandem with it. We thus find an urbanism that does not oppose fringe to center, home to workplace, but rather that is multi-centered, decentered, or fractal. X-urbia does not supplement the suburban city, but supplants it, changing it from the inside out.

Gandelsonas's main concern is the history of the American city, but in a tantalizing footnote, he suggests that X-urbanism, first developed in America, can now be exemplified by many cities in Asia, like Shanghai and Shenzhen — that is, that we are witnessing a kind of historical convergence, even though urban development in Asia may have followed a very different historical trajectory.[9] In making some comparisons between X-urbanism and any-space-whatever, keeping in mind the question of their relevance for the analysis of the Chinese city, we encounter three considerations.

First, there is the issue of visuality and its limits. Both Deleuze and Gandelsonas suggest in their own ways that the really important structural changes in urbanism may not produce any immediate visible difference. For example, at the visual level, there is not much difference between suburbia and

X-urbia, even though one is a radical mutation of the other; we seem to see the same houses, motorcars, and television sets. This suggests an important point for the analysis of Asian cities that new architecture has so obviously transformed visually, namely that we should not be seduced by the obvious and spectacular and erroneously focus attention exclusively on impressive architecture. Pudong, for example, is the district in Shanghai where the majority of new architecture is found, but Pudong is not Shanghai. Likewise, the Petronas Towers may bedazzle Kuala Lumpur with the light reflected from their aluminum-clad surfaces, but the Petronas Towers are not Kuala Lumpur. Paradoxically, it is the visual that can make Asian cities invisible.

Second, both X-urbanism and any-space-whatever suggest that the major changes in urbanism are initially registered and grasped at the affective level, in terms of a subjective, experiential response to space. For example, in many sitcoms—the classic one being *I Love Lucy*—the suburbs are depicted as the site of normalcy and quiet green spaces. By contrast, in the X-urban, as represented by David Lynch's *Blue Velvet*, the same white picket fences and manicured lawns are depicted as the scene of perversion and paranoia, where X marks the scene of a crime. Gandelsonas points to two of the most striking images of the X-urban: the gated communities where X-urbanites hide paranoically behind their electronic surveillance and alarm systems; and the TV docudrama *Cops*, in which the motorcar has morphed from a privileged means of suburban transport into the police car on the prowl for crime that lurks everywhere.

Third—and it is on this point that Deleuze and Gandelsonas significantly differ—the law of any-space-whatever is "fragmentation," and the fragment can be seen as a form of resistance to homogenization and assimilation into a whole. On the other hand, the law of the X-urban, we might say, is the fractal, something radically different. It is not the contestation of the whole, but rather the replication, on a smaller scale, of the whole. In many Asian cities today, we see the principle of replication at work, which supports Gandelsonas's intuition about the existence of X-urbanism in Asia. In Hong Kong new satellite towns come into existence through a process of replication as full-fledged, autonomous, multi-use urban centers. And if Pudong looks like a mini-Manhattan, and Macau like Las Vegas, and Silicon Valley is cloned in Bangalore and Kuala Lumpur's Cyberjaya, these are not instances of what used to be called Westernization, but, more accurately, instances of replication and the X-urban. As prefix, "x" suggests not just the unknown but also the figure of chiasmus, a critical point of crossover, where old boundaries are transgressed and everything needs to be reformulated, including familiar ideas like colonialism.

THE X-COLONIAL

Taken together, any-space-whatever and X-urbanism enable me to comment on the historical legacy that all Asian cities to some extent are burdened with: the legacy of colonialism and the postcolonial resistance to it. If any-space-whatever holds on importantly to some notion of resistance, thus making it an ally of postcolonial discourse, the X-urban with its problematics of replication points out just as importantly that resistance takes place in the context of mutations in urban form, and that it must take note of these changes and work out appropriate strategies, instead of repeating old radical pieties. This is another way of saying that the colonialism that must be dealt with may be called a kind of X-colonialism.

In this regard, it is the special position of Hong Kong before and after 1997 that provides the most illuminating case study of the X-colonial. Even in the days before 1997, when Hong Kong was still officially a colony, the colonialism there seemed to bear little resemblance to what is critiqued in textbooks. There was, on the one hand, the city's ambiguous relationship to China and, on the other hand, the gradual changeover from imperialist to globalist paradigms. Colonialism could therefore persist only if it adjusted to the new globalism by abandoning old imperial attitudes and even by taking on a benign appearance. This made colonialism in Hong Kong more difficult to represent and to critique. Narratives of greed and exploitation no longer seemed accurate. Colonialism was not where we thought it to be; and where we did not expect it, there we still found it. It became a form of X-colonialism, not a known and self-explanatory quantity like colonialism was, but something that needed to be explained, a ubiquitous but elusive presence. When Asian cities today, whether former colonies or not, seek to be integrated into the global system, there is every possibility that they, too, will have to deal with such elusive presences.

Once again, it is in the cinema that the most convincing representation

Outside the legislative-council building, Hong Kong. Photo by David Clarke.

of the X-colonial can be found, specifically in the Hong Kong cinema's affective response to urban space. In the films of Wong Kar-wai for example, we find again and again the evocation of some kind of invisible barrier between people, and human relations characteristically take the form of proximity without reciprocity—whether it is the case of the male lovers in *Happy Together*, who cannot be happy *and* together at the same time, or the case of the heterosexual couple in *In the Mood for Love*, who live in adjoining rooms in the same boarding house, but whose attraction for each other is based on the impossible premise that they do not want to be like their adulterous spouses, so that what pulls them together is exactly what keeps them apart.

In the situations portrayed in Wong's films there is an uncanny structural resemblance to what Manuel Castells has described as "the spatial logic specific to the Information Age," or the space of flows.[10] Castells emphasizes that the space of flows is not just a space of dispersal. Its main organizing unit is the network, which permits, simultaneously, centralization and decentralization. Thus, command-and-control institutions still congregate in cities like New York and London, while back offices spread into the suburbs, where they nevertheless form part of the network. Hence, the space of flows makes possible a "simultaneity of social practices without territorial contiguity," that is, a lot of things can happen at the same time, without their happening in the same place.[11] This action at a distance is, for Castells, a key spatial characteristic of the information age, but it is also the mirror image of Wong's films, although in them everything is reversed: we find "territorial contiguity without social practice," or closeness and inaction, wherein a lot of things don't happen, though people are in the same place.

Castells, too, has an argument about resistance: "Wherever there is domination," he writes, "there is resistance," and he suggests ways of turning the network against itself, of "grassrooting the space of flows."[12] He gives the example of the Champs Elysées, designed as an exclusive space in the nineteenth century, but taken over in the 1990s by young people from the *banlieue* as their own. What Castells fails to underline, but what his example shows, is that this process of appropriation took more than a century to achieve. This lag, or hysteresis, is something that also needs to be addressed by arguments about resistance. What resistance to the X-colonial, the network, or the global entails first of all is some way of dealing with the delays and inaction that Wong portrays so well, especially the kind of inaction that is produced by speed. It seems that the more instantaneous the technologies of speed become, the longer the hysteresis: this may be the contemporary form of uneven development.

THE POLITICAL ECONOMY OF THE FAKE

It is possible to look at the issue of globalization and the Asian city not only in terms of any-space-whatever, X-urbanism, and the X-colonial, but also from another angle: the fake. Many of the issues relating to Asian cities return in unexpected ways when we attempt a historical analysis of the fake. The fake is a symptom that enables us to address, rather than dismiss, some of the discrepancies of a rapidly developing and seemingly ineluctable global order. We can think of the fake as a social, cultural, and economic response, at a local and apparently trivial level, to the processes of globalization and to the uneven and often unequal relations that globalization has engendered. This is not to say, however, that we should romanticize the fake. Nor does it mean that we can overlook the many obvious objections to it. Many have argued that, morally speaking, faking is a form of cheating; economically speaking, it is a form of theft. From an aesthetic point of view, the objection is that

Not quite Kentucky Fried Chicken, Shanghai. Photo by David Clarke.

the fake is never as well made as the genuine article. Its social value, too, is highly dubious, as it can be seen to be a form of pretension. The list of protests can be easily extended, and in fact many of these objections are undeniably valid. The danger, though, is that indignation may make us lose sight of the structural and historical features of the fake, as well as the paradoxical role it plays in the context of globalization. Insofar as the fake points to unresolved problems in the world today, it should be analyzed, not dismissed. A preliminary historical analysis might help situate a problematic practice in a problematic space.

A good starting point is Orson Welles's *F for Fake* (1973), which should be as well known as *Citizen Kane* or *The Magnificent Ambersons* because its contemporary relevance is arguably even greater. *F for Fake* is a documentary about art forgers and forgeries. The audience is introduced to Elmyr de Hory, one of the most talented forgers of all time, whose works, signed with the names of famous artists, were once in all the great art museums of the world. Elmyr had turned to forgery to demonstrate the ignorance and pretense of the art experts and museums that had rejected his original work because they were impressed only by big names. Welles eventually reveals that the forger is not an isolated figure, that behind the forger is a whole series of other figures closely related to him. The series begins, ironically, with the art expert, whom Elmyr wryly observes is "god's gift to the forger," because without the expert who authenticates, the forger could never succeed in his deception: the knowledgeable expert is in collusion, however unwittingly, with the faker. The series continues with Elmyr's biographer, Clifford Irving, whose book, *Fake!*, not only makes Elmyr into a folk hero but also inspires Irving to try faking himself; Irving thus publishes a fake "authorized" biography of Howard Hughes, forcing the reclusive Hughes to issue a public denial. Then there is Welles himself, a great filmmaker and actor, for whom filmmaking and acting are no more than forms of fakery. The series continues, and does not stop even with the original artist himself, with Picasso, the most famous artist of the twentieth century. One of the most insightful moments into the nature of faking comes when an art dealer shows some Picassos to Picasso. "Fake!" Picasso says of the first painting. "Fake!" he says of the second, and again of the third. At this point, the art dealer feels he must protest. "But Pablo," he says, "I saw you painting that last one with my own eyes!" To which Picasso replies, "I can paint fake Picassos as well as anybody."

Welles's film makes several important points about the fake. First of all, it shows that just as there is always a series of figures behind the forger, the question of the fake never involves the fake alone. The contemporary fake, in particular, forces us to re-examine all the objects and processes around it, like legal systems, politics, technology, design culture, and globalization itself—including, of course, the globalization of media. Just as the global media circulates information about the latest commodities for Asian consumers to buy, so it brings information about these goods for counterfeiters to copy. The conditions that make the global commodity possible are the same ones that make the fake possible: digital reproduction, graphics software, distribution networks. Both belong to the same history, the history of information; both belong to the moment in which information is the most important commodity. This suggests a related point, namely the ability of the fake to act as a kind of historical marker. The production of fakes appears only when cities are just about to enter the world economy and become exposed to media representations of global commodities. Beijing, Shanghai,

Urban Shenzhen viewed at night from rural Hong Kong. Photo by David Clarke.

Guangzhou, and Shenzhen are just the best-known examples of Chinese cities that have reached this point of development following China's entry into the World Trade Organization.

Fake production ceases or diminishes when a city or nation becomes more integrated into the global establishment, at which point strict copyright laws begin to be passed, partly as a result of intellectual-property pressure from global companies and states. Hong Kong is at this stage, and fakes are now less common. The fake, then, is not without a certain value as a cultural symptom. Not only can it function as a historical marker of a city's relation to globalization and information, but the very fact that it is by definition a suspect object makes us take a suspicious or critical attitude to objects; hence, there is a certain negative value to the fake, what we might call the counter-value of the counterfeit.

A second point about the fake comes out most clearly in Picasso's statement that he can paint fake Picassos as well as anybody: the problem of the contemporary fake is not how close the fake is to the original, but how close the original is to the fake. The first scenario represents the usual way of understanding the fake and is not particularly disturbing, because even though it might be difficult to distinguish between fake and original, the *categories* of fake and original are still reassuringly in place, and the original is still the standard by which the fake is judged. In the second scenario the categories themselves come under fire, the standards by which the fake and original are judged disappear, and everything dissolves into a general confusion. The difference between the first and second scenarios can be clarified with an example from the world of watch making and watch faking. Some high-quality Chinese fake watches have gained a reputation for how well made they are. Chinese watch factories use Swiss movements (or *ébanches*, unfinished movements) supplied by ETA, the Swiss watch-movement factory (particularly popular movements like the ETA 2824, the Valjoux 7750, and the Unitas 6497) and provide watch cases for them. This exemplifies the first scenario: how close the fake is to the real thing. We catch a glimpse of the second scenario on learning that the majority of Swiss watch companies also buy ébanches—and often the same ébanches—from ETA, then simply case them, instead of making their own movements. Nicolas G. Hayek, the chairman of the Swatch Group, which owns ETA, recently caused a furor when he threatened to stop the supply of movements to all watch companies that did not belong to the Swatch Group.[13] This would have, in effect, put non-Swatch watch-making companies out of business, so they took Hayek to court on an antitrust charge. Hayek's counter-argument, interestingly, was that if ETA were to continue supplying these companies, it would discourage them from innovating and developing. This argument against a practice adopted by genuine watch companies is *exactly the same argument directed against fakes*. The case had the potential to destroy confidence in that quintessential global commodity, "the Swiss watch," and thus was played down. It was as if the aura of the Swiss watch was under attack, not from the outside, by the faked original, but from the inside, by what sounds like an oxymoron: the original fake, the original that does not have to wait to be faked, the original that is manufactured like the fake.[14] If we use the language of simulacra, then the original is also a simulacrum of the fake, not just the other way around. This switch, this reversibility, is the crucial confusion, but it is precisely under conditions of confusion that fakes are produced. Fakes do not just come from China and the Third World; in more sophisticated form, they can be found in the most unexpected places.

Hence the importance of a third point, which Welles's film also suggests in the ironic tone that runs throughout it: while moral and aesthetic judgements against the fake can easily be made, they are not very helpful for an analysis of the phenomenon, as they do more to obfuscate than to clarify. This is because the moral issues are hardly straightforward. For example, the United States, which now leads the world in the moral condemnation of fakes and in defense of intellectual-property rights, was one of the chief violators of intellectual-property rights in the nineteenth century, as China is today. American publishers reprinted Charles Dickens's novels and refused to pay him royalties, just as China now reproduces software and designer goods. Those who protest the loudest against intellectual-property-rights violations are those who stand to lose most by them: morality follows economics.

Take the big brand-name companies with their highly publicized campaigns against fakes. Do fakes hurt the big brands and reduce their profits, as these companies claim, or do fakes provide free advertising, and so increase company profits? The answer may well be a toss-up, suggesting that the real issues lie elsewhere: one protests loudly against the fake in order to send the message that one's product is real and authentic and valuable (what Jean Baudrillard calls a "deterrence strategy"), just as in the university, plagiarism is loudly condemned as the cardinal sin, more often than not by those who are least original. This is not to suggest that fakes can do no harm. There are, for example, fake foods and medicines. Fake milk powder caused the deaths of a number of Chinese infants, while fake Viagra has been known to lead to intense embarrassment. With regard to designer products, what the fake hurts most are not so much the big brands, but individual freelance artists and designers. Sadly, the only survival strategy, a desperate one, is to allow your publisher or distributor to release the original, then fake it yourself before the fakers get in on the act. Instead of taking a moral stand for or against the fake, then, it is more important to see the fake as the symptom of a set of social, economic, and cultural conditions, and to ask how these conditions might be changed—hence, the need to begin by bracketing moral and aesthetic judgments. Condemning a symptom will not make it go away.

The fake encourages an examination of the nature of consumption in times of confusion, which is characterized by a number of paradoxes. For instance, Thorsten Veblen analyzes the fake to exemplify his famous notion of "conspicuous consumption."[15] His study of conspicuous consumption

Not quite Crocodile, which is itself not quite Lacoste. Photo by David Clarke.

focuses much less on obvious displays of wealth than on how "the law of conspicuous waste guides consumption . . . chiefly at the second remove, by shaping the canons of taste and decency."[16] In such a culture, "we find things beautiful . . . somewhat in proportion as they are costly."[17] It is in this context that Veblen discusses the *sociological value* of the fake. The fake, he writes, "may be so close an imitation as to defy any but the closest scrutiny; and yet as soon as the counterfeit is detected, its aesthetic value, and its commercial value as well, declines precipitately. . . . It loses caste aesthetically because it falls to a lower pecuniary grade."[18] This dismissive attitude toward fakes, Veblen shows, is nothing more than an indirect expression ("at the second remove") of conspicuous consumption: objects are not costly because they are valuable; they are valuable because they are costly. Thus, the more costly something is, the higher automatically its value—an absurd principle that real-estate agents and high-end retailers in China today are happily redis-covering about the logic of consumption. Writing a little after Veblen, Walter Benjamin is equally paradoxical about the relation between consumption and taste. He argues that what today is called "taste" goes together with ignorance;

it is when the consumer is ignorant of how objects are produced that taste becomes important. And in the world of advanced design and high-tech products, ignorance is endemic, which helps explain why faking is everywhere. The consumer, Benjamin wrote around 1938, "is not usually knowledgeable when he appears as a buyer. . . . The more industry progresses, the more perfect are the imitations which it throws on the market. . . . In the same measure as the expertness of a customer declines, the importance of taste increases—both for him and for the manufacturer."[19] There is a relation therefore between taste-as-ignorance and the fake: the former provides a condition of possibility for the latter.

When consumption is consumption of the spectacle, as Guy Debord suggests, the confusions become even greater and the fake more dominant. Like Veblen, Debord notes that "it is the sale [of the artwork] which authenticates value."[20] Like Benjamin, he notes that "what is false creates taste. . . . And what is genuine is reconstructed as quickly as possible to resemble the false."[21] "Today," he concludes, "the tendency to replace the real with the artificial is ubiquitous. In this regard it is fortuitous that traffic pollution has necessitated the replacement of the Marly Horses in the Place de la Concorde, or the Roman statues in the doorway of Saint-Trophine in Arles by plastic replicas."[22] Another example is the "Chinese bureaucracy's laughable fake of the vast terracotta *industrial army* of the First Emperor, which so many visiting statesmen have been taken to admire *in situ*."[23] In other words, Debord is saying, a taste of the fake creates a taste for the fake, which is why in today's world "a financier can be a singer, a lawyer a police spy, a baker can parade his literary tastes, an actor can be president. . . . Anyone can join the spectacle. . . . Such picturesque examples also go to show that we should never trust someone because of their job."[24] And, as Paul Virilio asks, what happens when consumption takes place in the world of speed? This includes not just the relative speed of transport technologies (like cars and planes) but the absolute speed of today's information and reproductive technologies. What happens, Virilio answers, is that everything becomes fused and confused. Every invention has a specific way of going wrong; that is the sense Virilio gives to the *accident*, which both limits and defines the invention.[25] The accident of transatlantic voyages was the *Titanic*; of air travel, the plane crash; of nuclear energy, Chernobyl; of global finance, Enron. And the accident of reproductive technologies? The answer would have to be the fake. What these texts by Veblen, Benjamin, Debord, and Virilio have in common is a sense of how deeply entrenched the fake has become in many of the social practices and confusions of contemporary society.

If the problematic nature of consumption is one set of conditions for understanding the fake, the other important set of conditions is the changing nature of the commodity itself. This change in the commodity has often been described as a split in the commodity into manufactured goods on the one hand and service goods on the other: between (to simplify drastically) what is produced in factories and what is produced in design studios or offices. Service goods also include entertainment, travel, software, advertising, and so on, which are now important commodities. This does not mean, however, that service goods are not "material," in contrast to manufactured goods, or that an absolute division between goods and services exists. There nevertheless exists a class of service goods, which might be defined as objects with a large design or informational component built into them—for example, wristwatches, some kinds of furniture, computers, fashion—whose value is not mainly determined by the materials they are made of but by the amount of research and design necessary for their production, as well as all the work of promotion, distribution, and packaging. When the commodity in the form of service goods has a large cultural element built into it, it becomes increasingly difficult to speak, as we used to, of the "commodification of culture"; rather, it is a matter now of *the acculturation of the commodity*. This development in the nature of the commodity also has relevance for the fake. If today it is not only the artwork that is faked but also, and even more important, the commodity, that is because "artistry" is now a part of the commodity—often its most important and vulnerable part.

This split in the commodity into manufactured goods and service goods takes on a sociopolitical dimension when we relate it to the global division of labor. Many commodities are designed in one place, usually a "developed" country, and manufactured in another, usually a "developing" country. Nike shoes are a good example. Nike has no factories in the United States, only design and research units. Production is located abroad, in various Asian or East European countries. It has been argued, perhaps over-optimistically, that such an arrangement is actually beneficial to all concerned, an instance of the advantages of globalization. Not only do manufacturing countries receive much-needed foreign investments and benefits from technological transfers, but in the long run they could also develop their own designs. Richard Rose-crance argues, for example, that what the arrangement offers is a "new and productive partnership between 'head' nations, which design products, and 'body' nations, which manufacture them. Despite its apparent resemblance to territorial dominion in the past, however, the relationship between design-ing and producing nations does not entail a new imperialism of north over south. Body nations rapidly develop new ganglia that in time create heads of their own."[26] What the arrangement does entail, though, is that in the meanwhile developing countries have been cast in the role of workhorses or production units, with no guarantee that this "meanwhile" will not last a long time. Moreover, they are allowed to produce, but not to consume, as many of the commodities labeled "Made in China" and sold in the United States and Europe are not available for sale in China itself. It is at this juncture that the fake enters, almost like a postcolonial argument, to reverse this order of things. It produces objects labeled "Made in Italy" or "Made in France," the design centers of the world, and offers them for sale in China, at a fraction of the cost of "the real thing." Thus, the fake obtains economic advantages and effects its own version of "technology transfer"—not in the long term, but right now. It profits and learns through copying, and in its own way gestures toward leveling the difference between developed and developing countries. Ziauddin Sardar offers a version of such a postcolonial argument when he speaks of the fake as a form of resistance against exclusion from the global order of commodity consumption, and even as a form of "gentle subversion" against globalization itself. "Slight Malay bodies," he writes, "clad in fake de-signer jeans, fake T-shirts, wrists adorned with fake designer watches, clutch-ing fake designer bags and cloned mobile phones look as if they have wan-dered straight out of Beverly Hills for the pittance the get-up cost them. They are *in*-cluded, fashion and fancy, and not *ex*-cluded, marginalized onlookers. In the international politics of self and style they are fully empowered. And the transformation can be accomplished within the ambience and precincts of living history."[27]

Sardar's kind of postcolonial argument for the fake is in its own way as over-optimistic as Rosecrance's, not so much about the benefits of globalization itself as about the benefits of faking as a means of subverting global-ization. When something is faked, global order is not disturbed; in fact, the fake confirms, rather than subverts, the global division of labor, made worse now by the fact that it is developing countries that condemn *themselves* to the (fake) production of First World designs. The fake is not, as it is sometimes represented to be, capable of being politically subversive of the global order. There is a passive quality to the fake that makes it work as symptom, but not as subversion. Its value as symptom is that it reveals, in its own shabby and damaged way, a negative side of globalization that is usually well hidden under a rhetoric of cooperation and collaboration. But faking globalization is neither undermining it nor changing it.

FAKING GLOBALIZATION

It is when we turn to a globalizing China that the full complexity of the po-litical, economic, and design issues raised by the fake fully emerges. In Bei-jing the Hung Qiao Mall, where fake goods are retailed, stands next to the historic Temple of Heaven, where Chinese emperors used to make offerings to the gods for good harvests: side by side with the Temple of Heaven is the Temple of Fake Heaven, an emblem perhaps of China today, even more so than the presence of Starbucks in the Forbidden City. Some of the historical complexity and contradictions in the emblem can be found, too, in the fake. It is much too simplistic to say that China tolerates fakes because it has no respect for international law and intellectual-property rights. In the past so-cialist idealism might have been tolerant of fakes because of its belief in egali-tarianism and communitarianism; if "private property is theft," then fakes, in sharing even intellectual property, are a form of egalitarianism. But during the socialist era, lasting, say, into the 1970s, there was no fake production to speak of in China. It is in the era of market reform, when fake production is in fact more and more criminalized, that we see its golden age. The explanation for this paradox is that strange thing, the socialist market economy (which is the form globalization in China takes), wherein older social attitudes like egalitarianism jostle with the new. The official line today is that "egalitarian-ism" is a "feudal" hangover, but it is precisely this residual egalitarianism that allows the faker to operate without a bad conscience and the authorities to be a little too casual about copyright laws. However, emerging in the socialist market economy, together with the fake and in contradiction to it, is a new sense of private property and of the value of privacy in general: the discreet charm of the bourgeoisie. Every couple now wants its own private space and its own private means of transport. It is this new social attitude, as much as anything else, that has resulted in the greatest building boom in Chinese history, and in the sight of cities choked with traffic. The fake, which First World countries lament, and the building boom and automobile sales, which they applaud, *go together*. They are the contradictory aspects of a contradictory, transitional historic moment.

Enacting and enforcing stricter laws cannot be the answer, as they will have to contend with another "law": that if something can be faked, it will be. Laws are made to be broken, as the history of Prohibition shows. They even have the effect of romanticizing the fake and of endowing the act of buying fakes with a certain frisson. The only real solution must be not a punitive one, but one that benefits all parties. Can such a solution to the problem of the fake be found? Perhaps. To begin with, it would consist not of developing stricter laws, but of developing design culture. Moreover, the development of such a design culture in China would have to be the responsibility of all those involved in the fake, including those companies that regard themselves as its victims. These companies, in particular, would have to heed the warning of the fake and guard against complacency. When one's product can be reproduced almost to perfection and sold for often less than 10 percent of one's own price, one may have to reexamine the product and the design process. Products that are content to repeat themselves become so much more easy to copy.

On the Chinese side, the question of design culture comes into focus in an often-asked question: if fakers in China can produce such good fakes, why do they not produce genuine articles? Because of a shortsighted desire for quick profits, the answer often goes, but this economic explanation is not the whole story. The fake has to be situated not only in economics but also in culture and in design ethos. The fake is a species of *underground culture*; the underground is its ethos, is where it derives its energy and inventiveness from. As soon as the faker turns legitimate, as soon as he goes straight, it is as if he had to wear a (strait)jacket and tie, and all kinds of inhibitions set in. This rule applies to the different grades of fakes as well. The "quality" fake tends to be conservative and offers few complications, while the "ordinary" fake that tends to be experimental and inventive—so inventive, in the case of fake watches, that some watch designs first used in fake watches are now being copied by Swiss companies, an example of the original as a faking of the fake.

However, though some fakes are more inventive than others, their inventiveness is relative, as fakes on the whole are not inventive enough. They have too much respect and reverence for the global objects they imitate and hence cannot transform those objects or invent new ones. The fact that they can reproduce these objects to perfection shows how thoroughly they have studied and understood them; fakes are, as it were, the eternal understudies of the global commodity, never actors on the world stage. And the reason why the fake cannot be a new object is not because the fake is lawless and radical and needs to be legislated against, but because it is too rule-bound and conservative: it cannot falsify enough. This is a distinction that Welles's *F for Fake* was implicitly trying to draw by putting the artist and filmmaker next to the faker: the artist falsifies, the faker merely fakes—an important difference, in spite of a certain family resemblance. The fake is a way of relating to a global environment; it is an example of the seduction of global space and the objects found there. But such a space not only seduces; it can also betray and reduce to servitude. We might conclude, therefore, that the best way to go beyond the fake is not through legislation, but to encourage the development of design culture. And the first law of design culture is: more important than understanding the object is the ability to change it.

Should the United States encourage the development of design culture? Should Parsons set up shop in Beijing? Trying to answer these questions brings us face to face with one final twist in the relation of fakes to globalization. Design education may stop the fake in the long run, but it will also produce an even stronger China. China can already copy a vast range of products quickly, cheaply, and well. Once it can also design, it will be unstoppable—and this is already happening. The death of the fake in China will be the birth of an unrivaled economic giant. And do the United States, Europe, and Japan—all those who speak loudest against the fake—want to see that happen anytime soon?

NOTES

1. See Deleuze 1986.
2. Abbas 1997.
3. Ibid., 97.
4. Ibid., 109.
5. Ibid., 108.
6. Ibid., 121.
7. Ibid., 120.
8. See Gandelsonas 1999, esp. 1–43.
9. "In fact the latest form of this city transcends national frontiers paralleling the global economy. See the example of the new cities in Southeast Asia, in particular, the Pudong development area in China's Shanghai, and Shenzhen in the Pearl River Delta" (Gandelsonas 1999, 1).
10. See Castells 2000, 18–27.
11. Ibid., 19.
12. Ibid., 21.
13. See "What Is Nicolas G. Hayek Up To?" *Watch Time*, April 2003, 58–62; and "Perfect Fake."
14. Note that the fake does not destroy the aura of "the original," but rather enhances it: a fake-watch dealer I know once told me that her ambition was to sell enough fake Rolexes so she could raise enough money to buy a real one.
15. See Veblen 1931, esp. chap. 7 ("Dress as an Expression of the Pecuniary Culture," 167–87).
16. Ibid., 119.
17. Ibid., 169.
18. Ibid., 169.
19. Benjamin 1968, 105.
20. See Debord 1990, 50.
21. Ibid.
22. Ibid., 56.
23. Ibid., 51–52.
24. Ibid., 10–11.
25. See, for example, Virilio 2003.
26. Rosecrance 1999, xi.
27. Sardar 2000, 89.

MIDDLE EAST

Farha Ghannam

TWO DREAMS IN A GLOBAL CITY

CLASS AND SPACE IN URBAN EGYPT

Cairo's elite are anxious. They are concerned about their social clubs. According to the Arabic newspaper *al-Hayat*, several clubs that catered to the elite during the 1940s and 1950s have "deteriorated" over the years because they now attract the new rich.[1] Rather than being patronized only by the politically powerful and historically rich, famous clubs have been flooded by those who recently made their wealth abroad, especially in oil-producing countries. Several clubs have started raising their fees to increase profits and limit the number of their members, while others are instituting strict membership policies. Instead of relying only on financial abilities, some exclusive clubs (such as nadi al-Sayyarat, nadi al-ʾasima) monitor their members very carefully to make sure they are not only equipped with money but also with the taste that should match it. Family background, education, prominent careers, connections to current members, and relationships to the political system are all central to membership. Exclusive clubs also follow strict policy regarding dress code (e.g., no jeans), activities allowed on their premises (e.g., no wedding parties), and who is permitted to visit (e.g., no children). Unlike these old-school clubs, an increasing number of new clubs (such as al-Qatamiah

Heights) are emerging around Cairo to serve the new rich and satisfy their demands. These clubs (mainly American designed) cater simply to those who can afford their high membership fees, without regard to the family background and source of wealth.

This desire to separate the "authentic" from the "inauthentic," the "real" elites from the "fake" ones is part of the broader uncertainty haunting the life of the rich and the poor, men and women, and Cairo's old and new residents. Cairo's growing urbanization and globalization are challenging existing social divisions and presenting new possibilities for social mobility. Drawing boundaries, marking territory, fixing categories, and preventing undesirable encounters become central to the daily negotiations of these transformations.

The work of the French sociologist Pierre Bourdieu is useful in studying these issues. In particular, his discussion of class and its different fractions is valuable when one attempts to understand the uncertainties of Egypt's elite and the current form of social mobility, which is shaped by global forces and discourses.[2] Bourdieu argues that while material capital (wealth, property, job, money) differentiates between classes (the bourgeoisie versus the working class), cultural capital (education, knowledge of the arts, style of speech, language spoken, family upbringing) differentiates between fractions within the same class (the financially wealthy versus the highly educated). The concern over clubs in Cairo shows that to belong to a certain fraction, it is not enough to have material wealth alone. One also needs the cultural capital that would allow one to be accepted by the other members of a particular elite.

Bourdieu's emphasis on class fractions acquires more importance in the context of global cities, wherein capitals and signs of distinction tend to shift quickly. Transnational connections are increasingly central to the cultural, material, symbolic, and social capital of a fraction of the Egyptian elite. In addition to being linked nationally to government officials and policymakers, an emergent fraction of the Egyptian upper class is drawing on relations with multinational corporations and firms to reinforce their power and distinction. They are able to convert these links into symbolic and material capitals, which in turn support and reinforce the attempts of the Egyptian State to promote Cairo as a modern city and to reconfigure its role in the global era. Other groups, those with limited national and transitional connections, have to depend on more "localized" relationships and support systems.

I will look at some of these issues in the context of two settlements constructed on the outskirts of Cairo. One is being built on the western edge of the city, and the second is on its eastern edge. The first project, Dreamland, is highly celebrated in the media, enjoys governmental support, and builds on strong transitional affiliations. Started in 1995 as one of Cairo's many new luxurious residential areas, it has been built by and for the rich and promotes itself as an alternative to city life, pollution, and traffic problems. Basing itself on a clear separation from its immediate context and on what I call "refusal to indigenize," Dreamland privileges American styles and forms of design, division of individual units, and organization of public spaces. Dreamland and the amusement park within it, Dreampark, have created a machinery of media representation. They have their own newsletter, television station (called Dream TV), and website.[3] They run ads in national media, and several articles have been published on the project in newspapers and magazines. In fact, aside from a couple of short visits to the location, I derived all my data from various media, in particular the Internet.

The other settlement, which I call Amal, rarely appears in the media, at least not in any positive way. There are no visible signs to announce its name or mark its boundaries. One will not find it on any map. And to protect the privacy and well-being of my informants, I will not use the real name of the area. Instead, I give it the pseudonym Amal (hope) to acknowledge the aspirations and uncertainties embedded in its residents' daily life. Amal is one of many settlements spreading on the outskirts of Cairo to house millions of Cairons and rural migrants who cannot afford lodging inside the Egyptian capital. These "unplanned" areas are built by families and local contractors. No planners or architects are consulted. Residents of such areas do not have access to TV broadcasting, Internet connections, or newspapers. The data I present here is based on my knowledge of several families over the past thirteen years. I followed their movement from al-Zawiya al-Hamra, a low-income neighborhood in northern Cairo, where I have been working since 1993.

These two examples make it possible to address questions linked to class, power, and agency. To go beyond the claims of a growing homogenization or heterogenization of the globe, I shift attention to the actors who are negotiating global flows of capital, peoples, products, images, and discourses. How are the rich and the not-so-rich positioned in a global city? How is the relationship between the material and cultural capitals reconfigured? How is this reconfiguration linked to national and transnational forces?

CAIRO, THE MOTHER OF THE WORLD

The growing globalization of Cairo provides new possibilities for the capital, its administration, and residents, including more job opportunities and advances in means of communication.[4] Yet the demands of Cairo's growing population, investors, and tourists have put tremendous pressure on the city's resources and services, resulting in housing shortages, deteriorating sewage systems, increasing pollution, and the growing inefficiency of the transportation network, among other things. For example, the size of Cairo's population has exceeded all expectations. The Egyptian capital, which in 1900 had a population of 600,000, currently houses more than eight million inhabitants in the city proper and over sixteen million in Greater Cairo.[5] In short, Cairo is saturated, and many of its inhabitants are moving to new areas constructed around the city. Some of these areas, such as the satellite cities, have been initiated by the government. Others have been initiated by individual and groups (rich and poor) on the margins of Cairo. Both Dreamland and Amal are part of these initiatives, yet they are incorporated differently in the Egyptian national imagination and in the government's attempts to build a global, modern city attractive to capital and investors.

WELCOME TO DREAMLAND

Dreamland is the name of a project that is being constructed over 2,000 acres on Cairo's western edge.[6] The project is owned by Bahgat Group, which is headed by Ahmed Bahgat, who has a doctorate in engineering from the Georgia Institute of Technology and became wealthy by investing in telecommunications and household appliances.[7] He founded Bahgat Group in 1985, after returning from the United States (as highlighted on the group's website).[8] Bahgat tells a story of success in the United States, where he started with nothing, but managed to make a small fortune when he invented a watch that could signal the time of the Muslim prayers.[9] Despite the fact that he had several successful projects in the United States, he decided to return to Egypt after meeting President Mubarak in 1984. Mubarak told him, "If people like you don't come to Egypt, who is going to develop the country"?[10] Bahgat re-

Housing shortages, a deteriorating infrastructure, and high pollution are pushing the rich and the poor out of the city. Photo by the author.

turned to Egypt, and his national and transnational connections allowed him to become one of its richest and most successful businessmen.

Dreamland was started in 1995, with a projected cost of more than $200 million.[11] It has a huge theme park, golf courses, tennis courts, horse-racing tracks, residential areas, conference facilities, a hospital, health resorts (including a hospital and a fitness center), schools (offering American diplomas), a hotel (or, actually, several, if one includes the hotels that are nearby, but outside the boundaries of Dreamland), and shopping centers.[12] A fence marks its periphery, and its entrance is monitored by guards. Signs clearly announce its name and indicate its location. Golf and tennis tournaments on Dreamland's courts attract players from different parts of the globe, thus placing it on the national and international sports scene.

Dreamland's residential area, which is expected to accommodate 40,000 residents, is not yet finished, but an extensive ad campaign aims to attract potential buyers. Dreamland's website presents multimedia representations, including a video that shows lush green areas with swimming pools and small lakes. Various websites display the units available for sale: size, location, view, floor plan, number of rooms, and nearby facilities.[13] Fancy apartments, townhouses, and villas are designed and advertised to attract Egyptian expatriates, Arab travelers, foreign visitors, and "any one who would like to spend a weekend in the most beautiful city enjoying greenery scenes and various means of entertainment far away from pollution and noise."[14] Unlike in the United States and Brazil, the crime rate is very low in Cairo and thus cannot be used to effectively promote such projects.[15] Instead, Dreamland promoters link issues of pollution and hectic urban life to concerns about health and the future well-being of children and grandchildren.

FLEXIBLE URBANITY

Telephone, gas, electricity, satellite TV, and Internet connections are available in all Dreamland units. The residential area promises to combine the need for "absolute privacy" with the desire for various services, thus materializing the idea of "*al-fasil wa wasil*," or detachment and attachment, separation and connection.[16] Electronic communications are especially celebrated because they allow residents to "communicate with surrounding shops to request what they need without leaving home, something that does not exist any where else in the world."[17] Similar to Cairo's old elite, who excluded the new rich from their social clubs, Dreamland promises to provide the chance to fully separate oneself from others, interacting only when one so wishes. Dreamland offers what could be called "flexible urbanity," that is, benefiting from city life while avoiding living in it. It means having access to all the sources and facilities linked to life in Cairo (such as healthcare, sports facilities, schools, markets, entertainment facilities), yet, at the same time, being able to avoid its crowded streets, polluted air, and deteriorating infrastructure. Above all, Dreamland promises to control and limit interactions with other people, to regulate, that is, the very thing that many sociologists have seen as central to urban life.[18]

REFUSAL TO INDIGENIZE

Projects like Dreamland are based on what I call the "refusal to indigenize." They reject the Egyptianization, Arabization, or Islamicization of the new forms they are introducing. Dreamland promises to be a "self-contained community." It aims to exclude the poor, the urban, one's neighbors, and the history of Egypt. It tries to deny its wider context and to materialize an

Western forms and ancient themes in Dreamland. Photo by the author.

American dream on the Egyptian desert. The logic of Dreamland is based on lifting American motifs from their context and planting them in Egyptian soil, as is clearly reflected in Dreampark. The project's newsletter, *Dream*, celebrates the Disneyland style that the project aims to duplicate. The project as a whole, the newsletter emphasizes, has been designed and implemented with the help of foreign planners, especially American architects. Despite the fact that the designing firm, Forrec, suggested "ancient Egyptian archeological themes," the Egyptian manager of the project "preferred a North American Style." The chairman of Forrec stated, "We designed one theme area more as an ancient wonders of the world attraction, and not specifically Egyptian. The rest was influenced by the kinds of Hollywood television programs and movies that most of the world watches and understands."[19]

This fascination with American forms, designs, and names is part of a wide interest in the Western that one encounters among the upper class and in segments of the middle class. Having Western clothes, eating at Western restaurants, using Western furniture, speaking Western languages, and listening to Western music are all signs of distinction. For some, France represents civilization and progress; they send their children to French schools, speak French at home and with friends, and prefer French foods and habits.

Others send their children to German schools and tend to emphasize German connections, while still others embrace "Britishness." But most prefer the American way. Dreamland plays on these desires and seeks to provide a mini-America on the Egyptian desert.

While the designs are American, Dreamland's target customers are mainly rich Arabs and Egyptians who work in oil-producing countries. Dreamland has offices in Cairo, Saudi Arabia, Kuwait, Qatar, and Bahrain. There exists a hierarchy of economic and cultural centers, with the United States (among Western countries) tending to occupy a high position in terms of wealth and cultural capital (at least for a fraction of the upper class), while oil-producing countries tend to occupy high position in terms of wealth (or material capital) but less in terms of cultural capital (taste and symbolic capital). Thus, countries such as Saudi Arabia and Kuwait generate income for many people, yet many equate them with backwardness, laziness, ignorance, and extremism.

As I argue elsewhere, it is important to go beyond the current explicit or implicit view of globalization as flows between the West and the Rest.[20] This view has been taken for granted in previous scholarship, which has aimed to show that the globe is being "homogenized" or "Westernized," and is still largely present even in recent studies that aim to show the complexity of the articulation between global forces and local contexts. Such a view obscures intricate flows of money, products, ideas, and peoples that are central to the growing connectedness between different parts of the world (such as movement of peoples and goods between India and Saudi Arabia, or Kuwait and Egypt, or the Philippines, Saudi Arabia, and Egypt) and weakens the analytical potentials of the concept of "globalization." The problems with such a view are clearly seen in how globalization is frequently reduced into notions such as "neocolonialism," "McDonaldization," "cultural imperalism," or "Americanization."

An emphasis on a broader understanding of global processes, however, should not be understood as a negation of the inequalities that structure global flows. It is not accidental that the United States and its cultural forms are desired by the rich. But not all classes in Egypt desire these forms or aspire to acquire them. At the same time, people's access to global discourses, products, and images are also structured by factors such as class and gender. Lack of strong transitional connections could weaken claims to urban space

Amal, home of working-class families and new immigrants from the countryside. Photo by the author.

and might facilitate the marginalization of certain groups in their attempts to participate in the making of Cairo.

BUILDING THE DREAM

Amal is located on the side of Cairo opposite Dreamland. Three groups are actively building this settlement. First is a flux of families from rural Egypt who move to Cairo to improve their living conditions; a network of connections draws relatives, neighbors, and friends from the countryside to acquire land and build homes, whether they be elaborate and expensive structures or simple and cheap constructions. Second are the urban working-class and lower-middle-class families who cannot afford housing in Cairo or who are being pushed out of their current homes (for example, because their homes are too small or too old and about to collapse). The third group includes the families of semiskilled and unskilled workers who work in oil-producing countries; these workers often fail to make enough money to buy homes in Cairo proper, but manage to secure enough money to start building in new areas around the city.

I will now focus on the story of a family that I have known since 1993. The family's struggle to build the "dream home" reveals much about the social mobility that has become an important feature of Egypt's life in the past three decades. Although this family, through the education of their children, new job opportunities, and investments in real estate, has managed to accumulate enough material and cultural capital to move up the social ladder, their social mobility has been limited because they are excluded from both the national and international connections that Ahmed Bahgat enjoys. The location of their new home and the insecurity of their ownership continue to remind them of the misfit between their aspirations and self-image, on the one hand, and the material resources available to them, on the other hand.

UM ALI'S STORY: THE ART OF IMPROVISATION

Ever since I met Um Ali, in al-Zawiya al-Hamra during Ramadan in 1993, she has talked about her housing conditions and her plans to improve them. She was always aware of the significance of the housing unit, the organization of its space, and the quality of its furniture in the presentation of the self in her neighborhood.[21] She felt that her home, which consisted of one room in an apartment that she shared with another family, did not represent her status and aspirations. This room, which housed Um Ali, her husband, three daughters, and a son, was furnished with a cupboard, a sofa, and a big bed that took up most of the room. A small area was designated for daily meals, for receiving guests, and for the children to do their homework.

Um Ali moved to that room in the late 1970s, after getting married to one of her mother's distant relatives. For twenty-eight years, they lived in that same room while her husband worked two jobs and they tried to save as much as they could. Their aim was always to educate their children and to build a house. Um Ali's vision of her dream home was shaped by TV images and visits to middle- and upper-middle class neighborhoods, as well as by her experience in the countryside, where she had grown up. She often referred to her desire to live in a house rather than an apartment. She frequently described her birth family's spacious house and how she had had to learn to manage her body differently after moving to the small apartment in Cairo. "I could not turn in any direction without knocking down something," Um Ali chuckled. "I was used to my family's big house in the village, and it took me a while to learn how to live in a small room."

In 2002 Um Ali completed building the first story of her "dream house" in Amal, which, depending on traffic, was a one- to two-hour commute by public transportation from al-Zawiya. The process of building the house had started in the early 1980s, when Um Ali's family bought a piece of land, encouraged by two friends, Um Hakim and Um Batta. Um Hakim and her husband were the first to visit the area and buy land there. They then started helping their neighbors and friends, including Um Batta, to buy land there, too.[22] At the time, Abu Batta was working in Saudi Arabia and sending most of his salary to his wife, and the piece of land she bought was substantially larger than those bought by her other friends; she and her husband were planning to build several apartments for their children (one son and three daughters) to accommodate them after marriage. Um Ali, for her part, managed to convince her two married sisters (who are also her sisters-in-law) to share with her the cost of 120 square meters of land. They paid a local broker, who gave them "a document to prove their ownership."

In 1994 she decided to sell the shared lot and to buy her own piece. Over fourteen years, the price of the land had increased 500 percent. With the help of her friends and other neighbors in Amal, she found a buyer who paid in cash for the land. With their share of the money, Um Ali's family bought their own 60 square meters of land. They deposited the rest in the bank and then started planning the construction of their house. They found a local contractor. Since Abu Ali had two jobs and spent almost all of his time working, it was Um Ali who supervised construction and negotiated the shape of the structure to be erected. She helped carry construction material and provided (by carrying on her head) most of the water the crew needed. When necessary to continue construction, she sold her gold jewelry. She also formed savings associations (*gami'yat*) with friends, relatives, and neighbors. The last time I saw her house, in 2002, it consisted of two parts: one part houses Um Ali, her husband, and two unmarried daughters while the second houses her newly married son and his wife. While they all sleep in separate areas, they share the same kitchen and bathroom.

Building their house took more than seven years of continuous work. The family continues to work together to complete their house. The son, who studied Italian in college, now works for a tourist company in a coastal town in the Sinai Peninsula. He spends twenty days away from his new bride, then spends ten days with her and his family. Um Ali's older daughter works in a local hospital while the younger one is just starting college. Her middle daughter, after graduating with a degree in English, at the age of twenty-three, decided to marry a man at least twice her age. Despite the fact that he was already married and had two children who were older than she was, she was determined to marry him because she wanted "to live a better life." She currently lives with her newborn daughter in a middle-class neighborhood close to Amal. Abu Ali continues to work two jobs: as a mechanic in a government-owned company and ironing clothes for the neighbors in his original neighborhood. All family members continue to contribute parts of their income to the construction and improvement of the house.

DREAMS AND HOPES

Ahmed Bahgat states that of all his investments, Dreamland is his greatest source of pride because it's the biggest project of its kind and its facilities (especially its electronic connections) do not exist in any other part of the world.[23] Um Ali is similarly proud of her new home. As soon as you visit her, she takes you on a tour to show you the new rooms, the high roof, the spacious kitchen, the separate bathroom, and the new furniture. She will remind you and herself of her old home and laugh at how she and her family managed to live in that small room for such a long time.[24] As in ads for Dreamland, Um Ali and her children emphasize how the new area provides fresh air, in contrast to the pollution inside Cairo. They also appreciate the extra space and the quiet nights in Amal, compared to the crowded and noisy al-Zawiya al-Hamra.

However, unlike the highly celebrated Dreamland, Amal is considered an *ashwai* (random or unplanned) area. These unplanned areas represent a major part of the housing units for the working class and the lower-middle class. It is estimated that these settlements house around 70 percent of the total urban dwellings.[25] Still, in a hegemonic public discourse, *ashwai* areas are associated with crime, terrorism, and social disorder. Unplanned areas are described by officials, policymakers, and many intellectuals as "cancer cells," "devilish expansions," "ugly deformities," "shelters for criminals," and "breeders of terrorists."[26]

Um Ali is very well aware of these stereotypes. But she dismisses them

An unplanned neighborhood, viewed negatively by media and policymakers. Photo by the author.

and emphasizes the positive aspects of life in Amal. "Like my sisters, I was financially capable of moving into an apartment on the outskirts of Cairo. But I wanted my own house. I wanted a small garden and a space to keep some chickens and ducks." She also hopes to be able to build apartments for each of her children so that the whole family can live in the same house. She and her neighbors comment with pride on the developments in the area. "Amal used to be empty. Only sand and wild dogs used to exist in the area. We used to be very scared when we came here. But look now, all these buildings and shops." They all refer to a "moment of colonization" that is common to the production of localities in various contexts.[27] This reference highlights their sacrifices in building the area and gives legitimacy to their claims to the land. Amal has been developed primarily through the efforts of its residents. Local entrepreneurs, using their pickups, quickly linked the area to the main bus stop.[28] Similarly, water and electricity were first connected through private initiatives. Unauthorized pipes allowed water to be delivered to certain homes, then redistributed to the neighbors. When these pipes were disconnected, pickups and donkey carts started bringing water in big plastic containers to be sold on a daily basis. I was amazed by how quickly the area grew

Local water service. Photo by the author.

in the nine years between 1993 and 2002: mosques, pharmacies, highrises, grocery stores, furniture shops, bakeries, butcher shops, vegetable stands, and small gardens quickly spread throughout Amal. All of these changes have increased the vitality of the settlement and attest to the creative skills of Amal's residents and their contribution to the making of urban space.

URBAN ALL THE WAY

Yet Um Ali still feels uneasy about the new house. For one thing, the area and its location continue to remind her of the limited social mobility available to her and her children. The roads are not paved, sewage flows into the streets, trash litters sidewalks, and dirty stray dogs wander around—all are visible signs that frustrate Um Ali's desire to pass as a member of the middle class. She feels that her family has more cultural capital than their neighbors, but knows very well the limitations imposed on her by the lack of material capital. She tells me how when 'her son's boss wanted to visit them, she had to pretend she lived in her daughter's apartment in Nasser City, a middle-class neighborhood. She did not feel that her new neighborhood was suitable enough to receive the distinguished visitor. She delighted in describing how impressed the boss was with her daughter's neighborhood and apartment. She was happy that there was a fit between how she imagines herself and the material conditions reflected in her daughter's house.

Um Ali also feels unsure about the mixed population that forms Amal. The area, as she states, brings different people together. She is anxious about having to interact with people from different backgrounds, people that she does not know and cannot trust. She tells me of her fears of thieves and intruders. Her house has bars on its windows, and a huge metal door is kept locked most of the time.[29] Not unlike the Egyptian elite, Um Ali has a strong desire to be separate from the newcomers. Unlike them, however, Um Ali cannot afford to separate her family from their neighbors. In fact, the residents of Amal are the source of her strength. Their lack of national and transnational relationships reinforces their association with their immediate locality and "forces" them to cooperate with each other. While Bahgat is able to cooperate with German, American, and Japanese planners and companies, and enjoys the support of the government, Um Ali has to depend on her neighbors to protect her dream house. Despite the fact that her family acquired a document from the sellers confirming the purchase of the land and that most people around them recognize their claims to it, their "ownership" is not recognized by the government. Um Ali and her neighbors are not certain about the future of their homes. Their insecurity is exacerbated by regular newspaper reports about houses built without permits being demolished. In fact, government officials have tried (unsuccessfully) to demolish houses in Amal.

Immediately after she acquired her land, Um Ali needed the support of her neighbors. At first, she visited the area only a few times a year. But in 1998 she and her family gradually started moving to Amal. As soon as they had erected the first rooms and put a temporary roof on part of the structure, they began spending a night or two every week in Amal. Slowly, but in powerful ways, Um Ali was rooting her family in that area. She was quick to plant a tiny garden, with a few trees, some herbs, and flowers, in front of and inside the uncovered part of the structure. She also kept some chickens and ducks on the roof. These were markers of her presence and active participation in the making of that neighborhood.

Through these regular visits, Um Ali was also cultivating friendships in Amal and forging close relationships with several neighbors. These relationships were important for various reasons. First, they provided her with a social support system that facilitated her move from al-Zawiya al-Hamra. Second, the neighbors kept a close eye on Um Ali's place and protected it against intruders (including state officials). They told others about her "ownership" of the land and reported to her any suspicious individuals snooping around. Third, and perhaps most important, her neighbors provided information about the latest developments taking place in Amal. They kept her informed about any news or rumors (such as officials visiting the area or the institution of new public services). Such information was always discussed at length and shaped decisions about the future of individual homes and the settlement at large. Um Ali and her friend Um Hakim, for example, felt optimistic when they heard about the ditches being dug in the streets to connect the area to the sewage system. They both interpreted these ditches as clearly indicating the willingness of the government to grant legal home-ownership in the future. Such clues helped to minimize Um Ali's insecurity.

INCLUSIONS AND EXCLUSIONS

On several occasions, Um Ali and her neighbors discussed the best strategies for dealing with the government. They mentioned the possibility of bargaining with political figures during election times, consulting with lawyers about paying fines, and learning, from the experiences of other similar settlements, how to avoid demolition. But, above all, they emphasize the collective nature of Amal as the best defense against government attempts to fine or demolish their homes. Unlike Dreamland, Amal is built on inclusion. There are no clear borders, and many people manage to find homes for their families. If one is better-off, one can find a larger piece of land in a nice location. If one is poor, one can get a much smaller piece of land, rent a place, or even expand the borders of the settlement. While Um Ali feels anxious about the increasing mixing of the population of Amal, their presence also increases her sense of security about the future of her home. For her and her neighbors, there is power in numbers. "Look how many people live here? What are they going to do with all of us? They cannot just throw us out of here." She recalls with pride an incident in which bulldozers came to the area and tried to destroy some of the structures: women and children were sent to throw stones at the bulldozers, and the workers had to leave the area without removing anything.

Thus, while Dreamland promises to separate, Amal cannot survive without inclusion. There is a need to include more residents, expand personal networks, cooperate with neighbors, and relate to the city and its economic and social promises. While the rich are increasingly moving away from the city, the residents of Amal seek to be as close as possible to Cairo. As argued by Khalid Adham, Dreamland and other new elite spaces such as malls and gated communities all "provide a carefully controlled environment that is physically, economically and socially isolated from surrounding areas."[30] While the rich build walls to separate themselves from others, create new clubs and exclusive spaces, and move out of the city to avoid pollution and crowded streets, for Amal's residents the city continues to be the locus of desire, aspirations, and future success. It continues to be central to their access to jobs, education, and various other social and economic resources.

IMAGINING THE CITY IN A GLOBAL AGE

Dreamland is but one of Cairo's many new luxurious residential areas, which include projects such as Beverly Hills and California. There are strong indications that the developers of these new projects bought the land from the government for very little money (or never paid any money). Some argue that the land that was meant to be used to build housing for the poor and the middle class has been taken over by the rich for a fraction of its price.[31] Strong connections between developers and the government, according to some journalists and political analysts, have been also clearly reflected in the speed with which a road was constructed to connect Dreamland to Cairo. The newly built ring road allows people to travel from Cairo to the project in less than twenty minutes. And the metro will soon connect Dreamland to the center of Cairo—a trip of only ten minutes. But government support is also symbolically indicated by events such as President Mubarak (accompanied by his prime minister and several other ministers) inaugurating Dreamland, playing golf, and touring the project.

In addition to having strong connections with the state, Dreamland is able to utilize different media to market its products and enhance its cultural capital. Television and newspaper ads and articles and various websites have allowed the project to quickly become the daily life of many Egyptians. The English words *"Dreamland"* and *"Dreampark"* have been incorporated into the everyday vocabulary of Egyptians of various classes. Dreamland is largely viewed as contributing to the beauty, modernization, and globalization of the Egyptian capital. It also facilitates the broader project of the state, which seeks to create a modern nation and integrate the country within the global economy. Thus, while Bahgat could be considered part of what Timothy Mitchell calls "state-subsidized super-rich," it is also important to recognize how rich and connected men like Bahgat in turn "subsidize" the government and help it reinvent its power.[32] They not only aim to attract outside wealth (oil-producing countries) and to bring back wealthy Egyptians to settle down and invest their money in promoting the national economy; they also direct the flow of people out of Cairo, a process that the Egyptian government started with little success in the 1960s. The city has expanded beyond any expectations, and its infrastructure is not able to accommodate the demands of the national and global capital. The new cities constructed around Cairo have not been able to attract many working-class and middle-class families. So projects like Dreamland help redirect the flow of the population to new places around the Egyptian capital.

While Dreamland is viewed as contributing to the beauty, modernization, and globalization of the Egyptian capital, the housing units, small shops, and peddler carts of Amal are viewed as eyesores and cancer cells that have to be destroyed. While ʿashwai areas are often tolerated because they relieve the city and the government of the burden of housing the poor, their exclusion from transnational connections and their limited access to the media does not grant them the type of legitimacy a project like Dreamland is able to garner. Given their exclusion from meaningful national and transnational connections, Amal's residents mainly feel empowered by the collectivity that they themselves form. Um Ali's neighbors and community are central to her daily struggles and long-term plans. Interestingly enough, Um Ali also finds assurances in the presence of the foreign press. "The government," she repeats to bolster herself, "fears bad publicity. The government cannot destroy our houses. What would they tell foreign journalists? They do not care for their own people? No, they will not demolish our homes."

Amal and Dreamland highlight the strong link between social class, cultural capital, and new means of communication (including the Internet) in legitimizing and reinforcing various social inequalities. These means also allow the anthropologist access to specific types of data that are central to the analysis and critique of urban hierarchies. Ethnographic research, mainly participant-observation and in-depth interviews, has allowed me to capture some of the desires, relationships, and forces that have shaped Um Ali's attempts to build her family's dream home. These ethnographic methods are extremely important in understanding the concrete realities and daily practices of urban dwellers, especially those excluded from new forms of media, and the ability of such residents to actively draw on various local connections and global discourses in the making of their homes and identities. At the same time, websites, newspapers, pamphlets, and TV ads and programs are enabling specific populations to present and legitimize their views and projects. Looking at Dreamland's website and its various publications allowed me to understand specific aspects of this project and the connections that inform its public image and position in the national and global configurations of power, desire, and economic accumulation. Juxtaposing these types of information is integral to any critical understanding of how global images, forms, and discourses are being articulated with national and local forces in legitimizing projects, building homes, and accumulating material and cultural capital.

NOTES

1. *Al-Hayat*, 23 August 2003, 14.
2. Bourdieu 1984.
3. See "History," Bahgat Group, http://www.bahgat.com/history.htm.
4. As the capital of Egypt for more than one thousand years, Cairo — or Umm al-Dunya, the mother of the world, as it is often called — is the obvious political, economic, and cultural center of Egypt (for more on Cairo's history, please see Abu-Lughod 1971). As do many other capitals, Cairo plays a central role in linking Egypt with the rest of the globe.

    With regard to the idea of globalization, I am not assuming that Egypt was ever isolated from the rest of the world. Trade, travel, diplomacy, and pilgrimage have always connected Cairo with other cities (for more on this, see Rodenbeck 1998, Ghosh 1992). There has been, however, a remarkable increase in Cairo's connectedness with the rest of the world over the past fifty years. Modern means of communication and transportation in particular have had a profound impact on expanding and intensifying connections between the Egyptian capital and other Arab, African, and Western cities (see Ghannam 2002).
5. Ibrahim 1987, 93; *Al-Ahram Weekly*, 31 August–6 September 2002, 2. This centrality is clearly manifested in the fact that many people use the Arabic name for Egypt, Misr, to refer to Cairo, along with its Arabic name, al-Qahira, which means the Victorious. Over the years, Cairo has attracted a large number of migrants from the countryside

and from other cities. Containing around one-quarter of Egypt's population, Cairo is by far the largest city in the country and in Africa.

6. For an excellent discussion of the broader political and economic context of such projects, see Adham 2005.

7. *The Economist*, 20 March 1999, 6.

8. "History," Bahgat Group, http://www.bahgat.com/history.htm.

9. "Egyptian Online," Oracle ThinkQuest, http://library.thinkquest.org/.

10. Ibid.

11. Adham 2005.

12. Golf has suddenly become very important in Egypt. Courses are appearing around the country. The head of the Egyptian Golf Federation has stated that golf is gaining prominence because the greens help market new apartments and villas and attract European tourists, especially during the winter. Golfers are viewed as wealthy tourists who expect the best and are ready to pay for it (*Al-Ahram Weekly*, 16–22 November 2000, "Travel," 2).

13. Various websites relating to Dreamland are no longer accessible, but are listed on printouts on file with author (dated 27 September 2004).

14. *Dream*, December 1998, 17. *Dream* is Dreamland's newsletter.

15. Caldeira 2000.

16. *Dream*, January 1999, 8.

17. *Dream*, December 1998, 6.

18. See Sennett 1969.

19. *Shopping Centers Today*, 1 May 1999. See also http://www.icsc.org/ (visited 15 January 2008).

20. Ghannam 2002.

21. For more on this, see ibid.

22. Over time, Abu Hakim started charging for his services.

23. See "Egyptian Online," Oracle ThinkQuest, http://library.thinkquest.org/.

24. Um Ali is still not willing to give up her room in al-Zawiya al-Hamra. For one thing, Abu Ali still works in al-Zawiya and often spends the night in that room. In addition, leaving the room threatens to terminate her network and relationships in al-Zawiya. But above all, she still feels insecure about the new place and the legality of its ownership.

25. *Al-Ahram*, 26 June 2006, 11. Others estimate that up to 85 percent of Greater Cairo's residents live in "informal housing" (see Mitchell 2002, 287).

26. Ghannam 2002.

27. Appadurai 1996, 183.

28. To get to Um Ali's new place, you could take an autobus, one of the huge, government-owned buses. You would continue until the last stop, then take a privately owned and operated pickup. If you were a special visitor or looked dignified for one reason or another, you were given the front seat, next to the driver. The rest of the passengers

would be piled in the open trunk. These pickups ran frequently, and you could not but feel happy when you arrived safe and sound at your targeted location. The roads were not paved, but the pickup drivers did a good job of navigating the sandy (and often wet) roads while avoiding children, dogs, turkeys, and chickens, which appeared and disappeared randomly.

29. For more on the door and its social meaning, see Ghannam 2002.
30. Adham 2005, 7.
31. See Mitchell 2002.
32. Mitchell 2002, 286.

Orhan Pamuk

HÜZÜN—MELANCHOLY—TRISTESSE OF ISTANBUL

*H*üzün, the Turkish word for *melancholy*, has an Arabic root; when it appears in the Koran (as *huzn* in two verses and *hazen* in three others), it means much the same thing as the contemporary Turkish word. The Prophet Muhammad referred to the year in which he lost both his wife Hatice and his uncle, Ebu Talip, as *Senettul huzn*, or the year of melancholy; this confirms that the word is meant to convey a feeling of deep spiritual loss. But if *hüzün* begins its life as a word for loss and the spiritual agony and grief attending it, my own readings indicate a small philosophical fault line developing over the next few centuries of Islamic history. With time, we see the emergence of two very different *hüzün*s, each evoking a distinct philosophical tradition.

According to the first tradition, we experience the thing called *hüzün* when we have invested too much in worldly pleasures and material gain; the implication is, "If you hadn't involved yourself so deeply in this transitory world, if you were a good and true Muslim, you wouldn't care so much about your worldly losses." The second tradition, which rises out of Sufi mysticism, offers a more positive and compassionate understanding of the word and of the place of loss and grief in life. To the Sufis, *hüzün* is the spiritual anguish we feel because we cannot be close enough to Allah, because we cannot do enough for Allah in this world. A true Sufi follower would take no interest in worldly concerns like death, let alone goods or possessions; he suffers from grief, emptiness, and inadequacy because he can never be close enough to Allah, because his apprehension of Allah is not deep enough. Moreover, it is the absence, not the presence, of *hüzün* that causes him distress. It is the failure to experience *hüzün* that leads him to feel it; he suffers because he has not suffered enough, and it is by following this logic to its conclusion that Islamic culture has come to hold *hüzün* in high esteem. If *hüzün* has been central to Istanbul culture, poetry, and everyday life over the past two centuries, if it dominates our music, it must be at least partly because we see it as an honor. But to understand what *hüzün* has come to mean over the past century, to convey its enduring power, it is not enough to speak of the honor that Sufi tradition has brought to the word. To convey the spiritual importance of *hüzün* in the music of Istanbul over the last hundred years; to understand why *hüzün* dominates not just the mood of modern Turkish poetry but its symbolism, and why, like the great symbols of Divan poetry, it has suffered from overuse and even abuse; to understand the central importance of *hüzün* as a cultural concept conveying worldly failure, listlessness, and spiritual suffering, it is not enough to grasp the history of the word and the honor we attach to it. If I am to convey the intensity of the *hüzün* that Istanbul caused me to feel as a child, I must describe the history of the city following the destruction of the Ottoman Empire and, even more important, the way this history is reflected in the city's "beautiful" landscapes and its people. The *hüzün* of Istanbul is not just the mood evoked by its music and its poetry, it is a way of looking at life that implicates us all, not only a spiritual state but a state of mind that is ultimately as life affirming as it is negating.

To explore the ambiguities of the word, we must return to the thinkers who see *hüzün* not as a poetic concept or a state of grace, but as an illness. According to El Kindi, *hüzün* was associated not just with the loss or death of a loved one but also with other spiritual afflictions, like anger, love, rancor, and groundless fear. The philosopher-doctor Ibn Sina saw *hüzün* in the same broad terms, and this was why he suggested that the proper way of diagnosing a youth in the grip of a helpless passion was to ask the boy for the girl's name while taking his pulse. The approach outlined by these classic Islamic thinkers is similar to the one proposed in *The Anatomy of Melancholy*, Robert

Burton's enigmatic but entertaining tome of the early seventeenth century. (At some 1,500 pages, it makes Ibn Sina's great work, *Fi'l Huzn*, seem like a pamphlet.) Like Ibn Sina, Burton takes an encyclopedic view of the "black pain," listing fear of death, love, defeat, evil deeds, and any number of drinks and foods as its possible causes, and his list of cures ranges just as broadly. Combining medical science with philosophy, he advises his readers to seek relief in reason, work, resignation, virtue, discipline, and fasting—another interesting instance of common ground underlying these two texts that rise out of such very different cultural traditions.

So *hüzün* stems from the same "black passion" as melancholy, whose etymology refers to a basis in humors first conceived in Aristotle's day (*melaina kole*—black bile) and gives us the coloration normally associated with this feeling and the all-occluding pain it implies. But here we come to the essential difference between the two words. Burton, who was proud to be afflicted, believed that melancholy paved the way to a happy solitude; because it strengthened his imaginative powers, it was, from time to time, to be joyfully affirmed. It did not matter if melancholy was the result of solitude or its cause; in both instances, Burton saw solitude as the heart, the very essence, of melancholy. By contrast, while El Kindi saw *hüzün* both as a mystical state (engendered by the frustration of our common aim to be at one with Allah) and as an illness, solitude was not a desirable or even admissible condition. The central preoccupation, as with all classic Islamic thinkers, was the *cemaat*, or community of believers. He judged *hüzün* by the values of the *cemaat* and suggested remedies that return us to it; essentially, he saw *hüzün* as an experience at odds with the communal purpose.

My starting point was the emotion that a child might feel while looking through a steamy window. Now we begin to understand *hüzün* not as the melancholy of a solitary person but the black mood shared by millions of people together. What I am trying to explain is the *hüzün* of an entire city: of Istanbul.

Before I try to paint this feeling that is unique to Istanbul and that binds its people together, let us remember that the primary aim of a landscape painter is to awaken in the viewer the same feelings that the landscape evoked in the artist himself. This idea had an especially wide currency in the mid-nineteenth century among the Romantics. When Baudelaire identified the thing in the paintings of Eugène Delacroix that affected him most as their air of melancholy, he was using the word in a wholly positive way, as praise, like the Romantics and the Decadents who followed them. It was six years after Baudelaire set down his thoughts on Delacroix (in 1846) that his friend, the author and critic Théophile Gautier, paid a visit to Istanbul. Gautier's writings on the city would later imprint themselves deeply on Istanbul writers like Yahya Kemal and Tanpýnar; it is therefore worth noting that when Gautier described some of the city's views as melancholy in the extreme, he, too, meant it as praise.

But what I am trying to describe now is not the melancholy of Istanbul but the *hüzün* in which we see ourselves reflected, the *hüzün* we absorb with pride and share as a community. To feel this *hüzün* is to see the scenes, evoke the memories, in which the city itself becomes the very illustration, the very essence, of *hüzün*. I am speaking of the evenings when the sun sets early, of the fathers under the streetlamps in the back streets returning home carrying plastic bags. Of the old Bosphorus ferries moored to deserted stations in the middle of winter, where sleepy sailors scrub the decks, pail in hand and one eye on the black-and-white television in the distance; of the old booksellers who lurch from one financial crisis to the next and then wait shivering all day for a customer to appear; of the barbers who complain that men don't shave as much after an economic crisis; of the children who play ball between the cars on cobblestone streets; of the covered women who stand at remote bus stops clutching plastic shopping bags and speak to no one as they wait for the bus that never arrives; of the empty boathouses of the old Bosphorus villas; of the teahouses packed to the rafters with unemployed men; of the patient pimps striding up and down the city's greatest square on summer evenings in search of one last drunken tourist; of the broken seesaws in empty parks; of ship horns booming through the fog; of the wooden buildings whose every board creaked even when they were pashas' mansions, all the more now that they have become municipal headquarters; of the women peeking through their curtains as they wait for husbands who never manage to come home in the evening; of the old men selling thin religious treatises, prayer beads, and pilgrimage oils in the courtyards of mosques; of the tens of thousands of identical apartment-house entrances, their façades discolored by dirt, rust, soot, and dust; of the crowds rushing to catch ferries on winter evenings; of

Photo by Ara Güler.

Photo by Ara Güler.

the city walls, ruins since the end of the Byzantine Empire; of the markets that empty in the evenings; of the dervish lodges, the *tekkes*, that have crumbled; of the seagulls perched on rusty barges caked with moss and mussels, un-flinching under the pelting rain; of the tiny ribbons of smoke rising from the single chimney of a hundred-year-old mansion on the coldest day of the year; of the crowds of men fishing from the sides of the Galata Bridge; of the cold reading rooms of libraries; of the street photographers; of the smell of ex-haled breath in the movie theaters, once glittering affairs with gilded ceilings, now porn cinemas frequented by shamefaced men; of the avenues where you never see a woman alone after sunset; of the crowds gathering around the doors of the state-controlled brothels on one of those hot blustery days when the wind is coming from the south; of the young girls who queue at the doors of establishments selling cut-rate meat; of the holy messages spelled out in lights between the minarets of mosques on holidays that are missing letters where the bulbs have burned out; of the walls covered with frayed and blackened posters; of the tired old *dolmuşes*, fifties Chevrolets that would be museum pieces in any Western city but serve here as shared taxis, huffing and puffing up the city's narrow alleys and dirty thoroughfares; of the buses packed with passengers; of the mosques whose lead plates and rain gutters are forever being stolen; of the city cemeteries, which seem like gateways to a second world, and of their cypress trees; of the dim lights that you see of an evening on the boats crossing from Kadýköy to Karaköy; of the little children in the streets who try to sell the same packet of tissues to every passerby; of the clock towers no one ever notices; of the history books in which children read about the victories of the Ottoman Empire, and of the beatings these same children receive at home; of the days when everyone has to stay home so the electoral roll can be compiled or the census can be taken; of the days when a sudden curfew is announced to facilitate the search for terrorists and everyone sits at home fearfully awaiting "the officials"; of the readers' letters, squeezed into a corner of the paper and read by no one, announcing that the dome of the neighborhood mosque, having stood for some 375 years, has begun to cave in and asking why the state has not done something; of the underpasses in the most crowded intersections; of the overpasses in which every step is broken in a different way; of the girls who read Big Sister Güzin's column in *Freedom*, Turkey's most popular newspaper; of the beggars who accost you in the least likely places and those who stand in the same spot uttering the same appeal day after day; of the powerful whiffs of urine that hit you on crowded avenues, ships, passageways, and underpasses; of the man who has been selling postcards in the same spot for the past forty years; of the reddish-orange glint in the windows of Üsküdar at sunset; of the earliest hours of the morning, when everyone is asleep except for the fishermen heading out to sea; of that corner of Gülhane Park that calls itself a zoo but houses only two goats and three bored cats, languishing in cages; of the third-rate singers doing their best to imitate American vocalists and Turkish pop stars in cheap nightclubs, and of first-rate singers, too; of the bored high-school students in never-ending English classes where after six years no one has learned to say anything but "yes" and "no"; of the immigrants waiting on the Galata docks; of the fruits and vegetables, garbage and plastic bags and wastepaper, empty sacks, boxes, and chests strewn across abandoned street markets on a winter evening; of beautiful covered women timidly bargaining in the street markets; of young mothers struggling down streets with their three children; of all the ships in the sea sounding their horns at the same time as the city comes to a halt to salute the memory of Atatürk at 9:05 on the morning of November tenth; of a cobblestone staircase with so much asphalt poured over it that its steps have disappeared; of marble ruins that were for centuries glorious street fountains but now stand dry, their faucets stolen; of the apartment buildings in the side streets where during my childhood middle-class families—of doctors, lawyers, teachers, and their wives and children—would sit in their apartments listening to the radio in the evenings, and where today the same apartments are packed with knitting and button machines and young girls working all night long for the lowest wages in the city to meet urgent orders; of the view of the Golden Horn, looking toward Eyüp from the Galata Bridge; of the *simit* vendors on the pier who gaze at the view as they wait for customers; of everything being broken, worn out, past its prime; of the storks flying south from the Balkans and northern and western Europe as autumn nears, gazing down over the entire city as they waft over the Bosphorus and the islands of the Sea of Marmara; of the crowds of men smoking cigarettes after the national soccer matches, which during my childhood never failed to end in abject defeat: I speak of them all.

It is by seeing *hüzün*, by paying our respects to its manifestations in the

Photo by Ara Güler.

Photo by Selahattin Giz.

Photo by Ara Güler.

Photo by Ara Güler.

Photo by Hilmi Sahenk.

Photo by Ara Güler.

city's streets and views and people, that we at last come to sense it everywhere. On cold winter mornings, when the sun suddenly falls on the Bosphorus and that faint vapor begins to rise from the surface, the *hüzün* is so dense you can almost touch it, almost see it spread like a film over its people and its landscapes.

So there is a great metaphysical distance between *hüzün* and the melancholy of Burton's solitary individual; there is, however, an affinity between *hüzün* and another form of melancholy, described by Claude Lévi-Strauss in *Tristes Tropiques*. Lévi-Strauss's tropical cities bear little resemblance to Istanbul, which lies on the 41st parallel and where the climate is gentler, the terrain more familiar, the poverty not so harsh; but the fragility of people's lives in Istanbul, the way they treat one another and the distance they feel from the centers of the West, make Istanbul a city that newly arrived Westerners are at a loss to understand, and out of this loss they attribute to it a "mysterious air," thus identifying *hüzün* with the *tristesse* of Lévi-Strauss.

Tristesse is not a pain that affects a solitary individual; *hüzün* and *tristesse* both suggest a communal feeling, an atmosphere and a culture shared by millions. But the words and the feelings they describe are not identical, and if we are to pinpoint the difference it is not enough to say that Istanbul is much richer than Delhi or São Paolo. (If you go to the poor neighborhoods, the cities and the forms poverty takes are in fact all too similar.) The difference lies in the fact that in Istanbul the remains of a glorious past civilization are everywhere visible. No matter how ill-kept, no matter how neglected or hemmed in they are by concrete monstrosities, the great mosques and other monuments of the city, as well as the lesser detritus of empire in every side street and corner—the little arches, fountains, and neighborhood mosques—inflict heartache on all who live among them.

These are nothing like the remains of great empires to be seen in Western cities, preserved like museums of history and proudly displayed. The people of Istanbul simply carry on with their lives amid the ruins. Many Western writers and travelers find this charming. But for the city's more sensitive and attuned residents, these ruins are reminders that the present city is so poor and confused that it can never again dream of rising to its former heights of wealth, power, and culture. It is no more possible to take pride in these neglected dwellings, which dirt, dust, and mud have blended into their sur-

Photo by Ara Güler.

roundings, than it is to rejoice in the beautiful old wooden houses that as a child I watched burn down one by one.

While traveling through Switzerland, Dostoyevsky struggled to understand the inordinate pride Genevans took in their city. "They gaze at even the simplest objects, like street poles, as if they were the most splendid and glorious things on earth," wrote the West-hating chauvinist in one letter. So proud were the Genevans of their historic city that, even when asked the simplest directions, they'd say things like "Walk straight down this street, sir, past that elegant, magnificent bronze fountain." If an Istanbul resident were to do likewise, he might find himself uttering such instructions as are found in the story *Bedia and the Beautiful Eleni* by the great writer Ahmet Rasim (1865–1932): "Go past Ibrahim Pasha's *hamam*. Walk a little farther. On your right, looking out over the ruin you've just passed [the bath], you'll see a dilapidated house." Today's *Ýstanbullu* would be uneasy about everything the foreigner might see in those miserable streets.

A more confident resident might prefer to use the city's grocery stores and coffeehouses as his landmarks, now common practice, as these count among the greatest treasures of modern Istanbul. But the fastest flight from the *hüzün* of the ruins is to ignore all historical monuments and pay no attention to the names of buildings or their architectural particularities. For many Istanbul residents, poverty and ignorance have served them well to this end. History becomes a word with no meaning; they take stones from the city walls and add them to modern materials to make new buildings, or they go about restoring old buildings with concrete. But it catches up with them: by neglecting the past and severing their connection with it, the *hüzün* they feel in their mean and hollow efforts is all the greater. *Hüzün* rises out of the pain they feel for everything that has been lost, but it is also what compels them to invent new defeats and new ways to express their impoverishment.

The *tristesse* that Lévi-Strauss describes is what a Westerner might feel as he surveys those vast, poverty-stricken cities of the tropics, as he contemplates the huddled masses and their wretched lives. But he does not see the city through their eyes. *Tristesse* implies a guilt-ridden Westerner who seeks to assuage his pain by refusing to let cliché and prejudice color his impressions. *Hüzün*, on the other hand, is not a feeling that belongs to the outside observer. To varying degrees, classical Ottoman music, Turkish popu-

Photo by Ara Güler.

lar music, especially the *arabesque* music that became popular during the 1980s, are all expressions of this emotion, which we feel as something between physical pain and grief. And Westerners coming to the city often fail to notice it. Even Gérard de Nerval (whose own melancholy would eventually drive him to suicide) spoke of being greatly refreshed by the city's colors, its street life, its violence, and its rituals; he reported hearing women laughing in its cemeteries. Perhaps it is because he visited Istanbul before the city went into mourning, when the Ottoman Empire was still in its glory, or perhaps it was his need to escape his own melancholy that inspired him to decorate the many pages of *Voyage en Orient* with the bright Eastern fantasies.

Istanbul does not carry its *hüzün* as "an illness for which there is a cure" or "an unbidden pain from which we need to be delivered": it carries its *hüzün* by choice. And so it finds its way back to the melancholy of Burton, who held that "All other pleasures are empty. / None are as sweet as melancholy"; echoing its self-denigrating wit, it dares to boast of its importance in Istanbul life. Likewise, the *hüzün* in Turkish poetry after the foundation of the Republic, as it too expresses the same grief that no one can or would wish to escape, an ache that finally saves our souls and also gives them depth. For the poet, *hüzün* is the smoky window between him and the world. The screen he projects over life is painful because life itself is painful. So it is, also, for the residents of Istanbul as they resign themselves to poverty and depression. Imbued still with the honor accorded it in Sufi literature, *hüzün* gives their resignation an air of dignity, but it also explains why it is their choice to embrace failure, indecision, defeat, and poverty so philosophically and with such pride, suggesting that *hüzün* is not the outcome of life's worries and great losses, but their principal cause. So it was for the heroes of the Turkish films of my childhood and youth, and also for many of my real-life heroes during the same period: they all gave the impression that because of this *hüzün* they'd been carrying around in their hearts since birth, they could not appear desirous in the face of money, success, or the women they loved. *Hüzün* does not just paralyze the inhabitants of Istanbul; it also gives them poetic license to be paralyzed.

No such feeling operates in heroes like Balzac's Rastignac, who in his furious ambition comes to convey, even glorify, the spirit of the modern city. The *hüzün* of Istanbul suggests nothing of an individual standing against society; on the contrary, it suggests an erosion of the will to stand against the values and mores of the community and encourages us to be content with little, honoring the virtues of harmony, uniformity, humility. *Hüzün* teaches endurance in times of poverty and deprivation; it also encourages us to read life and the history of the city in reverse. It allows the people of Istanbul to think of defeat and poverty not as a historical end point, but as an honorable beginning, fixed long before they were born. So the honor we derive from it can be rather misleading. But it does suggest that Istanbul does not bear its *hüzün* as an incurable illness that has spread throughout the city, as an immutable poverty to be endured like grief, or even as an awkward and perplexing failure to be viewed and judged in black and white; it bears its *hüzün* with honor.

As early as 1580, Montaigne argued that there was no honor in the emo-

Photo by Ara Güler.

tion he called *tristesse*. (He used this word even though he knew himself to be a melancholic; years later, Flaubert, likewise diagnosed, would do the same.) Montaigne saw *tristesse* as the enemy of self-reliant rationalism and individualism. *Tristesse*, in his view, did not deserve to be set in capital letters alongside the great virtues, Wisdom, Virtue, and Conscience; he approved of the Italian association of *tristezza* with all manner of madness and injury, the source of countless evils.

Montaigne's own sorrow was as solitary as mourning, eating away at the mind of a man who lives alone with his books. But the *hüzün* of Istanbul is something the entire city feels together and affirms as one. Just like the heroes of Tanpýnar's *Peace*, the greatest novel ever written about Istanbul: because of the *hüzün* they derive from the city's history, they are broken and condemned to defeat. It is *hüzün* which ordains that no love will end peacefully. Just as in the old black-and-white films—even in the most affecting and authentic love stories—if the setting is Istanbul, it is clear from the start that the *hüzün* the boy has carried with him since birth will lead the story into melodrama.

In these black-and-white films, as in works of "high art" like Tanpýnar's

Photo by Ara Güler.

Peace, the moment of identification is always the same. It is when the heroes have withdrawn into themselves, when they have failed to show enough determination or enterprise, submitting instead to the conditions imposed on them by history and society, that we embrace them, and at that same moment so does the whole city. No matter how picturesque, how famous the scenery in the drama unfolding on the city's black-and-white streets, it too will shimmer with *hüzün*. Sometimes, when I am changing channels on television and happen upon one of these films at some random point in the middle, a curious thought occurs to me. When I see the hero walking along the cobblestones of a poor neighborhood, gazing up at the lights in the windows of a wooden house and thinking of his beloved, who is of course about to marry someone else, or when the hero answers a rich and powerful factory owner with humble pride and, resolving to accept life as it is, turns to gaze at a black-

and-white Bosphorus, it seems to me that *hüzün* does not come from the hero's broken, painful story or from his failure to win the hand of the woman he loves; rather, it is almost as if the *hüzün* that infuses the city's sights and streets and famous views has seeped into the hero's heart to break his will. It then seems that to know the hero's story and share his melancholy I need only to look at the view. For the heroes of these popular films, as for the heroes of Tanpýnar's *Peace*, there are only two ways to face the impasse: either they go for a walk along the Bosphorus or they head off into the back streets of the city to gaze at its ruins.

The hero's only resort is the communal resort. But for those Istanbul writers and poets who are excited by Western culture and wish to engage with the contemporary world, the matter is more complex still. Along with the sense of community that *hüzün* brings, they also aspire to the rationalism of Montaigne and to the emotional solitude of Thoreau. In the early years of the twentieth century, some drew upon all these influences to create an image of Istanbul that is, it must be said, still part of the city and so part of my story, too. I wrote this book in constant—and sometimes fierce—dialogue with four lonely authors who (after voracious reading, long hesitant discussion, and meandering walks strewn with coincidences) gave modern Istanbul its melancholy.

BIBLIOGRAPHY

Abbas, Ackbar. 1997. *Hong Kong: Culture and the Politics of Disappearance*. Minneapolis: University of Minnesota Press.

Abu-Lughod, Janet. 1971. *Cairo: 1001 Years of the City of the Victorious*. Princeton: Princeton University Press.

Adham, Khaled. 2005. "Globalization, Neoliberalism, and New Spaces of Capital in Cairo." *Traditional Dwellings and Settlements Review* 17.1: 1–14.

Adorno, Theodor W. 1991. *The Culture Industry: Selected Essays on Mass Culture*. London: Routledge.

Agier, Michel. 2002. "Between War and City: Towards an Urban Anthropology of Refugee Camps." *Ethnography* 3: 317–41.

Amin, Ash. 2002. "Spatialities of Globalization." *Environment and Planning A* 34: 385–99.

Anderson, Benedict. 1991. *Imagined Communities: Reflections on the Origin and Spread of Nationalism*. London: Verso.

Appadurai, Arjun. 1996. *Modernity at Large: Cultural Dimensions of Globalization*. Minneapolis: University of Minnesota Press.

———. 2000. "Spectral Housing and Urban Cleansing: Notes on Millennial Mumbai." *Public Culture* 12.3.

———. 2001. "Deep Democracy: Urban Governmentality and the Horizon of Politics." *Environment and Urbanization* 13.2 (October): 23–43.

Arlt, Roberto. 1993. *Aguafuertes porteñas: Buenos Aires, vida cotidiana*. Buenos Aires: Alianza.

Arrighi, Giovanni. 1994. *The Long Twentieth Century: Money, Power, and the Origins of Our Times*. London: Verso.

Athanasiou, Athena. 2003. "Technologies of Humanness, Aporias of Biopolitics, and the Cut Body of Humanity." *Differences* 14: 125–62.

Benjamin, Walter. 1968. *Charles Baudelaire*. Translated by Harry Zohn. New York: New Left Books.

Bennett, Tony. 1988. "The Exhibitionary Complex." *New Formations* 4 (spring): 73–102.

Berry, Sara. 1997. "Tomatoes, Land and Hearsay: Property and History in Asante in the Time of Structural Adjustment." *World Development* 25: 1,225–41.

Biaya, T. K. 2001. "Parallel Society in the Democratic Republic of Congo." In *Shifting African Identities*, ed. Simon Bekker, Martine Dodds, and Meshack Khosa. Pretoria: Human Sciences Research Council.

Bombay First–McKinsey Report. 2003. *Vision Mumbai: Transforming Mumbai into a World-class City*. Mumbai: Bombay First / McKinsey and Company.

Borges, Jorge Luis. 1943. *Poemas*. Buenos Aires: Losada.

Borja, Jordi, and Manuel Castells. 1997. *Local y global: La gestión de las ciudades en la era de la información*. Madrid: United Nations for Human Settlements (Habitat) / Taurus.

Bourdieu, Pierre. 1984. *Distinction: A Social Critique of the Judgement of Taste*. Translated by Richard Nice. Cambridge, Mass.: Harvard University Press.

———. 1993. *The Field of Cultural Production: Essays on Art and Literature*. Edited by Randal Johnson. New York: Columbia University Press.

Branco, Pedro Paulo Martoni. 1999. "Informação e missão institucional: Pesquisa desvenda economia paulista." *São Paulo em Perspectiva* 13.1–2: 3–17.

Brant, Vinícius Caldeira, et al. 1989. *São Paulo: Trabalhar e viver*. São Paulo: Brasiliense.

Bredekamp, Horst. 1995. *The Lure of Antiquity and the Cult of the Machine: The Kunstkammer and the Evolution of Nature, Art, and Technology*. Translated by Allison Brown. Princeton: Markus Wiener Publishers.

Brenner, Neil. 1999. "Beyond State-centrism? Space, Territoriality and Geographical Scale in Globalization Studies." *Theory and Society* 28: 39–78.

Brenner, Neil, and Roger Keil, eds. 2006. *The Global Cities Reader*. New York: Routledge.

Burnett-Hurst, A. R. 1925. *Labour and Housing in Bombay: A Study in Economic Conditions of the Wage-Earning Classes in Bombay*. London: P. S. King.

Caldeira, Teresa P. R. 2000. *City of Walls: Crime, Segregation, and Citizenship in São Paulo*. Berkeley: University of California Press.

———. 2003. "Urban Planning, Democratization, and Neoliberalism in São Paulo." Paper presented at the invited session "Critiquing the Modern State 3: Latin America and the Caribbean," 102d meeting of the American Anthropological Association, Chicago.

Caldeira, Teresa P. R., and James Holston. 1999. "Democracy and Violence in Brazil." *Comparative Studies in Society and History* 41.4: 691–729.

————. 2005. "State and Urban Space in Brazil: From Modernist Planning to Democratic Interventions." In *Global Assemblages: Technology, Politics, and Ethics as Anthropological Problems*, ed. Aihwa Ong and Stephen J. Collier, 393–416. London: Blackwell.

Calvino, Italo. 1974. *Invisible Cities*. Translated by William Weaver. New York: Harcourt, Brace, Jovanovich.

————. 1983. "Italo Calvino on Invisible Cities." *Columbia* 8: 37–42.

Cardoso, Adalberto, and Alvaro Comin. 1995. "Câmaras setoriais, modernização produtiva e democratização nas relações capital-trabalho: A experiência do setor automobilístico no Brasil." In *A Máquina e o Equilibrista*, ed. Nadya Castro. Rio de Janeiro: Paz e Terra.

Castells, Manuel. 1995. *La ciudad informacional*. Madrid: Alianza.

————. 1996. *The Rise of the Network Society*. Vol. 1. Oxford: Blackwell.

————. 2000. "Grassrooting the Space of Flows." In *Cities in the Telecommunication Age*, ed. James O. Wheeler, Yuko Aoyama, and Barney Warf. New York: Routledge.

Cesari, Jocelyn. 1999. "The Re-Islamisation of Muslim Migration in Europe." In *Islam, Modernism and the West: Cultural and Political Relations at the End of the Millennium*, ed. Gema Martin Muñoz, 211–33. London: Zed Books.

————. 2003. "Muslim Minorities in Europe: The Silent Revolution." In *Modernizing Islam: Religion in the Public Sphere in the Middle East and in Europe*, ed. John Esposito and Francois Burgat, 251–69. Brunswick, N.J.: Rutgers University Press.

Chakrabarty, Dipesh. 2000. *Provincializing Europe: Postcolonial Thought and Historical Difference*. Princeton: Princeton University Press.

Chandavarkar, Rajnarayan. 1994. *The Origins of Industrial Capitalism in India*. Cambridge: Cambridge University Press.

————. 1998. *Imperial Power and Popular Politics*. Cambridge: Cambridge University Press.

Chatterjee, Partha. 2003. "Are Indian Cities Becoming Bourgeois at Last?" In *Body.City: Siting Contemporary Culture in India*, ed. Indira Chandrashekhar and Peter C. Ceel. New Delhi: Tulika / House of World Cultures.

————. 2004. *The Politics of the Governed: Reflections on Popular Politics in Most of the World*. New York: Columbia University Press.

Clifford, James. 1997. *Routes: Travel and Translation in the Late Twentieth Century*. Cambridge, Mass.: Harvard University Press.

Comin, Alvaro, and Claudio Amitrano. 2003. "Economia e emprego: A trajetória recente da região metropolitana de São Paulo." *Estudos Cebrap* 66: 53–76.

Conklin, Alice. 1997. *A Mission to Civilize: The Republican Idea of Empire in France and West Africa 1895–1930*. Stanford, Calif.: Stanford University Press.

Cox, Kenneth. 2001. "Territoriality, Politics and the 'Urban.'" *Political Geography* 20: 745–62.

Dai Jinhua. 2002. *Cinema and Desire: Feminist Marxism and Cultural Politics in the Work of Dai Jinghua*. Edited by Jing Wang and Tani E. Barlow. London: Verso.

Daireaux, Émile. 1988. *Vida y costumbres en el Plata*. Vol. 1. Buenos Aires: Félix Lajouane.

Dean, Mitchell. 1999. *Governmentality: Power and Rule in Modern Society*. London: Sage.

Dean, Warren. 1969. *The Industrialization of São Paulo 1880–1945*. Austin: University of Texas Press.

De Boeck, Filip. 2000. "Borderland Breccia: The Mutant Hero and the Historical Imagination of a Central-African Diamond Frontier." *Colonialism and Colonial History* 1: 1–44.

———. 2003. "Kinshasa: Tales of the 'Invisible City' and the Second World." In *Under Siege: Four African Cities: Freetown, Johannesburg, Kinshasa, Lagos: Documenta 11, Platform 4*, ed. Okwui Enwezor, Carlos Basualdo, and Uta Meta Bauer, 243–85. Kassel, Germany: Hatje Cantz Publishers.

Debord, Guy. 1990. *Comments on the Society of the Spectacle*. Translated by Malcolm Imrie. London: Verso.

———. 1994. *Society of the Spectacle*. Translated by Donald Nicholson-Smith. New York: Zone Books.

de Certeau, Michel. 1984. *The Practice of Everyday Life*. Minneapolis: University of Minnesota Press.

Deleuze, Gilles. 1986. *Cinema 1: The Movement Image*. Translated by Hugh Tomlinson and Barbara Habberjam. Minneapolis: University of Minnesota Press.

Dreier, Katherine. 1920. *Five Months in the Argentine from a Woman's Point of View 1918 to 1919*. New York: Frederic Fairchild Sherman.

During, Simon. 2005. *Cultural Studies: A Critical Introduction*. London: Routledge.

Dwivedi, Sharada, and Rahul Mehrotra. 1995. *Bombay: The Cities Within*. Bombay: India Book House.

Edwardes, S. M. 1909. *Gazetteer of Bombay City and Island*. Bombay: Government Press.

———. 1923. *Bombay City Police: A Historical Sketch 1672–1916*. London: Humphrey Milford / Oxford University Press.

Esherick, Joseph W., ed. 2000. *Remaking the Chinese City: Modernity and National Identity 1900–1950*. Honolulu: University of Hawaii Press.

Fanthorpe, Richard. 2001. "Neither Citizen or Subject: 'Lumpen' Agency and the Legacy of Native Administration in Sierra Leone." *African Affairs* 100: 363–88.

Feldman, Allen. 2004. "Securocratic Wars of Public Safety: Globalized Policing as Scopic Regime." *Interventions* 6: 330–50.

Ferguson, James. 1999. *Expectations of Modernity: Myths and Meanings of Urban Life on the Zambian Copperbelt*. Berkeley: University of California Press.

Fernandes, Rubem César. 1994. *Privado, porém público: O terceiro setor na América Latina*. Rio de Janeiro: Relume-Dumará.

Fiori Arantes, Otilia Beatriz. 2000. "Pasen y vean . . . Imagen y city-marketing en las nuevas estrategias." *Punto de Vista* 66 (April): 19.

Fix, Mariana. 2001. *Parceiros da Exclusão*. São Paulo: Boitempo Editorial.

Foucault, Michel. 1986. "Of Other Spaces." *Diacritics* 16.1: 22–27.

Friedman, John. 1986. "The World City Hypothesis." *Development and Change* 17.1: 69–84.

Frúgoli Jr., Heitor. 2000. *Centralidade em São Paulo: Trajetórias, conflitos e negociações na metrópole*. São Paulo: Cortez / Edusp / Fapesp.

Furthman, Jules. 1973. "*Morocco*" and "*Shanghai Express*": *Two Films by Josef von Sternberg*. New York: Simon and Schuster.

Galloway, Anne. 2004. "Intimations of Everyday Life: Ubiquitous Computing and the City." *Cultural Studies* 18: 384–408.

Gandelsonas, Mario. 1999. *X-Urbanism*. New York: Princeton Architectural Press.

Gaonkar, Dilip Parameshwar, ed. 1999. "Alter/Native Modernities." Special issue, *Public Culture* 11.1.

Garcia, Joana. 2004. *O Negócio do Social*. Rio de Janeiro: Zahar.

García Canclini, Néstor, coord. 1994. *Los nuevos espectadores: Cine, televisión y video en México*. Mexico City: CONACULTA-IMCINE.

———. 1995. *Hybrid Cultures: Strategies for Entering and Leaving Modernity*. Translated by Christopher L. Chiappari and Sylvia Lopez. Minneapolis: University of Minnesota Press.

García Canclini, Néstor, Alejandro Castellanos, and Ana Rosas Mantecón. 1996. *La ciudad de los viajeros: Travesías e imaginarios urbanos: México 1940-2000*. Mexico City: Universidad Autónoma Metropolitana / Grijalbo.

García Canclini, Néstor, et al. 1998. *Cultura y comunicación en la ciudad de México*. Mexico City: Universidad Autónoma Metropolitana / Grijalbo.

García Montero, Luis. 1972. *Luna en el sur*. Sevilla: Editorial Renacimiento.

Ghannam, Farha. 2002. *Remaking the Modern: Space, Relocation, and the Politics of Identity in a Global Cairo*. Berkeley: University of California Press.

Ghose, Rina. 2003. "Community Participation, Spatial Knowledge Production, and GIS Use in Inner-city Revitalization." *Urban Technology* 10: 39–60.

Ghosh, Amitav. 1992. *In an Antique Land*. New York: Vintage Books.

Gore, Charles, and David Pratten. 2003. "The Politics of Plunder: The Rhetorics of Order and Disorder in Southern Nigeria." *African Affairs* 101: 211–40.

Gorelik, Adrián. 1998. *La grilla y el parquet*. Buenos Aires: Universidad Nacional de Quilmes.

———. 2002. "Imaginarios urbanos e imaginación urbana." *BazarAmericano* (June–July), http://www.bazaramericano.com/bazar/articulos/imaginarios_gorelik.htm.

Graham, Stephen, and Simon Martin. 2001. *Splintering Urbanism: Networked Infrastructure, Technological Mobilities and the Urban Condition*. London: Routledge.

Gupta, Akhil, and James Ferguson. 1997. *Culture, Power, Place: Explorations in Critical Anthropology*. Durham, N.C.: Duke University Press.

Habermas, Jürgen. 1984. *The Theory of Communicative Action*. Vol. 2. Boston: Beacon.

Hall, Stuart. 2001a. "The Local and the Global: Globalization and Ethnicity." In *Culture*,

Globalization, and the World System, ed. Anthony King, 19–39. Minneapolis: University of Minnesota Press.

———. 2001b. "Museums of Modern Art and the End of History." *Modernity and Difference*. London: Institute of International Visual Arts.

Hannerz, Ulf. 1996. *Transnational Connections: Culture, People, Places.* London: Routledge.

Hansen, Thomas. 2001. *Wages of Violence: Naming and Identity in Mumbai.* Princeton: Princeton University Press.

Hardin, Rebecca. 2001. "Concessionary Politics in the Western Congo Basin: History and Culture in Forest Use." Working Paper Series. Institutions and Governance Program, World Resources Institute and Central Africa Regional Program for the Environment. Washington: World Resources Institute. http://pubs.wri.org/pubs/.

Hardt, Michael, and Antonio Negri. 2000. *Empire.* Cambridge, Mass.: Harvard University Press.

———. 2004. *Multitude: War and Democracy in the Age of Empire.* New York: Penguin.

Harvey, David. 1989. *The Condition of Postmodernity: An Enquiry into the Origin of Social Change.* Oxford: Blackwell, 1989.

Herbst, Jeffrey. 2000. *States and Power in Africa: Comparative Lessons in Authority and Control.* Princeton: Princeton University Press.

Hirst, Paul, and Grahame Thompson. 1996. *Globalization in Question: The International Economy and the Possibilities of Governance.* Cambridge, U.K.: Polity Press.

Holston, James. 1989. *The Modernist City: An Anthropological Critique of Brasília.* Chicago: University of Chicago Press.

———, ed. 1999. *Cities and Citizenship.* Durham, N.C.: Duke University Press.

Holston, James, and Arjun Appadurai. 1999. "Introduction: Cities and Citizenship." In *Cities and Citizenship*, ed. James Holston, 1–18. Durham, N.C.: Duke University Press.

Hopkins, A. G. 2002. *Globalization in World History.* London: Pimlico.

Horkheimer, Max, and Theodor W. Adorno. 2002. *Dialectic of Enlightenment.* Translated by Edmund Jephcott. Stanford, Calif.: Stanford University Press.

Hosagrahar, Jyoti. 2005. *Indigenous Modernities: Negotiating Architecture and Urbanism.* London: Routledge.

Huyssen, Andreas. 2005. "Geographies of Modernism in a Globalizing World." In *Geographies of Modernism: Literatures, Cultures, Spaces*, ed. Peter Brooker and Andrew Thacker, 6–18. London: Routledge. [Longer version in *New German Critique* 100 (winter 2007): 189–207.]

Ibrahim, S. E. 1987. "Cairo: A Sociological Profile." In *Urban Crisis and Social Movements*, ed. Salim Nasr and Theodor Hanf, 87–99. Beirut: Euro-Arab Social Research Group.

Jameson, Fredric. 1994. "Remapping Taipei." In New Chinese Cinemas: Forms, Identities, Politics, ed. Nick Browne et al., 117–50. New York: Cambridge University Press.

———. 2002. *A Singular Modernity: Essays on the Ontology of the Present*. London: Verso.

Khosla, Romi. 2002. *The Loneliness of a Long Distant Future: Dilemmas of Contemporary Architecture*. New Delhi: Tulika.

King, Anthony D. 1976. *Colonial Urban Development: Culture, Social Power and Environment*. London: Routledge.

———. 1990. *Urbanism, Colonialism, and the World Economy*. London: Routledge.

———. 1997. *Culture, Globalization, and the World System: Contemporary Conditions for the Representation of Identity*. Rev. ed. Minneapolis: University of Minnesota Press.

———. 2004. *Spaces of Global Cultures: Architecture, Urbanism, Identity*. London: Routledge.

Knauft, Bruce M., ed. 2002. *Critically Modern: Alternatives, Alterities, Anthropologies* Bloomington: Indiana University Press.

Kong, Shuyn. 2003. "Big Shot from Beijing." *Asian Cinema* 14.1: 183–86.

Koolhaas, Rem. 1978. *Delirious New York: A Retroactive Manifesto for Manhattan*. New York: Oxford University Press.

Kosambi, Meera. 1986. *Bombay in Transition: The Growth and Ecology of a Colonial City, 1880–1980*. Stockholm: Almqvist and Wiksell International.

———. 1995. "British Bombay and Marathi Mumbai." In *Bombay: Mosaic of Modern Culture*, ed. Sujata Patel and Alice Thorner. Bombay: Oxford University Press.

Lao She. 1979. *Rickshaw: The Novel Lo-t'o Hsiang Tzu*. Trans. Jean M. James. Honolulu: University of Hawaii Press.

Latham, Alan, and Derek McCormack. 2004. "Moving Cities: Rethinking the Materialities of Urban Geographies." *Progress in Human Geography* 28: 701–24.

Lee, Leo Ou-fan. 1999. *Shanghai Modern: The Flowering of a New Urban Culture in China 1930–1945*. Cambridge, Mass.: Harvard University Press.

Lefebvre, Henri. 1971. *Everyday Life in the Modern World*. New York: Harper and Row.

———. 1991a. *The Critique of Everyday Life*. Translated by John Moore. London: Verso.

———. 1991b. *The Production of Space*. Translated by Donald Nicholson-Smith. Oxford: Blackwell.

Leme, Maria Carolina, and Ciro Biderman. 1997. "O mapa das desigualdades no estado de São Paulo." *Novos Estudos Cebrap* 49: 181–211.

Levin, Thomas, Ursula Frohne, and Peter Weibel, eds. 2002. CTRL *[Space]: Rhetorics of Surveillance from Bentham to Big Brother*. Cambridge: Massachusetts Institute of Technology Press.

Lin, Xiaoping. 2002. "New Chinese Cinema of the 'Sixth Generation': A Distant Cry of Forsaken Children." *Third Text* 16.3: 261–84.

Liu, Lydia H. 1995. *Translingual Practice: Literature, National Culture, and Translated Modernity—China, 1900–1937*. Stanford, Calif.: Stanford University Press.

Lo, Kwai-cheung. 2001. "Transnationalization of the Local in Hong Kong Cinema." In *At Full Speed: Hong Kong Cinema in a Borderless World*, ed. Esther C. M. Yau, 261–76. Minneapolis: University of Minnesota Press.

Lu, Tonglin. 2006. "Trapped Freedom and Localized Globalism." In *From Underground to Independent: Alternative Film Culture in Contemporary China*, ed. Paul G. Pickowicz and Yingjin Zhang, 123–41. Lanham, Md.: Rowman and Littlefield.

Lyotard, Jean-François. 1983. "Answering the Question: What Is Postmodernism?" In *Innovation/Renovation*, ed. Ihab Hasan and Sally Hassan. Madison: University of Wisconsin Press.

MacGaffey, Janet, and Remy Bazenguissa-Ganga. 1999. *Congo-Paris: Transnational Traders on the Margins of the Law*. Bloomington: Indiana University Press / International Africa Institute, London.

Macleod, Gordon, and Mark Goodwin. 1999. "Reconstructing an Urban and Regional Political Economy: On the State, Politics, Scale and Explanation." *Political Geography* 18: 697–730.

Madgavkar, Govind Narayan. 1961 [1863]. *Mumbaiche Varnan*. Edited by N. T. Phatak. 2d ed. Bombay: Marathi Granth-Sangrahalaya.

Mamdani, Mahmood. 1996. *Citizen and Subject*. Cape Town: David Philip.

Mandaville, Peter. 2000. "Information Technology and the Changing Boundaries of European Islam." In *Paroles d'islam: Individus, sociétés et discours dans l'islam européen contemporain*, ed. Felice Dassetto, 281–97. Paris: Maisonneuve-Larose.

Marcuse, Peter, and Ronald van Kempen, eds. 2000. *Globalizing Cities: A New Spatial Order*. Oxford: Blackwell.

Marques, Eduardo, and Haroldo Torres. 2000. "São Paulo no contexto do sistema mundial de cidades." *Novos Estudos Cebrap* 56: 139–68.

Masselos, Jim. 1982. "Change and Custom in the Format of the Bombay Mohurrum during the Nineteenth and Twentieth Centuries." *South Asia* (New Series) 5.2.

Massumi, Brian. 2002. *A Shock to Thought: Expressions after Deleuze and Guattari*. London: Routledge.

McCarthy, Helen, and Paul Miller. 2003. *London Calling: How Mobile Technologies Will Transform Our Capital City*. London: Demos.

McLuhan, Marshall. 1964. *Understanding Media: The Extensions of Man*. New York: McGraw-Hill.

Mehrotra, Rahul. 2002. "Bazaar City: A Metaphor for South Asian Urbanism." *Kapital and Karma*, ed. Angelika Fitz. Vienna: Kunsthalle.

———. 2004. "Planning for Conservation: Looking at Bombay's Historic Fort Area." *Future Anterior* 1.2 (fall): 25–31.

Melo, Marcus C. 1995. "State Retreat, Governance and Metropolitan Restructuring in Brazil." *International Journal of Urban and Regional Research* 19.3: 342–57.

Meyer, Regina Maria Prosperi. 1991. Metrópole e urbanismo: São Paulo anos 50. Ph.D. diss., Faculdade de Arquitetura e Urbanismo, Universidade de São Paulo.

Mistry, Rohinton. 2002. *Family Matters*. New York: Knopf.

Mitchell, Timothy. 1989. "The World as Exhibition." *Comparative Studies in Society and History* 31.2: 217–36.

———, ed. 2000. *Questions of Modernity*. London: University of Minnesota Press.

———. 2002. *Rules of the Experts: Egypt, Techno-politics, Modernity*. Berkeley: University of California Press.

Monsiváis, Carlos. 1995. *Los rituales del caos*. Mexico City: Era.

Morse, Richard M. 1970. *Formação Histórica de São Paulo*. São Paulo: Difel.

Ndebele, Njabulo. 1998. "Game Lodges and Leisure Colonialists." In *Blank: Architecture, Apartheid and After*, ed. Hilton Judin and Ivan Vladislavic. Rotterdam: Netherlands Architectural Institute Publishers.

Nielsen, Jorgen. 1999. *Towards a European Islam*. Houndmills, U.K.: Macmillan / Centre for Research in Ethnic Relations, University of Warwick.

Nielsen, Tom, Neils Albertsen, and Peter Hemmersam, eds. 2004. *Urban Mutations: Periodization, Scale and Mobility*. Aarhus, Denmark: Arkitekskolens Forlag.

Nordstrom, Carolyn. 2003. *Shadow Powers: The Illegal, the Illicit, and the Invisible*. Los Angeles: University of California Press.

Ong, Aihwa. 1999. *Flexible Citizenship: The Cultural Logics of Transnationality*. Durham, N.C.: Duke University Press.

Osborne, Thomas, and Nikolas Rose. 1999. "Governing Cities: Notes on the Spatialisation of Virtue." *Environment and Planning D: Society and Space* 17: 737–60.

Pamuk, Orhan. 2005. *Istanbul: Memories and the City*. Translated by Maureen Freely. New York: Knopf.

Pang, Lailewau. 2002. *Building a New China in Cinema: The Chinese Left-wing Cinema Movement, 1932–1957*. Lanham, Md.: Rowman and Littlefield.

Paoli, Maria Célia. 1999. "Apresentação e introdução." In *Os sentidos da democracia: Políticas do dissenso e hegemonia global*, ed. Maria Célia Paoli and Francisco de Oliveira, 7–23. São Paulo: Nedic / Fapesp / Editora Vozes.

———. 2001. "As privações da cidadania: Política sem direitos, sociedade sem mundo." Paper presented at the 25th annual meeting of the Associação Nacional de Pós-Graduação e Pesquisa em Ciências Sociais, Caxambu, Minas Gerais, Brazil.

"Perfect Fake." *QP* 8: 37–41.

Perulli, Paolo. 1995. *Atlas Metropolitano: El cambio social en las grandes ciudades*. Madrid: Alianza.

Philo, Chris. 2000. "Foucault's Geography." In *Thinking Space*, ed. Mike Crang and Nigel Thrift, 205–38. London: Routledge.

Pieterse, Jan Nederveen. 2004. *Globalization and Culture: Global Mélange*. Lanham, Md.: Rowman and Littlefield.

PNUD-IPEA. 1996. *Relatório para o Desenvolvimento Humano no Brasil*. Brasília: PNUD-IPEA.

Prakash, Gyan. 2002. "The Urban Turn." In *Sarai Reader 2002: The Cities of Everyday Life*. New Delhi: Sarai.

Pratt, Mary Louise. 1992. *Imperial Eyes: Travel Writing and Transculturation*. London: Routledge.

Raeymaekers, Timothy. 2002. *Network War: An Introduction to Congo's Privatised Conflict Economy*. Amsterdam: NOVIB (Nederlandse Organisatie voor Internationale Ontwikkelingssamenwerking).

Raftopolous, Brian, and Tsueneo Yoshikuni, eds. 1999. *Sites of Struggle: Essays in Zimbabwe's Urban History*. Harare: Weaver Press.

Rama, Ángel. 1984. "La ciudad letrada." In *Estudios críticos*, ed. Mabel Moraña. Pittsburgh: University of Pittsburgh Press / Instituto Internacional de Literatura Iberoamericana.

Ribot, Jesse. 2000. *African Decentralization: Local Actors, Powers and Accountability*. Paper no. 8. Geneva: United Nations Research Institute for Social Development Program on Democracy, Governance and Human Rights.

Robertson, R. 1994. "Globalisation or Glocalisation?" *International Communication* 1.1: 33–52.

Robin, Régine. 2001. *Berlin Chantiers: Essai sur les passés fragiles*. Cameron: Stock Editions.

Robinson, Jennifer. 1998. "Global and World Cities: A View from off the Map." *International Journal of Urban and Regional Research* 26.3: 378–93.

———. 2006. *Ordinary Cities: Between Modernity and Development*. London: Routledge.

Rodenbeck, Max. 1998. *Cairo: The City Victorious*. Cairo: American University in Cairo Press.

Roitman, Janet. 1998. "The Garrison-entrepot." *Cahiers d'Etudes africaines* 150–52: 297–329.

———. 2003. "Unsanctioned Wealth, or the Productivity of Debt in Northern Cameroon." *Public Culture* 15: 211–37.

Rolnik, Raquel et al. N.d. *São Paulo: Crise e Mudança*. São Paulo: Brasiliense.

Rose, Nikolas. 1996. "Governing 'Advanced' Liberal Democracies." In *Foucault and Political Reason: Liberalism, Neo-liberalism and Rationalities of Government*, ed. Andrew Barry, Thomas Osborne, and Nikolas Rose, 37–64. Chicago: University of Chicago Press.

Rosecrance, Richard. 1999. *The Rise of the Virtual State*. New York: Basic Books.

Rushdie, Salman. 1995. *The Moor's Last Sigh*. London: Jonathan Cape.

Rydell, Robert W. 1984. *All the World's a Fair: Visions of Empire at American International Expositions, 1876–1916*. Chicago: University of Chicago Press.

———. 1993. *World of Fairs: The Century-of-Progress Expositions*. Chicago: University of Chicago Press.

Said, Edward. 1978. *Orientalism*. New York: Random House.

Saint-Blancat, Catherine. 2002. "Islam in Diaspora: Between Reterritorialization and Extraterritoriality." *International Journal of Urban and Regional Research* 26: 138–51.

Saraiva, Camila, and Eduardo Marques. 2004. "A dinâmica social das favelas da região metropolitana de São Paulo." Centro de Estudos da Metrópole, http://www.centrodametropole.org.br/textos.html.

Sardar, Ziauddin. 2000. *The Consumption of Kuala Lumpur*. London: Reaktion Books.

Sarlo, Beatriz. 1999. *La máquina cultural*. Buenos Aires: Planeta.

———. 2000. "The Modern City: Buenos Aires, the Peripheral Metropolis." In *Through the Kaleidoscope: The Experience of Modernity in Latin America*, ed. Vivian Schelling. London: Verso.

Sassen, Saskia. 1991. *The Global City: New York, London, Tokyo*. Princeton: Princeton University Press.

Sennett, Richard. 1969. *Classic Essays on the Culture of Cities*. New York: Meredith Corporation.

Shetty, Prasad. 2005. "Stories of Entrepreneurship." Short Term Independent Research Fellowship Programme, Sarai–CSDS, New Delhi, August. Unpublished.

Shields, Rob. 1991. *Places on the Margin: Alternate Geographies of Modernity*. London: Routledge.

Singer, Paul. 1984. "Interpretação do Brasil: Uma experiência histórica de desenvolvimento." In *História geral da civilização Brasileira*, vol. 3, *O Brasil Republicano, 4 Economia e Cultura (1930–1964)*, ed. Boris Fausto, 211–45. São Paulo: Difel.

Sklair, Leslie. 1998. "The Transnational Capitalist Class and Global Capitalism." *Political Power and Social Theory* 12: 3–43.

Sklarew, Bruce H., Bonnie S. Kaufman, Ellen Handler Spitz, and Diane Borden, eds. 1998. *Bertolucci's "The Last Emperor": Multiple Takes*. Detroit, Mich.: Wayne State University Press.

Smith, Michael Peter. 2001. *Transnational Urbanism: Locating Globalization*. Oxford: Blackwell.

———. 2002. "Power in Place: Retheorizing the Local and the Global." In *Understanding the City*, ed. John Eade and Christopher Mele, 109–30. Oxford: Blackwell.

Soja, Edward. 1989. *Postmodern Geographies*. London: Verso.

South African Institute of Race Relations. 1999. *South Africa in Transition*. Johannesburg: South African Institute of Race Relations.

Spivak, Gayatri Chakravorty. 2003. *Death of a Discipline*. New York: Columbia University Press.

Stevens, G. W. 1915. "All India in Miniature." In *The Charm of Bombay: An Anthology of Writing in Praise of the First City in India*, ed. R. P. Karkaria. Bombay: D. B. Tarporevala and Sons.

Sundaram, Ravi. 2001. "Recycling Modernity: Pirate Electronic Cultures in India." In *Sarai Reader 2001: The Public Domain*. New Delhi: Sarai.

Taylor, Charles. 2004. *Modern Social Imaginaries*. Durham, N.C.: Duke University Press.

Thomas, Nicholas. 1994. *Colonialism's Culture*. Princeton: Princeton University Press.

Till, Christopher. 1995. Foreword to *Africus: Johannesburg Biennale*. Johannesburg: Transitional Metropolitan Council.

Tindall, Gillian. 1992. *City of Gold*. New Delhi: Penguin Books.

Urry, John. 2002. "Mobility and Proximity." *Sociology* 36: 255–74.

Varma, Rashmi. 2004. "Provincializing the Global City: From Bombay to Mumbai." *Social Text* 22.4: 65–89.

Veblen, Thorsten. 1931. *The Theory of the Leisure Class*. New York: Viking.

Venkatraman, Vinay, and Stefano Mirti. 2005. "Network Design." *Domus* 887 (December).

Virilio, Paul. 2003. *Unknown Quantity*. Translated by Chris Turner. London: Thames and Hudson.

Wacha, D. E. 1920. *Shells from the Sands of Bombay*. Bombay: Bombay Chronicle Press.

Wallerstein, Immanuel. 1979. *The Capitalist World Economy: Essays*. Cambridge: Cambridge University Press.

Wang, Shujen. 2003. "Big Shot's Funeral: China, Sony, and the WTO." *Asian Cinema* 14.2: 145–54.

Wark, McKenzie. 2004. *A Hacker's Manifesto*. Cambridge: Massachusetts Institute of Technology Press.

Welch Guerra, Max y Jordi Borja. 2001. "Buenos Aires en perspectiva: Berlín y Barcelona." *Punto de Vista* 71 (December).

Williams, Raymond. 1973. *The Country and the City*. Oxford: Oxford University Press.

Xu, Jian. 2005. "Representing Rural Migrants in the City: Experimentalism in Wang Xiaoshuai's *So Close to Paradise* and *Beijing Bicycle*." *Screen* 46.4: 433–49.

Zermeño, Sergio. 2001. "La democracia impertinente: Comités vecinales en una cultura estatal." Paper presented at the international symposium "Reabrir espacios públicos: Políticas culturales y ciudadanía," Universidad Autónoma Metropolitana, Mexico City, 24–26 September.

Zhang, Yingjin. 1996. *The City in Modern Chinese Literature and Film: Configurations of Space, Time, and Gender*. Stanford, Calif.: Stanford University Press.

———, ed. 1999. *Cinema and Urban Culture in Shanghai, 1922–1943*. Stanford, Calif.: Stanford University Press.

———. 2002. *Screening China: Critical Interventions, Cinematic Reconfigurations, and the Transnational Imaginary in Contemporary Chinese Cinema*. Ann Arbor: University of Michigan Center for Chinese Studies.

———. 2006. *Shenshi Zhongguo: Cong xuekeshi jiaodu guancha Zhongguo dianying yu wenxue yanjiu* (China in focus: Studies of Chinese cinema and literature in the perspective of academic history). Nanjing: Nanjing daxue chubanshe.

Zhang, Zhen. 2005. *An Amorous History of the Silver Screen: Shanghai Cinema, 1896-1937*. Chicago: University of Chicago Press.

Žižek, Slavoj. 2000. *The Fragile Absolute, Or, Why Is the Christian Legacy Worth Fighting For?* London: Verso.

CONTRIBUTORS

Ackbar Abbas now teaches literature, cultural theory, and film at the University of California, Irvine. Previously he was chair of comparative literature and the co-director of the Center for the Study of Globalization and Cultures (CSGC) at the University of Hong Kong. *Hong Kong: Culture and the Politics of Disappearance* was published in 1997.

Teresa P. R. Caldeira is a professor in the Department of City and Regional Planning at the University of California, Berkeley. Her research has focused on the interconnections among urban violence, spatial segregation, and democratization. Currently, she is studying new experiments in urban policy, as well as youth cultures in Brazil. *City of Walls: Crime, Segregation, and Citizenship in São Paulo* (2000) won the 2001 Senior Book Award of the American Ethnological Society.

Néstor García Canclini is the director of the Urban Culture Studies Program at the Universidad Autónoma Metropolitana in Mexico. He has taught at the University of Texas, Austin, Duke University, Stanford University, the Universidad de Barcelona, the Universidad de Buenos Aires, and the Universidad de São Paulo. He received a Guggenheim Fellowship and the Premio Casa de las Américas. In 1992 *Hybrid Cultures* won the Latin American Studies Association award for best book on Latin America. His other works include *Consumers and Citizens* (2001), *The Imagined Globalization* (Duke University Press, forthcoming), and *Diferentes, desiguales y desconectados: Mapas de la interculturalidad* (2004).

Okwui Enwezor is the dean of academic affairs and the senior vice president at the San Francisco Art Institute, as well as an adjunct curator at the

International Center of Photography, New York. He has held positions as a visiting professor in art history at the University of Pittsburgh, Columbia University, New York University, the University of Illinois, Urbana-Champaign, and the University of Umea, Sweden. Enwezor was the artistic director of Documenta 11, Kassel, the Second Johannesburg Biennale, and the Second International Biennial of Contemporary Art, Seville. His publications include *Reading the Contemporary: African Art from Theory to the Marketplace* and *Mega Exhibitions: Antinomies of a Transnational Global Form* (1999). He coedited the four-volume publication of *Documenta 11 Platforms: Democracy Unrealized; Experiments with Truth: Transitional Justice and the Processes of Truth and Reconciliation; Créolité and Creolization; Under Siege: Four African Cities, Freetown, Johannesburg, Kinshasa, Lagos* (2002). He received the Peter Norton Curatorial Award in 1998 and the Agnes Gund Award for Curatorial Excellence in 2007. In 2006 he received the Frank Jewett Mather Award for Criticism by the College Art Association, as well as an award for Best International Photography Book of the Year for his exhibition catalog *Snap Judgments: New Positions in Contemporary African Photography* (2006).

Farha Ghannam is an associate professor of anthropology at Swarthmore College. She is the author of *Remaking the Modern: Space, Relocation, and the Politics of Identity in a Global Cairo* (2002).

Andreas Huyssen is the Villard Professor of German and Comparative Literature and the chair of the Department of Germanic Languages at Columbia University. He is the founding director of Columbia's Center for Comparative Literature and Society (1998–2003) and one of the founding editors of *New German Critique* (since 1974). His books, which have been translated into several languages, include *After the Great Divide: Modernism, Mass Culture, Postmodernism* (1986), *Twilight Memories: Marking Time in a Culture of Amnesia* (1995), and *Present Pasts: Urban Palimpsests and the Politics of Memory* (2003).

Hilton Judin is an independent curator and architect who developed, in collaboration with the History Workshop of the University of the Witwatersrand, a research and exhibition project of official archive documents and video testimonies: "[setting apart]" (1994). With Nina Cohen, he designed the "Living Landscape Project" in Clanwilliam for the Archaeology Department of the University of Cape Town (1996) and the Nelson Mandela Museum in the Eastern Cape for the Department of Arts, Culture, Science and Technology (2000). In 1997–98 he curated "Blank: Architecture, Apartheid and After," a research project for the Netherlands Architecture Institute, which later became a book with more than sixty contributors, including researchers, writers, photographers, and filmmakers.

Rahul Mehrotra is an architect who trained at the Ahmedabad School of Architecture and at Harvard University. He established a private practice in 1990, and his projects range from interior design and architecture to urban planning and conservation. He coauthored, with Sharada Dwivedi, *Bombay: The Cities Within* (1996), which covers Bombay's urban history from the 1600s to the present. He edited, for the Union of International Architects, *The Architecture of the 20th Century in the South Asian Region* (2000), which earmarks the end of the twentieth century. He currently divides his time between Mumbai and MIT, where he teaches.

Orhan Pamuk is a novelist from Istanbul, Turkey. His books *The Black Book*, *White Castle*, *Snow*, *Istanbul*, *My Name Is Red*, and *The New Life* have been translated into more than fifty languages. He teaches at Columbia University and is an honorary foreign member of the American Academy of Arts and Letters. His essays, short pieces, and scholarly articles are collected in *Other Colors*. He received the Nobel Prize in Literature in 2006.

Gyan Prakash is the Dayton-Stockton Professor of History at Princeton University and a member of the Subaltern Studies Editorial Collective. He is also the director of Shelby Cullom Davis Center for Historical Studies. He is the author of *Bonded Histories* (1990) and *Another Reason: Science and the Imagination of Modern India* (1999). He has also edited several volumes of essays on colonial history, including *After Colonialism* (1995). He is currently researching and writing a book on the urban imaginaries of Bombay.

Beatriz Sarlo has served as the editor of the independent cultural journal *Punto de Vista* since 1978. She has been a professor in the Universidad de Buenos Aires and has taught extensively in the United States at Columbia University, the University of California, Berkeley, the University of Minnesota, and the University of Maryland. She was named Simón Bolívar Professor of Latin American Studies at the University of Cambridge; she was also a Woodrow Wilson Fellow and a Guggenheim Fellow. Currently, she is a senior researcher at Consejo Nacional de Investigaciones Científicas y Técnicas (CONICET). She is the author of many books and essays on literature, culture, urban studies, and ideologies. Publications in English include *Borges: A Writer on the Edge* (1993) and *Scenes from Postmodern Life* (2001). Sarlo also publishes a weekly column in the Sunday magazine *Clarín*, one of Latin America's most widely read newspapers.

AbdouMaliq Simone is an urbanist in the broad sense that his work focuses on various communities, powers, cultural expressions, governance and planning discourses, spaces, and times in cities across the world. Simone is presently a professor of sociology at Goldsmiths College, University of London, and has taught at New School University, the University of Khartoum, the University of Ghana, the University of the Western Cape, the University of the Witwatersrand, and the City University of New York. He has also worked for several African nongovernmental organizations and regional institutions, including the Council for the Development of Social Science Research in Africa and the United Nations Centre for Human Settlements. His key publications include *In Whose Image? Political Islam and Urban Practices in Sudan* (1994) and *For the City Yet to Come: Changing Urban Life in Four African Cities* (Duke University Press, 2004).

Yingjin Zhang is the director of the Chinese Studies Program and a professor of Chinese literature and film, comparative literature, and cultural studies at the University of California, San Diego. He is the author of *The City in Modern Chinese Literature and Film: Configurations of Space, Time, and Gender* (1996), *Screening China: Critical Interventions, Cinematic Reconfigurations, and the Transnational Imaginary in Contemporary Chinese Cinema* (2002), and *Chinese National Cinema* (2004); a coauthor of *Encyclopedia of Chinese Film* (1998); editor of *China in a Polycentric World: Essays in Chinese Comparative Literature* (1998) and *Cinema and Urban Culture in Shanghai, 1922–1943* (1999); and coeditor of *From Underground to Independent: Alternative Film Culture in Contemporary China* (2006).

INDEX

Andreas Huyssen is the Villard Professor of German and Comparative Literature and the chair of the Department of Germanic Languages at Columbia University.

Library of Congress Cataloging-in-Publication Data
Other cities, other worlds : urban imaginaries in a globalizing age /
edited by Andreas Huyssen.
p. cm.
"The essays that make up this volume were first presented as formal lectures in a
year-long graduate research seminar in 2001–2002 at Columbia University"—Introd.
Includes bibliographical references and index.
ISBN 978-0-8223-4248-9 (cloth : alk. paper)
ISBN 978-0-8223-4271-7 (pbk. : alk. paper)
1. Cities and towns—Developing countries.
2. Urbanization—Developing countries.
3. Urban geography—Developing countries.
4. Globalization—Social aspects—Developing countries.
I. Huyssen, Andreas.
HT149.5.O84 2008
307.7609172'4—dc22   2008028435